Cleeve Hill

CLEEVE HILL
The History of the Common and its People

new edition

DAVID H ALDRED

First published in 1990
This new edition published in the United Kingdom in 2023
by The Hobnob Press,
8 Lock Warehouse, Severn Road, Gloucester GL1 2GA
www.hobnobpress.co.uk

© David Aldred, text and images, 2023

The Author hereby asserts his moral rights to be identified as the Author of the Work.

All rights reserved. No part of this publication may be reproduced, stored in a retrieval system, or transmitted in any form or by any means, electronic, mechanical, photocopying, recording or otherwise, without the prior permission of the publisher and copyright holder.

British Library Cataloguing in Publication Data
A catalogue record for this book is available from the British Library

ISBN 978-1-914407-55-0 paperback
ISBN 978-1-914407-56-7 caseboiund

Typeset in Chaparral Pro, 11/14 pt
Typesetting and origination by John Chandler

CONTENTS

Preface to the first edition	vii
Preface to the new edition	ix
Introduction	xi
1 The Making of the Human Landscape (before c.400AD)	1
2 The Boundaries are Defined (c.400AD-1086)	29
3 Searching for Hidden Landscapes (1086-c.1520)	54
4 Conflict in the Community (c.1520-1818)	86
5 Cheltenham Moves out of Town (1818-1859)	129
6 The Common under Threat (1818-1890)	154
7 The 'Cotswold Health Resort' (1890-1918)	177
8 The Development of the Cotswold Health Resort since 1918	221
The Final Word	266
First Edition Acknowledgements	267
New Edition Acknowledgements	269
Glossary	271
Index of Places	273

PREFACE TO THE FIRST EDITION

This book tells the story of a landscape and of the people who have played a part in its creation. Cleeve Hill lies some four miles north-east of Cheltenham in Gloucestershire. It reaches a height of 1,083 ft (330 m) — the highest point of the Cotswolds — and is considered, technically, a mountain. Rising out of the Severn Vale its common of over one thousand acres can be seen for miles. It not only shelters the vale physically from the east but also metaphorically provides a backcloth to the lives of the people who live and work at its feet.

Cleeve Hill has fascinated me for most of my life, and yet when I began to investigate its past I found very little had been written about it. As L.D. Stamp and W.G. Hoskins noted in 1963, common land has not attracted much attention from historians or historical geographers. Although written nearly thirty years ago their statement still has validity. This book is intended in some small way to add to our limited knowledge of the subject.

The aim is not only to explain the development of a human landscape as I interpret the evidence, but also to explain how the landscape itself can be read for the clues to its own past. It is a book to read at home and take on walks over the hill. It is a book of local interest and yet it should have a wider value to students of landscape history, and the general reader, as a rare example of a full length history of an extensive area of common pasture. To this purpose I have borne in mind the need at all times to set the history of the hill into its wider contexts, for only in such contexts can its history be fully understood. Local history must not become parochial history.

I have arranged the chapters around themes. The general themes of conflict, continuity and change link with the more detailed themes of grazing, quarrying, woodland and settlement. The choice of themes is necessarily subjective but they seem to me to provide the best structure for arranging the evidence to give coherence to the history and prevent its fragmenting into a series of unrelated episodes.

In order to keep the story flowing, I have chosen a number of conventions that need some explanation here. Footnotes have been replaced by a section on further reading at the end of each chapter. Acknowledgements for the illustrations have been included in the captions. Where none appears the illustrations are my own. I have generally kept the historic measurements as they were used at the time. Readers not totally familiar with such measurements, or their metric equivalents, might wish to know that 1 mile = 1.6 km; 1 acre = 0.4 hectare; 240d. = 20s. = £1 = 100p.

As any author will acknowledge, such pieces of research would not be possible without the generous help and cooperation of many people. I am pleased to make those acknowledgements either in the captions or at the end of the book. However, a special acknowledgement needs to made here. In 1958 my parents made a decision to move us from Manchester to Woodmancote. Without that decision I would never have come to know Cleeve Hill and this book would never have been written. It seems appropriate, therefore, to dedicate this book to them.

David H. Aldred
November 1990

PREFACE TO THE NEW EDITION

Thirty-three years have passed since the first edition of this book. It has long been out of print and yet the growth in population in the local area, particularly in Bishop's Cleeve, and the increased use of the common for recreation after the covid epidemic of 2020-21 has encouraged me to review and expand on my original work. I have also been able to amend errors and re-consider conclusions.

Extensive archaeological investigations and findings in Bishop's Cleeve since 1990 have enabled me to put the early history of the hill and its common into a firmer and wider context than was previously possible in Chapter 1. The middle sections of the book have been altered the least. Chapter 5 has been lengthened as more evidence for the races has become available whilst Chapter 7 has been greatly expanded by using the census returns which have now been published online. Chapter 8, the 'Postscript' in the original book, has been expanded the greatest. The availability of the minutes of the Board of Conservators from 1890 to 2014 has led to a detailed study of the common which was not previously possible and this has provided the backbone of the chapter. During the period covered by the chapter the Board of Conservators was renamed Cleeve Common Trust in 2017 and I will use the terms appropriate to the dates.

I have used as many of the original illustrations as possible, some appearing here in colour. However many of the scenes recorded over thirty years ago have changed considerably and so there are many new photographs and illustrations. I have acknowledged sources in the captions when they were not taken by me or from my own collection of images.

Finally, the first edition was dedicated to my parents who are sadly no longer with us. This new addition is dedicated in thanks to the

Trust, its members, staff and volunteers whose careful management and enthusiasm ensure Cleeve Common continues to be a special place for all its visitors.

David Aldred
November 2023

INTRODUCTION

> Common land is any land over which there are rights of common.
> B. Harris and G. Ryan, *An outline law relating to Common Land*, 1967

Cleeve Common rises above the treelined slopes of Cleeve Hill. Together they create a prominent landscape feature which provides a backdrop to the lives of the people living at its foot and a distinctive shape which is visible for miles around. This book seeks to explain the

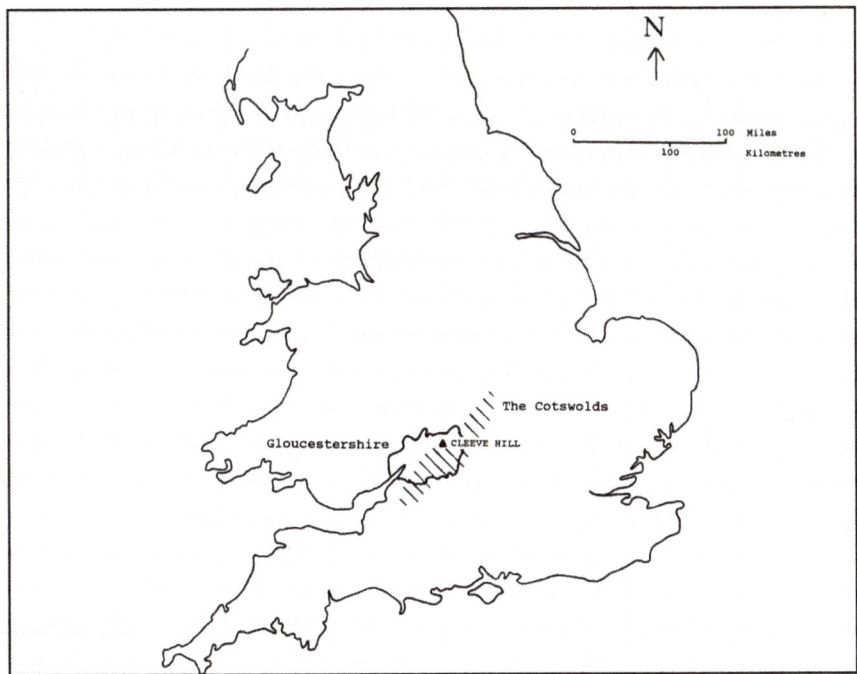

Location map of Cleeve Hill

development of that landscape in general, and the history of its common in particular. Cleeve Common is valued today as a semi-wild scarce resource where open space attracts visitors by its 'otherness', its fresh air, wide-ranging views and, from April to November, the many sheep which still serve as a reminder of its historical importance as a grazing ground.

Sheep on the common between April and November provide a living link to the common's historical importance

Today it is a major surviving example of a lowland common. Common land now covers only three per cent of England, but Cleeve Common represents nearly twenty per cent of the area of the historic parishes of Bishop's Cleeve, Southam and Brockhampton and Woodmancote to which it is attached. In 1990 I wrote that the history of such common land had been strangely neglected. Since then the subject has received much more attention by historians as can be found in the further reading at the end of this Introduction, despite the continuing lack of historical records relating to such commons compared to the records concerned with arable land which grew life-giving crops. People needed to know who held the land which grew crops and therefore many records were created over a long period of time. On the other hand, common pasture generated far fewer records and in many places all traces of such land have disappeared, leaving areas like Cleeve Common as fortunate survivors.

Cleeve Common was created by the coming together of two separate forces for change in the landscape: the natural geology and geomorphology, and the work of human beings. This Introduction sets the scene by discussing both these forces, starting with the geology and geomorphology.

Cleeve Hill was formed around 180 million years ago as the seabed of a shallow sea, created from shells, corals and carbonate of lime. Then the land was folded upwards, higher in the west than in the east, to create that famous scarp which today runs from Bath to Chipping Campden with its gentle dip slope stretching eastwards as the Cotswolds. The scarp is gradually being eroded towards the east, cut into by fast-flowing streams flowing through on their way to the vale to reach the River Severn. The process is continuous but barely discernible. It will, in time, separate Cleeve from Nottingham Hill, and leave the latter a true

Beds of freestone and peagrit at Castle rock

outlier like Langley or more distant Bredon. The erosive power of water can be seen on the common itself which is now cut by the northward-running valleys of Dry Bottom and Watery Bottom.

This timescale is slow beyond comprehension, but the recorded human story has been affected by the underlying geology in significant ways. The limestone, called Inferior Oolite, has been exploited for centuries: the smooth, good quality freestone as a superior building material; coarser limestones and pea grits, also used for building but also for field walls, road stone and lime for mortar; and the sands, gravels

The sand hole by the White Way

and grits, which have been extracted for a variety of purposes, from use in the pottery industry, polishing marble and creating footpaths. The exploitation of these minerals for over 2,000 years has changed the appearance of the common and created its famous outline as seen from the vale.

The limestone itself soaks up the rainfall and results in a quick-drying surface which, in combination with continued animal grazing, has inhibited regeneration of trees after the original clearance and in more recent times has provided a good turf for horse racing and training. However, bands of clay lie between the limestone beds in many places. Here the water cannot pass, and so it emerges as a spring – the one in Watery Bottom above the Washpool, which is the source of the River

The Washpool

Isbourne, and the one which runs down part of Stockwell Lane are both good examples. In other places the clay becomes waterlogged and slumps down the slope. This accounts for the instability of the land bordering the B4632, and has caused great problems for builders, householders and the highway authorities. However, the slumping created a ledge running along the slope which provided a convenient route for the present road when it was laid out in 1823. So the geology has provided people with the opportunity to exploit and develop a natural resource. What use have they made of it?

The proper answer to that question forms the content of this book, but here it is necessary to consider the nature of common land, for there are many misconceptions about it, and the quotation at the beginning of this chapter indicates clearly the problem of finding a

An attempt to prevent land slippage along the B4632 in September 1985

meaningful definition. Two popular misconceptions concern common land, that it is not owned by anyone, and that everyone has rights to it. Common land is private land over which third parties, usually referred to as 'commoners' have rights in law. This was enshrined in law by the Statute of Merton as long ago as 1236. Cleeve Common is still privately owned but in many other places local authorities have bought commons, especially in the large centres of population, to ensure free access for the inhabitants. Traditionally, rights to the use of common land have been limited to commoners who were people of the manor with land in the manor, who used the common for animal grazing, for collecting fuel, and in certain places for grazing pigs in woodland. Only the lord had rights to the minerals lying under the soil and so on Cleeve Common the quarries were worked under licence from the lord. Rights of way and then increased access for others to enjoy the open spaces became established by usage over the years. In the second half of the nineteenth century preserving access to common land which was under pressure from recreational users, especially around London in places such as Wimbledon, Epping Forest, Hampstead Heath and Berkhamsted, led to the setting up in 1865 of the Commons, Open Spaces and Footpaths Preservation Society to lobby for legislation. The most important piece of legislation resulting from this pressure was the 1876 Commons Act which allowed uses of any common to be regulated by law, if requested by a sufficient number of people. By 1914 36 applications had been made under the act, one of which was for Cleeve. This led to the act of 1890 by which Cheltenham Corporation began to pay £50 per annum for the right of its inhabitants to have free access. The details of this can be read in Chapter 6.

The general concern for the preservation of commons in the nineteenth century clearly reflected the threat they were perceived to be under. There are almost a million acres surviving in England and Wales today, which is

In 1990 these signs stood at the entrances to the common reflecting the terms on the 1890 act

The signs today are less forbidding but also less informative about what activities are permitted on the common

barely one tenth of the estimated acreage 300 years ago and half of those which do survive are smaller than two and a half acres. Most of the commons disappeared between 1750 and 1860 by being enclosed and taken into private ownership for the exclusive use of the landowners when open fields were remodelled into modern enclosed fields, usually by acts of parliament. The commoners were compensated for the loss of their common rights by being granted small plots of land which were too small for grazing their animals. Many observers regretted this treatment of the lower orders but were powerless to stop it happening. Cleeve Common survived because the large number of 148 people insisted on their rights of common when the open fields of the parish were enclosed. This was completed in 1847. Many other local commons were subdivided as private property and subsequently ploughed as a result of similar enclosures. This happened to the common on Nottingham Hill with the enclosure of Gotherington in 1807, and Prestbury and Sevenhampton's share of Cleeve Down disappeared as common land at their enclosure in 1732 and 1814 respectively. Written records indicate how relatively easy it is for us to trace the disappearance of common land with reasonable certainty. Conversely they remind us how difficult it is to trace its origins. This is one of the questions the early part of the book attempts to answer in relation to Cleeve, but what can be said more generally about the origins of common?

There is no clear date by which they could be said to have come into existence. One of the problems facing historians is that the type of land most frequently described today as common land is, strictly speaking, common pasture. The arable open fields were also common fields because the villagers had rights over them, for example the right to graze their animals on the fallow fields which were left untilled to regain their goodness as part of the annual crop rotation. As a result it is difficult to distinguish between the term 'common' applied to these fields from the 'common' referring to the common pasture or 'waste', although other types of land use could also be held in common: Tewkesbury Ham is still a common meadow today and the name Sherwood is a reminder that Sherwood Forest was centred on a wood in which the people of Nottinghamshire had woodland rights, first recorded in 958AD.

Another problem concerns the nature of the record. It has so far been impossible to recognise common land from archaeological evidence and the earliest written recordings are not particularly helpful. They might have been made only when the existing rights were under threat. However there is clear evidence that the concept of common grazing land predated the Norman Conquest of 1066. Early references were made to common land in the laws of King Edgar (959AD- 975AD). Stamp and Hoskins recorded that by the early thirteenth century Dartmoor provided common grazing for the whole of Devon, except the boroughs of Barnstaple and Totnes which were founded in the tenth century, presumably after the time by which the rights to Dartmoor had been established. The earliest date we possess for Cleeve Hill as common grazing land is 1150 (see Chapter 3).

In theory the uses of common land have been controlled by custom and byelaw. Much of this book is concerned with such cases. Probably the greatest need to control usage has been to prevent overgrazing, by limiting the number of animals any one person could turn out on the common pasture. This was known as 'stinting'. It first appears when records became generally available from the early thirteenth century and probably reflected a growth of pressure on common lands throughout England. At different times and in different

Rock House behind the tree on the left and Cleeve Lodge by the trees on the far right are examples of houses built on land taken from the common

places different figures were employed to regulate stinting. People in Bishop's Cleeve, Southam and Woodmancote could place as many animals on the common as they could keep on their land in the vale during the winter months. The many attempts to enforce this at different times in the past was a clear indication that the stints were not being observed. Anything which prevented the commoners from enjoying their rights was considered anti-community, particularly encroachments on to the common which reduced the land for communal grazing. The traditional beliefs that the builders of a house constructed overnight with smoke issuing from the chimney by morning could claim squatters' rights probably explains some of the encroachments on the edges of Cleeve Common. The manorial courts had varying success in removing such enclosures from the late seventeenth century onwards and these often ended in charging a rent for their continued existence. The late nineteenth and early twentieth century expansion of Cleeve Hill as the

Dr J.H. Garrett's map, drawn to accompany From a Cotswold Height *(1919) still remains a useful guide to the common and its approaches (J.V. Garrett)*

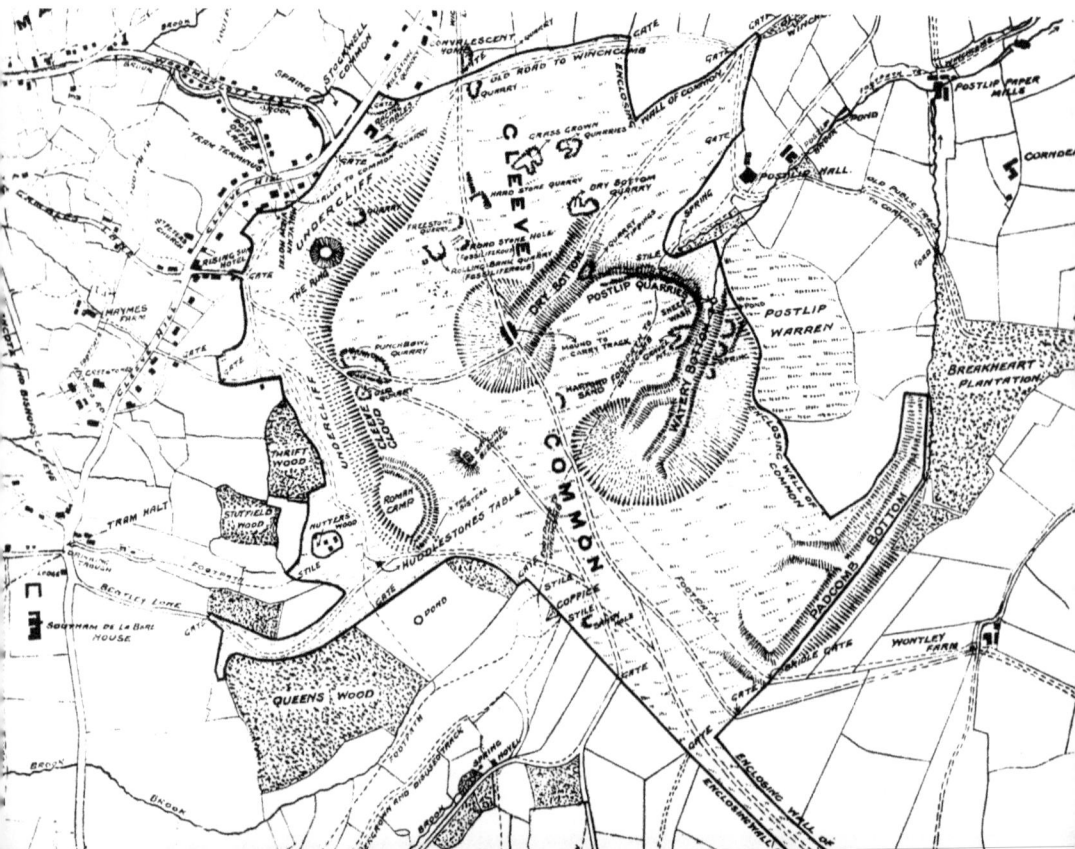

'Cotswold Health Resort' exploited some of these encroachments on the common.

There is nothing unusual about the history of Cleeve Common when it is set into its wider historical context. It has been a valued resource for grazing, quarrying and recreation including horse racing and golf. It has come under the influence of the neighbouring large centre of population to become 'Cheltenham's lung'. Its management over the centuries always attempted to reconcile these potentially conflicting uses whilst today the emphasis is on conservation, recreation and education. This is a story which can be repeated time and again in lowland England but the individual factors which have moulded the history of Cleeve Hill and its common is a story worth telling for its own sake.

FURTHER READING

The most readable account of the underlying geology of Cleeve Hill and the Cotswolds is still *Geology explained in the Severn Vale and Cotswolds,* by W. Dreghorn (David & Charles, Newton Abbot, 1967). The most detailed and scholarly is *A Handbook of the Geology of Cheltenham and Neighbourhood,* by L. Richardson (Norman, Sawyer & Co., Cheltenham, 1904). The British Geological Survey's website https://www.bgs.ac.uk is the most comprehensive.

For commons in general the standard reference work remains *The Common Lands of England and Wales,* by L.D. Stamp and W.G. Hoskins (Collins, London, 1963). *Common Land and Enclosure,* by E.C.K. Gonner (1912; reprinted by F. Cass, London, 1966) is only for the committed. *English Commons and Forests,* by G. Shaw-Le Fèvre (Cassell, London, 1894) traces the development of the fight to preserve commons in the nineteenth century, and is written by a founder member of the Commons, Open Spaces and Footpaths Preservation Society. Since 1990 many articles and books have been written on all aspects of common land. These findings have been summarised in *Common Land in Britain* by Angus J.L. Winchester (Boydell, Woodbridge, Suffolk, 2022). Of particular interest is Alan Everitt's chapter 'Common Land' in Joan Thirsk (ed.), *The English Rural Landscape,* (Oxford University Press, Oxford, 2000). *The Common Land Forum Report* (Cheltenham, 1986) was produced by the Countryside Commission for England and Wales to make recommendations on the future management of commons. It includes much of general interest.

The Cleeve Common Trust's website http://www.cleevecommon.org.uk contains current information on the common. The county council has a website with details of the common lands in the county at https://www.gloucestershire.gov.uk/business-property-and-economy/land-and-property/common-land-and-village-greens. *Gloucestershire Commons: Their History, Wildlife and Future* (Gloucestershire Trust for Nature Conservancy, Stonehouse, 1989) provides a useful summary of the county's commons at that date. Many local historical studies make incidental references to commons and wastes. The Victoria County History of Gloucestershire, which is slowly covering the county's parishes, often includes relevant references in its sections entitled 'Economic History', which are included in every parish study. The county common closest to Cleeve in its form and function is at Minchinhampton, dealt with in *Minchinhampton and Avening,* by A.T. Playne (1915; reprinted by Alan Sutton Publishing, Gloucester, 1978). There are many books on the Forest of Dean. Those by Dr Cyril Hart cover its history, but the position of common land in the Forest is altogether different from Cleeve Common.

Apart from the first edition of this book, three books have been written about Cleeve Common. The classic account is *From a Cotswold Height*, by Dr J.H. Garrett (J.J. Banks, Cheltenham, 1919; reprinted by Alan Sutton Publishing, Gloucester, 1988) which describes a series of walks made over and around the common in the early years of the twentieth century. Unfortunately for the historian the best descriptions are those of the area's natural history, which has since changed rather less than its social and economic history. Readers interested in this aspect of the common should refer to Dr Garrett's book for a comprehensive treatment of a subject not covered in detail here. In 1993 his son Dr J.V. Garrett followed literally in his father's footsteps with *Cleeve Common and the North Cotswolds* (Thornhill Press, Parkend, 1993). *Cleeve Common, Glos., Rights and Regulations over this Common*, by J.F. Daubeny (Army & Navy Cooperative Society, London, 1900) consists mostly of legal clauses, as it was an attempt to clarify the legal obligations of the then Lady of the Manor *vis-à-vis* the powers of the Conservators. It does, however, contain some useful, if incidental, contemporary information. Hugh Denham's *The Woodmancote Book* (privately published, 1997) includes many interesting episodes on the history of Cleeve Hill.

The history of Cleeve Hill and its common is discussed briefly in 'When Cleeve ceased to be common' in my article in *Gloucestershire and Avon Life* (October, 1977). Sections of two of my books in Alan Sutton Publishing's 'The British Isles in Old Photographs' series contain many postcard and other views of the common at the turn of the last century; they are *Bishop's Cleeve to Winchcombe in Old Photographs* (1987) and *Around Bishop's Cleeve and Winchcombe in Old Photographs* (1989). My book *A History of Bishop's Cleeve and Woodmancote* (Amberley Publishing, Stroud, 2009) contains a general account of the development of Cleeve Hill as a health resort in Chapter 7. More historic illustrations can be found in Amberley's *Through Time* series compiled by myself and my late friend Tim Curr: *In and Around Bishop's Cleeve* (2009) and *In and Around Bishop's Cleeve: A second selection* (2010).

N.B. Throughout the FURTHER READING sections I have only given actual website addresses where they might not be obvious from the references. All the websites were accessible at the time of writing. There is also a glossary at the end of the book to explain historical terms.

1
THE MAKING OF THE HUMAN LANDSCAPE
(BEFORE c.400AD)

> Before, however, entering on the authenticated incidents recorded of the eighth century, it will be interesting to trace back, briefly, (so far as is practicable through so long a vista of remote ages) some of the facts presented to us by the discoveries of ancient British and Roman remains.
>
> E. Dent, *The Annals of Winchcombe and Sudeley*, 1877

Some Early Problems

Every story has a beginning. Emma Dent quite clearly believed that her story began with 'the authenticated incidents recorded of the eighth century'. Almost a century and a half of archaeological research have yielded much knowledge of prehistory so that it now deserves greater mention than a footnote attached to a story based largely on the written word, but our knowledge is still incomplete. Understanding still depends upon the recognition and interpretation of fragmentary pieces of evidence, and parallels which can never provide conclusive answers. For this reason the first few millenia of Cleeve Hill's history take up no more space than a single chapter, while the rest of the book is taken up with developments since *c*.400AD.

Prehistory is divided conventionally into different ages. These are simple conveniences for the prehistorian and archaeologist, but they do give a structure to the early part of the story and will be used here for that purpose. By following chronological divisions it is easier to identify the recurring themes which are echoed in the area's later history.

The basis of this chapter is the evidence of the landscape itself as there are no written records to support its interpretation. But the landscape yields its clues only grudgingly and has to be handled with care. Knowledge of the hill's history has emerged from a small number of actual excavations, dating back to 1863; from careful examination of surviving features; and from stray finds which have been reported and recorded. This type of information creates three problems: firstly, how should this material be interpreted in order to look behind it to the people who made it and moulded the landscape? Secondly, how typical are the features which survive? How accurate is the picture we can paint from necessarily fragmentary and incomplete evidence? These considerations need to be kept in mind, but they must not be allowed to undermine the conclusion that the evidence quite clearly points to prehistory as the period in which the present general features of Cleeve Hill and its common were formed.

The First Clearances

No evidence has yet been found for human activity on the hill before the final retreat of the glaciers in the last Ice Age over twelve thousand years ago. They had stretched down to the Bredon Hill area, and as the weather warmed, the countryside became colonized by birch and pine, then hazel and oak with lesser numbers of elm and lime. There are some indications that trees were being cleared, at least on a small scale, soon after the glaciers retreated. Small scatters of tiny flints dating from the Mesolithic period (*c.*9600BC-*c.*4000BC) have been found in the area. Flint does not occur naturally on the Cotswolds and its discovery must indicate human presence. The archaeological investigation of Haymes Romano-British settlement in 1975 (see below) uncovered three such flints.

More recently in 2014 investigations by Worcestershire Archaeology at Yew Tree Farm at the bottom of nearby Bushcombe Lane discovered a larger number. The report contained a noteworthy conclusion that these, and later Romano-British and Medieval finds were mixed up together as a result of the soil slumping that had occurred down the hill slope for centuries. A similar problem was found at Haymes. This complicates the archaeological investigations on the hill slopes as artefacts are not only moved from their original location but can be covered by a depth of earth. Further evidence undoubtedly lies under the pastoral land use of the common and its surrounding fields, but we can only draw supported conclusions from what has been found.

When Cotswold Archaeology excavated the Cleevelands around Dean Farm to the north west of Bishop's Cleeve's centre before its development for housing in 2014-16, it reported that a few Mesolithic flints had been found. A single possible flint had been discovered during the excavations near the surgery in Stoke Road in 1997. Such evidence might be slight but it does indicate that there was already enough tree clearance for people to be moving about in the vale, as well as on the hill slopes and so presumably on the hill itself. People lived as hunter-gatherers, never staying long in the same place.

The earliest period for which there is more than fragmentary evidence in the landscape is the Neolithic period (*c.*4000BC-*c.*2000BC), when farming was first introduced into the area. Although not situated on the common, Belas Knap long barrow is close enough to be used as an indication of what was happening in the upland landscape of which the common is a part. The name itself, 'Belas' from *bel*, a beacon, and 'Knap' meaning a hilltop, describes its position well. It is one of seventy known long barrows on the Cotswolds and at nearly fifty metres long and four metres high is one of the largest. However, don't think it has always looked as it does today. Edward J. Burrow's sketch records its condition

Burrow's sketch of Belas Knap of 1913 shows the extent of the modern reconstruction after the excavations of 1928-30

in 1913. It had already been excavated in 1863 and 1865 but our knowledge comes mostly from excavations in 1928 and 1930 before the present structure was built in 1930-31 as part of a national government scheme to give employment to the unemployed. Comparing it to other Cotswold long barrows, notably the one at Hazleton near Northleach, excavated in 1979-83, the dry stone walling around the false entrance which faces north probably continued around the whole structure, surmounted by turf on the roof.

The false entrance at the northern end of Belas Knap

Professor Timothy Darvill, the expert on Cotswold long barrows, thinks that the stones of the false entrance could be part of a portal dolmen tomb, which was excavated in 1863 and 1865 when the bones of a young man and five children aged under eight were discovered together with horse and pig bones, flint and pottery. The archaeologists also found what might have been the remains of another burial under the centre of the long barrow as they found a broken circle of stones and ash in the soil. It seems these burials dated from a few hundred years before the long barrow was built on what therefore was already considered to be sacred ground. Carbon-14 dating of the bones in the long barrow itself indicated it might only have been in use for approximately three hundred years before *c.*3600BC. This led Professor Darvill to conclude it might have been the last resting place of a single extended family. Archaeologists continue to debate the reasons for the building and siting of long barrows, because the area devoted to the actual burials is so small; at Belas Knap less than five per cent of the total area. Were they territorial markers indicating ownership or guardianship of land and resources, legitimised by the bones of the ancestors? So what can the long barrow tell us about the development of the landscape on Cleeve Hill?

When Alan Saville excavated the long barrow at Hazleton, he showed it had been built in a sizeable woodland clearing. The situation at Belas Knap seems to have been very similar. To the east trees still grow on the slope at Humblebee above which the barrow is located. However, to the south and east of the barrow, field walking has produced flint scatters across the plateau which extends to Cleeve Common and Wontley, indicating clearance of the trees. Grave goods of flint sickle blades and a flint saw were found inside the tombs, indicating crops were being grown. Fragments of pottery indicated storage and preparation of food. Animals were represented by bones of horse and pig; the latter suggesting (controlled) use of woodland for hunting, or pasture for domesticated breeds. Woodland still remains uncleared on the scarp faces, but by *c.*3500BC, when Belas Knap appears to have gone out of use, the eastern plateau attached to Cleeve Hill had already been cleared of woodland and was developing its open aspect. How far might the clearances have extended?

Scatters of worked flint picked up between the edge of the common and Wontley suggest that it might be only the present pasture use of the common which prevents us picking up flints from across the common itself. Timothy Darvill considers that spurs of land, such as that extending south and east from Belas Knap to Cleeve Common were among the first areas to be cleared of trees. The excavations at the King's Beeches above Rising Sun Lane in 1902 (see below) recovered three flints and further investigation towards the Stables Quarry at the same time produced a few more. More spectacularly, sixty seven flints were retrieved at Haymes Romano-British settlement site by 1985, indicating activity in the Neolithic period following on (although not necessarily

Flints found in the field immediately to the south of Belas Knap

continuously) from the earlier Mesolithic period at this place. So these flint scatters would support the conclusion that clearances had taken place across the hill and parts of its upper slopes, and that continuity of land use as pasture and arable made it difficult for trees to re-establish themselves. It might be that its use as pasture followed only after exhaustion of the soil by arable farming, as happened on other upland areas such as Dartmoor or on the chalk downlands of southern England at the end of the Bronze Age, although no clear landscape evidence for this has been found on the common. However, we know from the excavations of Belas Knap from 1863 to 1865 that quantities of Iron Age and Romano-British pottery were found adjacent to the site. This could suggest a movement back to arable use by c.500BC, for the sherds of pottery came from the manure from the farmyard, even if any farm was occupied for only part of the year when the animals grazed on the upland; another feature identified from excavated sites in the south and west of England.

We know more about how the landscape changed in the Neolithic period than about the people responsible for the changes. As long ago as 1985 Alastair Marshall of the Cotswold Archaeological Research Group concluded that by careful field walking he had found a sufficient number of flints in the field immediately to the south of Belas Knap to conclude there had been a small settlement on that spur of land during the Neolithic period. Stray finds of flints over many years suggest the vale itself had large clearings by at least c.2000 BC. Investigations in 2020 by Cotswold Archaeology of the former allotment site alongside the A435 to the north of Bishop's Cleeve drew the conclusion there was sufficient evidence from flint and pottery to suggest there had been a temporary small early Neolithic settlement. A few flints were also found on the Cleevelands site and the excavators hypothesised that people were already moving between vale and hill.

The Landscape Takes its Present Form

It is impossible to consider any of these prehistoric periods in any detail; one can only hope to identify trends in the development of the landscape. People continued to exploit the potential of the hill. During the Neolithic period and the Bronze Age (c.2000BC-c.800BC) the climate was significantly warmer than that of today, thus making life at the higher altitude of Cleeve rather more hospitable for growing

The possible round barrow lies to the left of The Ring

crops and living there. Much of the evidence we possess for the Bronze Age has come from grave goods, buried with the people to serve them in the next world, from a number of known round barrows. These were scattered when the barrows were destroyed and no obvious barrows still survive on Cleeve Hill. The greater number of round barrows than of long barrows suggests an increase in population and groups were competing for land; some three hundred round barrows are known to have existed in Gloucestershire. They might also have been territorial markers giving legitimacy to claims to territories like the long barrows. However, unlike long barrows they were usually the last resting place of the ashes of a single individual as cremation was used.

Readers familiar with the large numbers of well-preserved round barrows on the Wiltshire Downs will be disappointed with the evidence from Cleeve Hill. Only one structure remotely looks like a barrow today, the round platform adjacent to 'The Ring' earthwork, east of Rising Sun Lane. Although it was recorded in 1884 on the first large scale Ordnance Survey map as a round barrow, the 1976 inventory of the Royal Commission on Historical Monuments (RCHM) described it as the possible site of a later Iron Age hut. Only careful excavation will throw

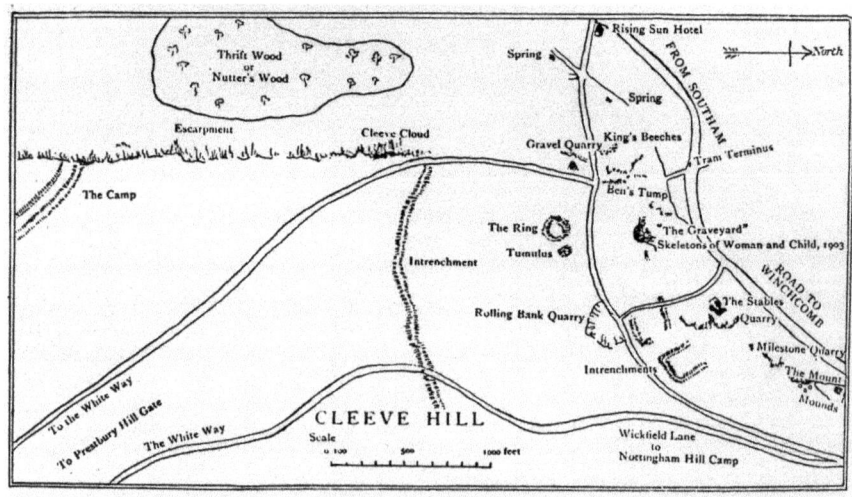

Fig. 2.—SKETCH-MAP OF THE NORTH-WEST PORTION OF THE CLEEVE-HILL PLATEAU.

This sketch map drawn to accompany G.W.S. Brewer's report on his excavations at the King's Beeches provides a valuable, if impressionistic, record of the archaeological features on the common in 1904 and marks 'mounds'

further light on the matter. Most of our knowledge of the round barrows, therefore, comes from the writings of earlier historians.

In 1779 the county historian Samuel Rudder recorded four barrows lying equidistant between Nottingham Hill and Cleeve Hill 'camps'. One had recently been opened to yield a large quantity of human bones, 'broken and crumbled'. John Goding's *Norman's History of Cheltenham*, written in 1863, made further reference to them, and they were obviously still visible in 1902 when the archaeologist at the King's Beeches, G.W.S. Brewer picked up scattered bones, and recorded the barrows on his map as 'mounds'. Shortly after this date the barrows were destroyed by the expansion of Milestone Quarry, the excavator of

Milestone Quarry. The bush in the centre of the photograph indicates the approximate position of the round barrows

which, Arthur Yiend, was ordered to stop its expansion in 1911 for safety reasons, as it had begun to encroach onto the track at its eastern edge. When the archaeologist O.G.S. Crawford visited in November 1920 he reported he could find no trace of the barrows. It is just possible that part of the most easterly barrow still survives as a low mound, although it is now covered by more recent debris. Some of the stray finds made during the nineteenth century (and now in Cheltenham Museum) might have come from these barrows. The finds included several bronze axes, a miniature dagger and what is probably a large-socketed axe. Their use was probably funereal as accompaniments into the after life rather than practical.

Bronze Age finds including a spearhead (marked '6') found on Cleeve Hill and illustrated in Emma Dent's Annals of Winchcombe and Sudeley *(1877)*

In 1931 a little-known find of pottery and a lower jaw bone, said to have been those of an old woman, was made by workmen digging a trench for water pipes where the former public conveniences, now Lou's Views, were later built near the top of Stockwell Lane. This could have been another Bronze Age, or possible Iron Age, burial. In 1924 a miniature dagger and plough share were found on the hill and handed in to Cheltenham Museum. Later, in 1971, the Ordnance Survey reported the finds of two miniature bronze figurines on the hill. These are likely to have come from religious sites but unfortunately the find locations were not recorded.

These burials could allow the interpretation that the hill and vale were being linked. The archaeological excavations in and around Bishop's Cleeve, especially in the last thirty or so years as the village has expanded, have greatly increased our understanding of this part of the vale in the Bronze Age. Small settlements were found at the Tesco site by Wessex Archaeology in 1998 and 2004, at the Homelands to the west of Gotherington Lane by Headland Archaeology in 2015 and at the Cleevelands site already noted. From each of these sites the round barrows by Milestone Quarry would have been visible. Archaeologists sometimes consider that during the Bronze Age land could be divided metaphorically into land for the living and land for the dead. People lived in the vale and buried their dead on the hill to where they could look up to their ancestors. Could this have been the situation here at least during part of the Bronze Age? However, other burials have also been discovered in the vale by excavation. In 2015 Worcestershire Archaeology uncovered an early Bronze Age cremation in the field opposite Cheltenham North rugby ground along Stoke Road. In 2021 Cotswold Archaeology found another in an adjacent field. At the Cleevelands site a small middle Bronze Age cemetery was unearthed during the excavations. A field

The view from Milestone Quarry evidences that the round barrows would have been seen from the area which is now Bishop's Cleeve

to the west of Lower Farm, off the bypass, was called Burrows Piece in the 1839 Tithe award which suggests a round barrow and early Bronze Age pottery was found in the immediate vicinity when an Anglo-Saxon cemetery was discovered in 1969. On the hill itself two early eleventh-century charters make reference to two round barrows along West Down, which have since disappeared and neither were visible from Bishop's Cleeve (see Chapter Two). Timothy Darvill has identified the remains of a round barrow in the field to the west of Belas Knap, but again this is not visible from Bishop's Cleeve or its surrounding area in the vale. However, it may have been deliberately sited near Belas Knap.

Further evidence dating from the Bronze Age has been found on Nottingham Hill. In his introduction to the *Landboc* of Winchcombe Abbey, published in 1892, the Reverend David Royce referred to three round barrows on the hill. No trace can be found of them today, but in 1972 ploughing within the site of the Iron Age camp disturbed a hoard of twenty five Bronze Age objects hidden in a wooden box, including three bronze swords. Now in Cheltenham Museum, they have been dated between *c.*1700BC to *c.*700BC and they provide evidence that Nottingham Hill had been cleared of woodland by the late Bronze Age.

Nottingham Hill hillfort showing the overgrown ramparts in the foreground and Granna (or Grinnell) Lane cutting across the plateau. Until enclosure in 1807 this area, then of Gotherington, like Cleeve, was common pasture

So there is sufficient evidence to draw a conclusion that by *c.*800BC the countryside was probably open and exploited both on the hilltop plateau and in the vale. People moved around in the landscape. Tin and copper came from the south-west; flint from the south-east; people drove animals to and from pastures. Many of the routes marked on the map on page 46 were probably in use during the Bronze Age, particularly the route coming up Nottingham Hill as Granna or Grinnell Lane and across Cleeve as the White Way before forking, the south-eastern route following West Down and the more southerly route passing on to Ham Hill and through Dowdeswell. Although the evidence for use of all the routes from the vale up the scarp is clearer for the Iron Age, it is unlikely they were new creations in that period, for Cleeve Hill had already become a valuable resource. Timothy Darvill has suggested that the ditch and bank known as the Cross Dyke, running across the hill from near the top of Rising Sun Lane through Dry Bottom to Postlip Quarries dates from the Bronze Age rather than the Iron Age as previously thought. Although no excavations have taken place, careful study indicates it was built in three different sections. It runs up the scarp as a major feature in the landscape and runs down as a lesser feature towards Postlip along the western slope of Dry Bottom, possibly signifying that its main function was to be seen as a boundary marker from the vale. There is a linear ditch and bank running off the common and above Postlip Hall which might be a continuation of the Cross Dyke. From parallels elsewhere, particularly Icomb Hill near Stow-on-the-Wold, Professor Darvill considers it divided the area into two territories. Its existence indicated this area of upland was already considered a valuable contested resource. Thus by the end of the Bronze Age *c.*800BC the landscape was

The Cross Dyke is at its most impressive above the Rising Sun

The bank and ditch lessen as they reach its summit

filling and boundaries needed to be created. Cleeve and much of its later common already had connections with the settlements in the vale. With its limestone barrows standing in open pasture and visible for miles and with the Cross Dyke also visible for miles around, it must have formed an impressive landscape, but one which quite clearly had strong links to the territory directly at the bottom of the scarp rather than those along the dip slope, which later became known as Charlton Abbots, Postlip and Sevenhampton. By *c.*800BC we could say that there was now enough evidence to draw the tentative conclusion that the territory around Bishop's Cleeve had successfully staked its claim to its hill.

The First Settlements

It is not until the Iron Age (*c.*800BC-43AD) that there appears the first direct evidence of people living on the hill. That evidence comes from an archaeological dig when gravel digging cut into a settlement platform at the King's Beeches in 1902. This revealed clear evidence about life on Cleeve Hill during the Iron Age. Here was a place where pottery was actually made judging by the number of pits containing clay and shaped stones for fashioning pots, in addition to the finished pottery. The pottery has been dated to between the sixth century BC and the first century AD. Some pieces have been identified as Severn Valley ware, showing links with the vale and even further afield as Malvern. Post holes and fragments of daub indicated wooden structures had been built there, but there was no evidence of fortification. Other finds indicated the type of economy which existed then. Many sheep bones were found, including a high proportion of bones from lambs, suggesting they were kept for food. They would have grazed on the upland pasture. Numerous pig bones were discovered. Many of these were from young pigs, which again suggested domesticated animals with nearby woodland providing their pannage. Shells from a woodland species of snail confirmed that woodland must have been close at hand for snails do not travel far,

The King's Beeches stand out on a patch of green, seen from Woodmancote

even during a full, natural lifespan. There was indirect evidence that the settlers possessed dogs from the gnaw marks on many bones, but direct evidence was limited to only one bone and two teeth. Similarly the only evidence for arable farming was indirect, the remains of cattle teeth which could have indicated plough oxen. Although the remains of a horse were found the archaeologists concluded it was more likely to have been for riding than hauling. Here, then, was a small community, with access to pasture and woodland, dependent on farming but still hunting, for the remains of red and roe deer were also found. All the finds were sealed by quarry waste which contained three Roman denarii minted in London in 293AD. Not only do they tell us a date by which the settlement had been abandoned, but give us the earliest evidence for quarrying on the hill, possibly connected to the site at Haymes, although the stone used in Belas Knap indicates quarrying took place in that vicinity in the Neolithic period.

In his report on the excavation, the archaeologist G.W.S. Brewer also noted other Iron Age finds which he included on his map. Unfortunately we know nothing about 'The Graveyard' but Iron Age finds from 'The Stables Quarry' were placed in Cheltenham Museum where they later became unfortunately mixed up with the finds from the King's Beeches. The pottery was very similar, indicating a contemporary date. The stables' site was also undefined, possibly extending to the platform fifty metres to the south of the stables where more Iron Age, and also Romano-British, pottery was picked up in 1972 when a water pipe cut across its south-west corner. We can imagine here another small settlement consisting of a few timber-built huts with thatched roofs sitting in the landscape rather than dominating it, but farming it in a way not unfamiliar today.

Geophysical investigations by the local archaeological society, Gloucestershire Archaeology (GlosArch, formerly Gadarg), of the earthwork known as 'The Ring' in 2019 and 2020 tentatively concluded it could have been the site of a small late Iron Age or Romano-British settlement as traces of two possible building platforms and a hearth were discovered. The investigations were made difficult by the building of a green when the golf course was laid out at the end of the nineteenth century (see Chapter 7). All the possible Iron Age monuments on the hill were examined and planned in the RCHM's Inventory on Iron Age and

CLEEVE HILL

Romano-British monuments in the Gloucestershire Cotswolds, which appeared in 1976 and gives a useful summary of knowledge about the period as it stood in the mid-1970s.

General awareness of the Iron Age in the popular mind is still dominated by hillforts. Some thirty five are spread along the Cotswold scarp from Bath to Chipping Campden; two of them lie in our area of study. Above Nutterswood the hillfort as it can be seen today encloses three acres but it has been estimated a third of the size has been lost through quarrying. In 1779 Samuel Rudder was able to record an entrance fronting the scarp edge which has now gone. Comparison with the excavated hillfort on Crickley Hill fourteen miles to the south-west, would suggest an early Iron Age hillfort, dating from before c.400BC, with a single bank and ditch, developed into a double bank and ditch two or three centuries later. Two sherds of pottery confirm its existence at least between c.700BC and c.400BC. Further geophysical investigations by GlosArch in 2019 and 2022 found evidence of roundhouses, a large number of pits either for storage or indicating postholes for structures and one rectangular building, but as at The Ring investigations were

Cleeve Cloud hillfort showing clearly the extent of damage by quarrying. The large circular feature near the edge is the remains of an enclosure to protect saplings. The golf green cutting the ramparts is also visible towards the top of this aerial view

The hillfort being surveyed by members of GlosArch. The commanding position of the hillfort over the vale can be clearly seen

hampered by another late nineteenth-century golf green. What was its purpose? It can be seen breaking the skyline of the common for miles around. From its position on the hill it has a 180° view of the Severn vale and Cotswold scarp. It was built to be seen and to see; a key land mark in the landscape. Do the large number of pits indicate it served as a storage area for grain? Was it a place of gathering for trade and exchange of livestock? There is no evidence of any high status buildings for a local élite and it is unlikely to have had a religious significance. One function it could not have fulfilled is one of defence, for the ground to the north east rises above it. Nevertheless for the sake of clarity here, it will be referred to as a hillfort.

Artist's impression of an Iron Age roundhouse (M. Aldred)

The ramparts of Nottingham Hill, sketched in 1913 before they became covered with undergrowth

What of the hillfort on Nottingham Hill, the scene of the burial of the Bronze Age hoard? Timothy Darvill considers it to have been an early Iron Age hilltop enclosure built for storing produce and keeping animals. The excavations of 1972 discovered a hearth, storage pits and a trackway which indicated some habitation but it was not possible to decide with certainty a date for this. Its size of 120 acres makes it a different type of hillfort to Cleeve and the two could have been complementary, although the one on Nottingham Hill had earlier origins and could have gone out of use before that on Cleeve Hill was started. If the parallel with Crickley again holds strong, then the hillforts went out of use by c.400BC. The reasons for this change are unclear, except that around this time the large fortified hillforts such as Uley Bury and Salmonsbury camp at Bourton-on-the-Water were developed, possibly suggesting the development of a more hierarchical society, with leaders controlling ever-increasing territories leading ultimately to the emergence of the Dobunni tribe in c.100BC, with their centre at Bagenden near Cirencester. The territory of Cleeve, never isolated from other areas in Britain, became increasingly integrated into a wider political world. Throughout the history of Cleeve Hill this wider context cannot be ignored.

During the Iron Age, if not before, the vale had fully developed as an agrarian landscape. As Bishop's Cleeve has spread away from its historic centre, more Iron Age farmsteads have been discovered than were known when this book first appeared in 1990. At that time only Gilder's Paddock site had been excavated and reported upon. Charles Parry of the county council's archaeological unit led the investigations which found evidence of small paddocks and pits dating to the late Iron Age. Since then, further excavations in 1998 and 2004 on the Tesco site discovered two round houses dated to the middle Iron Age. In 2003 and 2004 Cotswold Archaeology discovered more middle Iron Age ditches and pits on the site of Maxwell Place on Church Road which seemed to link up with those of Gilder's Paddock. Away from the village centre, in 2006 Birmingham University uncovered the remains of a farmstead before the development of Greenacre Way by Bovis Homes. Two middle Iron Age roundhouses were found at the excavations at the Cleevelands in 2014-16. In the trial trenches by Worcestershire Archaeology along Stoke Road in 2015, a number of Iron Age features were discovered. The widening evidence for the nature of the landscape during the Iron Age allowed Cotswold Archaeology to conclude that the local landscape comprised dispersed farmsteads surrounded by arable and open grazing and divided into fields by hedges. In places it was subjected to flooding and so the farmsteads were found on the patches of sands and gravels which dotted the vale.

There are probably more settlement sites to be found in the area but they are not likely to change this pattern. That they were linked to the hill seems obvious from the observation that steep holloways from the vale from Bushcombe Lane in the north to Bentley Lane in the south led directly to a known Iron Age site on the hill. This happened along the whole of the Cotswold edge. On Cleeve Hill they can be traced back to the ancient ridgeway, now the A38, running between Tewkesbury and

Housing along Stockwell Lane easily masks its sunken nature

Gloucester. There is also Granna or Grinnell Lane, climbing Nottingham Hill from Gotherington, possibly linking the Midlands via a river crossing at Tewkesbury, to the south east. Locally, the lanes support an hypothesis that the hill was used by the small settlements in the vale, as the constant traffic caused the surface of these routes led to the formation of the holloways. Then, as now, animals would have been taken to pasture on the upland during the summer. This linkage of vale and hill is supported by archaeological finds at nearby Beckford in the vale where excavations in the 1970s produced first-century BC pottery exactly the same as that found in the hillfort on Bredon Hill.

The Iron Age was an interlude of perhaps eight centuries when continuity of land use and landscape appearance remained stable. The continuing similar needs of farmers possessed of similar technologies would not have changed the landscape dramatically. Elites might have been behind the development of the hillforts, which were occupied and then abandoned over perhaps no more than four hundred years. This does suggest, however, an intensifying competition for territories and their attendant rights to the land which seems to have emerged in the Bronze Age and which has continued in one form or another down to the present day. They remind us that when this part of the territory of the Dobunni came under the influence of the invading Roman armies and became a distant part of the vast Roman Empire shortly after the invasion of Britain in 43AD, the landscape was already developed and its people settled.

The arrival of Roman influences cannot be traced from the archaeological record. Iron Age pottery and timber buildings continued to be produced and most of the population continued to live in traditional ways. Richard Reece, a leading authority on the Cotswolds during the Roman period, called it 'a veneer of Roman culture'. Villas gradually developed as centres of large estates, but the relationship of any villa to the existing farmsteads around it is not totally clear. Perhaps their produce sustained the villa estate and provided a surplus to sell. Consequently some of the 'Iron Age' pottery found on the hill could well date from the Roman period. It may be assumed that the appearance of the hill, pasture above and then areas of woodland along the scarp which rose out of a cultivated vale, changed little during the first centuries AD, although there might have been some regeneration of woodland on the scarp at the end of the period and into the early Saxon period, if parallels in other places are applicable.

Reference has already been made to some Romano-British (43AD-c.400AD) features, thirty sherds of Romano-British pottery and two third-century Roman coins found at Belas Knap led Timothy Darvill to conclude people then seemed to have an interest in what they perceived to be an historic site. A scatter of pottery, carried out with the manure, between there and Wontley perhaps indicated arable cultivation. A few sherds of similar pottery were found near the Stables Quarry and the three coins found at the King's Beeches gave evidence of quarrying at the end of the third century AD. Stone from the hill had been used in the construction and maintenance of the only Romano-British period settlement site on the hill, at Haymes. It was first discovered in 1974 when a water pipeline cut through the upper part of Weir Mead (see map on page 112), and it was completely destroyed in 1985 when the Severn-Trent Water Authority built a reservoir over the site. At these dates the site was excavated by Bernard and Barbara Rawes, two well-known amateur archaeologists, on whose observations the following conclusions are based.

The view looking eastward across the site of Haymes Romano-British settlement shortly before the building of the reservoir in 1985. The excavations took place in the middle distance

The excavations presented a very confused picture because of the soil slumping which had taken place since the site had been abandoned. No clear foundations of buildings were found, but from the finds Bernard thought there may have been three. Baked clay and daub, pottery and stone tiles provided the clues together with a large sill stone which represented a doorway into a building which Bernard considered may have been a temple, possibly a household shrine, during the second century, based on the deposits of the eighteen second-century brooches found close by. Fragments of slag were found, indicating some iron smelting. The evidence of coins indicated occupation from the early second century to the end of the fourth century AD, but the flints dated to the Mesolithic, late Neolithic and early Bronze Ages, together with middle Iron Age brooches and pottery, also suggested an earlier occupation.

The massive sill-stone excavated at Haymes in 1985, which Bernard Rawes felt might have been at the entrance to a shrine (J. Rawes)

Romano-British pottery stretched from the second century to the fifth century with most dating from the second and third centuries. One small blue glass bead was dated to the sixth or seventh centuries, possibly from Sweden or Ireland. This would provide evidence for the continuing use of the site into the Anglo-Saxon period (c.400AD-1066AD), although Bernard made no further comment in his report.

All the evidence points to the existence of a small settlement. There was no direct evidence for arable farming, but the large number of animal bones suggested grazing on the open downland. Dogs were also well represented and were presumably used in sheep farming. Cattle and horses needed pasture, while the presence of pigs' bones, and fragments of bone from red and fallow deer confirm the existence of woodland, as we would expect, although the presence of the flints suggests the immediate area had been cleared for thousands of years. The settlement was probably surrounded by paddocks and small fields, protected by ditches, fences and hedges. Animals continued to graze on the uplands. It is tempting to link this farmstead with the earlier Iron Age settlements

Bronze pins and a seal-box lid; some of the artefacts found at Haymes and now in Cheltenham Museum (J. Rawes)

on the hill, but there is no direct evidence.

What is more certain is that the inhabitants at Haymes would have looked across the vale which had changed little in general appearance for centuries. Bernard likened the farmstead to that found at Tredington when the M5 motorway was built through the area in 1969. This was almost the first archaeological indication that the vale had been cleared of trees and used for farming, confirming that the long-held belief, that when the Anglo-Saxons appeared they were the first to clear the vale of its trees, was erroneous. The developments at Bishop's Cleeve outlined above and which have occurred since Bernard wrote his report, have confirmed just how extensively settled the area had become, with dispersed timber-framed, thatched farmsteads surrounded by animals and crops in paddocks and fields separated by ditches, hedges and fences. Five Romano-British farmsteads were discovered on or near the line of the bypass after its construction started in 1989. Further farmsteads and associated field systems were found at the Iron Age sites listed above at Tesco, Church Road and Home Farm where Charles Parry concluded that the Iron Age activities at Gilder's Paddock had moved across what is now Cheltenham Road to the other side. Somewhere, possibly under or very close to Cleeve Hall, a high-status 'villa' had developed by *c.*300AD for archaeologists have found fragments of wall plaster, hypocaust tiles and high-status Samian pottery spread across the area to the north of the hall. They hypothesised that it had developed out of an earlier late Iron Age farmstead and might have become the centre of an estate which incorporated the other Iron Age farmsteads found in and around the present village. To find its location still presents them with a challenge.

Continuing uncertainties

Much of the discussion in this chapter has focused on the interpretation of chance observations and finds. On the uplands only at Belas Knap, the King's Beeches and Haymes has any serious archaeological research been carried out, and the former two sites were investigated many years ago when techniques for retrieving evidence were much less advanced than they are today. Large scale Ordnance Survey maps from early last century marked 'Ben's Tump' immediately north of the King's Beeches as a possible long barrow. More recent investigations suggest the shape is solely a consequence of adjacent quarrying and its associated trackways. On the other hand we do have knowledge of other finds made in the nineteenth century which are potentially very significant, but which are now lost. In 1811 the *Cheltenham Chronicle* reported the discovery of two large earthenware pots containing gold and silver coins from the end of the fourth century AD 'at Cleeve', presumably on the hill. Half a century later the *Gloucester Journal* recorded the finding by quarrymen around the Nutterswood hillfort of 'soldiers' graves', presumably skeletons in stone coffins, together with some coins, mostly dating from the reign of the third Caesar (Tiberius [14AD-37AD]), plus burnt bones, the foundations of 'a Roman dwelling' and some other relics which they sold to strangers. This took place in 1863. Lord Ellenborough, the lord of Southam manor, stopped the quarrying to carry out a proper investigation but no later report has ever been discovered and the finds were lost. Also in 1863 J. Goding's *Norman's History of Cheltenham* recorded the discovery of a Dobunnic coin (coins were issued between *c.*50 BC and the Roman invasion), a lance head and a human skeleton during quarrying in the entrenchments of Nottingham Hill. No further record of these finds exists, but they do provide possible evidence for a re-occupation of that hillfort at the end of the Iron Age.

In the first edition of this book I had put forward the view that the large figure of a horse carved on the scarp near the hillfort and visible from Cheltenham, about which we learn from Emma Dent's account in the *Winchcombe and Sudeley Record* of March 1891, might have dated back to the Iron Age, although she wrote that it had been cut to honour the visit of King George III to Cheltenham in 1788. She explained how a gang of labourers made an annual visit, starting with breakfast at the Rising Sun Hotel, to recut it. It was so big that it was reputed it could be seen from Gloucester. Thomas Yiend, a quarry man on the hill, related to Emma how he had worked the quarries since 1851 and could remember workmen coming each year to re-cut it. "When these payments ceased there was nothing left to save it from the ruthless hands of the quarrymen", Thomas concluded. I noted in the first edition that a careful investigation of Cheltenham Museum's archive on the 1788 royal visit had produced no reference to the figure. Since then an article found in the *Cheltenham Examiner* of 5 May 1852 complicates the story. Under the heading 'The "Brown Horse" of Cheltenham' the article describes how the outline of a brown horse cut into the hill above Queen's Wood, similar to the white horse of the Wiltshire Downs, was 'worthy of a passing notice', although not quite completed and the view from the town was such that its legs 'are supposed to be understood'. Seen from various places in the town, from the Tewkesbury Road, from Bayshill and from Lansdown, it was the brain child of John Yearsley, who ran a boarding house and wine business in Clarence Street from where he could look across St Mary's churchyard to the hill. A number of workmen were employed on the task who were then treated to 'a good supper with copious draughts of home-brewed', provided no doubt by John Yearsley. Writing forty years later, had Emma Dent relied on hearsay or had there once been two horses on the hill? If so, neither dated back to the Iron Age.

In 2010 a water pipeline was laid across the common from the golf club towards Wontley (See Chapter 8). During a watching brief the archaeologist found what was considered to be the remains of a hedge approximately a quarter of a mile north of the pylons and also, near the boundary of the common at Wontley, two banks and ditches but in none of these locations was there any material to date the features. Sadly nothing of significance was found when the pipe line cut the Cross Dyke so that its dating remains uncertain.

Conclusion

This outline of the earliest developments on Cleeve Hill has enabled the limited evidence to be used to hypothesise that by the Bronze Age at the latest the landscape of the hill as an area of mainly open pasture had largely taken its present form. Although further finds and discoveries will continue to be made on the hill, it is very unlikely they will change the view that by *c.*400AD the present land uses of the common, open pasture for grazing, quarrying and settlement, were in existence, together with the woodlands on the scarp face. This chapter has allowed the introduction of some fundamental concepts underpinning this study: continuity, change and conflict over a scarce economic resource. The major themes of land use, settlement patterns and boundaries will be considered in more detail as the evidence for them becomes more plentiful in the succeeding centuries.

FURTHER READING

Much of this chapter has been based upon my interpretation of a variety of archaeological reports, linking them to the present landscape as relevant. The best starting points for this period are undoubtedly Timothy Darvill's *Prehistoric Gloucestershire: Second Edition* (Amberley Publishing, Stroud, 2011) and Tim Copeland's *Roman Gloucestershire* (The History Press, Stroud, 2011). Alan Saville (ed.), *Archaeology in Gloucestershire* (Cheltenham Art Gallery and Museums, and Bristol and Gloucestershire Archaeological Society, Cheltenham, 1984) is still a useful summary, which was updated in 2006 as *Twenty-Five Years of Archaeology in Gloucestershire* (Cotswold Archaeology; Bristol and Gloucestershire Archaeological Report No.3). This also has relevance for later periods.

Iron Age & Romano-British Monuments in the Gloucestershire Cotswolds (RCHM [England], London, 1976) has very detailed plans with comments on the prehistoric features on the common. The latest investigations into The Ring and hillfort can be found in Phillip Cox, Mike Milward, Les Comtesse, 'Cleeve Cloud Iron Age hillfort and The Ring, Southam, Gloucestershire: Re-assessment by remote sensing and geophysical survey' in *Glevensis No. 55* (Gloucestershire Archaeology, 2022).

There is a comprehensive list, with descriptions of all but the very recent discoveries of the archaeological finds and sites in the area, in the Gloucestershire County Council: Historic Environment Record Archive, accessed at https://www.heritagegateway.org.uk/gateway/ and typing in the place name in the search box. Most of the sites can be found under 'Bishop's Cleeve' and 'Southam'.

The report of the King's Beeches excavations can be found in the *Proceedings of the Cotteswold Naturalists' Field Club* Volume 15 (1904), which can be read online. Many articles have been written in the *Transactions of the Bristol and Gloucestershire Archaeological Society*. Volumes over five years old can be read in full online at the society's website. The major articles used here have been from Volumes 51/2 (1929/30) on Belas Knap; Volume 96 (1978) on the finds from the King's Beeches; Volume 104 (1986) on Haymes; Volume 116 (1998) on Home Farm; Volume 117 (1999) on Gilder's Paddock; Volume 125 (2007) on the Tesco site; Volume 131 (2013) on the Cleeve Hall site; Volume 132 (2014) on Stoke Road near Cheltenham North; Volume 138 (2020) on The Homelands and Volume 139 (2021) on the Cleevelands. There are also individual special reports, viz: *Bristol and Gloucestershire Archaeological Society Report 1* (2002) on the site in Stoke Road by the surgery and *Report 5* (2007) on Church Road. Brief reports on archaeological investigations during the past year are provided in the annual *Transactions*. The report on the pipeline of 2010 is lodged with Cheltenham Art Gallery and Museum. I owe this reference to Tim Copeland.

The Cleeve Common Trust has produced a self-guided archaeological walk across the common which identifies the main sites. A summary can also be found at https://uniofglos.blog/history/2017/11/13/the-archaeology-of-cleeve-common/

2
THE BOUNDARIES ARE DEFINED
(c.400AD-1086)

This syndon tha landgemaeru to Clife.
(These are the bounds of Cleeve)
  G.B. Grundy, *Saxon Charters and Field Names of Gloucestershire*, part 1,
1935

Sources and Contexts

The six hundred years following the Roman occupation of the area are important in the evolution of Cleeve Hill and its common, for it is during this period that the boundaries of the common were first recorded. In general, however, there is a lack of evidence for the period between the decline of Roman Britain and Domesday and it is necessary to use a broader context to understand more clearly the changes, continuities and conflicts of the period.

A long-held traditional view of the Anglo-Saxon invasions dating back to the Victorian era is of a people slaughtering the remaining Romano-British population or driving them to Wales and the West Country, taking over an empty landscape where they built their villages and managed open fields, leaving the margins of their territories as woodland and waste. They brought cataclysm and change into the landscape. Superficially the development of the Cleeve area fits this model. Many place-names undoubtedly date from the Saxon period: Cleeve itself ('at the cliff'), Cockbury (Cocca's camp), Padcombe (Pata's valley), Wontley (Honta's burial mound). The woodland lay away from the arable on the scarp slopes, and the so-called waste, Cleeve Common, ran to the territorial boundary. This follows a commonly accepted perception of the period as 'the Dark Ages', but the reality was very different.

The previous chapter has shown how the landscape was well-developed by the time of the decline of the Roman influence in the fifth century. The Anglo-Saxon 'invasions' led to a political and cultural takeover of an existing population by a relatively small number of people. In places Romano-British leaders, such as the legendary King Arthur, resisted the westward advance, but overall there was no mass slaughter, no resettlement of the existing population and no instant foundation of new villages. In Gloucester and Cirencester there is clear evidence of these Romano-British centres still existing as settlements long after the traditional end of the Roman period in 410AD, and being of enough significance to be recorded as falling to the Saxons after the Battle of Dyrham in 577AD.

Since the first edition of this book in 1990, the archaeological excavations arising from the development of Bishop's Cleeve have also thrown more light on the vale and the hill between the end of the Romano-British period and the arrival of the Normans. In 1990 the archaeological evidence and historical context were limited. One coin dated to *c.*390AD, found by Bernard Rawes on the Haymes settlement site, provided a latest date for Romano-British occupation on the hill, but the single blue glass bead from the sixth or seventh century provides evidence of a human presence on the site in the early Saxon period. In 1969 a possible sixth-century Saxon cemetery was excavated during gravel digging in the field to the west of Lower Farm off the bypass on the eastern edge of the present Grundon site. Unfortunately a report was not produced until 2000 by which time some of the finds, especially bones, had been lost. Neil Holbrook of Cotswold Archaeology, who compiled the report, found evidence for twenty individuals and using the grave goods associated with them concluded the cemetery had been in use for a relatively short time *c.*525AD-*c.*575AD. Where it was possible to give an age to the skeletons the youngest was five and the oldest forty five. He used the grave goods to conclude these people were Saxons, rather then Angles, but it was impossible to decide whether these people were really incomers or inhabitants of the area who had adopted the new life style. Neil also concluded that the presence of a small community meant that the local field systems dating back to the Iron Age would still have been used. The modern developments in and around the village have thrown light on this continuity.

One of the major problems facing archaeologists working on this period is that the nature of the evidence changed considerably. As the Romano-British systems broke down, commercially-produced pottery ceased, to be largely replaced by vessels of wood and leather which rot over time and so are rarely found in excavations. Saxon pottery was of very poor quality and little has been found. Masonry buildings ceased, to be replaced by timber and thatch, which again don't survive. Nevertheless the excavations in and around the centre of Bishop's Cleeve have thrown more light on this period than was known in 1990. Excavations at Home Farm found one sherd, or piece, of hand-made Anglo-Saxon pottery, at the bottom of a boundary ditch dug in the fourth century, of a type which suggested strongly the boundary was still in use up to the eighth century. Eighteen sherds were found at the same site in the upper fills of other ditches. On the Tesco site a large number of 238 sherds of pottery were discovered, some again at the bottom of an earlier ditch but most as part of the filling of two small streams. The sherd of pottery found in the nearby Stoke Road excavations by a semi-circle of postholes allowed the archaeologists to conclude here had been some sort of construction, they weren't sure what, dated to between the seventh and ninth centuries. Although the pottery is difficult to date, it suggests that people were still living in small farmsteads in the area in and around the present village, but how might this relate to Cleeve Hill?

At present the bead from Haymes is the only tangible evidence we have that people were on the hill, but it must be remembered that the evidence for this period has largely rotted away. However, we can make some inferences from what has been found in the vale. Animals were kept there and it would be very likely that the open pasture continued to be used for grazing. Timber for construction, as evidenced at Stoke Road, and wood for handles, wattles and fuel was still needed and so the woodlands on the hill continued to be exploited. We are more certain that quarrying continued because at Home Farm the excavators discovered a possible Saxon lamp, a trough and a large slab, all made from the sort of stone found on the hill.

Turning from the archaeological evidence which is very slight and open to interpretation, we know much more about the hill from the earliest surviving piece of written evidence, a charter granting land, which has been dated to 777AD-779AD. It is a grant of a unit of land by Ealdred, a sub-king of the Hwicce, to a *monasterium* at Cleeve with the permission of the famous King Offa of Mercia. The *monasterium* was not a monastery but an important minster church from which the priests would go out to Christianise the surrounding area. In the grant Offa freed the land from paying him an annual tax to support his army which meant all the profits from the land could go to the *monasterium*. What was the context of the grant?

Until c.800AD Bishop's Cleeve lay in the kingdom of the Hwicce. Its origins are obscure but Margaret Gelling, who was one of the country's leading place-name scholars, suggested the word means an 'ark' or 'chest'. The description suits the area around Winchcombe, lying in a valley bottom between surrounding hills. The area of Cleeve lay near the heartland of the Hwiccan territory. The origins of the kingdom are obscure. Some historians have used the close relationship of the finds of Dobunnic coins from before the Roman invasion with the territory of the Hwicce to postulate the kingdom arose out of the territory of the tribe. As Della Hooke, from Birmingham University, pointed out the boundaries of the tribe are unknown. She favoured an origin as a kingdom set up by the kings of Mercia to control a mixed population of British and Anglo-Saxon people in the seventh century. In the eighth century the rulers of the Hwicce were being described as sub-kings but by the early ninth century they were being referred to as *ealdermen* – of royal birth but subject to the authority of the king, in this case the king of Mercia, the large kingdom covering most of central England and so by that date there had ceased to be a separate Hwiccan kingdom.

In 679AD the bishopric of Worcester was established to formalise the conversion of the people of the Hwicce to Christianity. Bishop's Cleeve continued as part of this diocese until 1561. Within the Worcester bishopric, many minster churches were created to evangelize the area. Cleeve was one of these places as were Beckford, Cheltenham and Winchcombe. This suggests that there were a sufficient number of people living in the area to make such a venture worthwhile. At some time before 777AD-779AD the Hwiccan kings had granted part of the land they lived on to support a minster at Cleeve, presumably through rents and produce. A church dedicated to St Michael the Archangel was built, presumably on the same site as the existing church, although its oldest parts only date back to the end of the twelfth century. The choice of dedication is an interesting one because churches dedicated to St Michael seem to be associated with high ground. Historians are agreed that this was Cleeve Hill, which would have reinforced the importance of the hill in the perceptions of the people. Then between 777AD and 779AD, a further grant of land was made to the minster. The details are that Ealdred granted fifteen *mansiones*, or hides, of land at a place called *Timbingctun,* lying adjacent to the estate already held by the minster *aet Clife*. Here is the earliest recording of the name 'Cleeve', which means the place at the cliff i.e. the cliff-like face of Cleeve Hill. *Timbingctun* can be translated as the settlement of the people/family of an unknown man called *Tymba*. *Timbingctun* is described as lying under *Wendlesclif,* i.e. the rock of the mountain, on the north side of the brook called *Tyrl*. Although the name applied to an estate or area of land and not a

This view above Southam illustrates how Timbingctun estate was centred here rather on Bishop's Cleeve, as Dr Grundy had supposed. The scarp remains heavily wooded even today

settlement, it was clearly the area around Southam, but this earlier name for the estate has completely disappeared. In these descriptions there is probably sufficient evidence to conclude part at least of the exposed rocks of Cleeve Cloud had been created by quarrying. There is also crucial evidence that the boundaries of the estate were already well known, for in addition to the location as north of the *Tyrl*, now Hyde Brook, the phrase 'with its own boundaries' was added, although at this date the pasture land on Cleeve Hill might have been shared by the surrounding communities. The two combined estates became the basis of the ancient ecclesiastical parish of Bishop's Cleeve, covering also Brockhampton, Gotherington, Southam, Stoke Orchard and Woodmancote. It lasted as an important land unit for over a thousand years.

There are two further points for discussion which arise from the above charter. The first is very speculative. Did these two estates granted to the minster have as their origins the territories associated with the Romano-British villas at Haymes and the one presumed to have existed near the centre of Bishop's Cleeve? We will probably never know

The two ploughed fields in the middle and on the left formed Muckmead

but it remains a possibility. In both places evidence dating from this early Anglo-Saxon period has been found. The second point concerns the disappearance of *Timbingctun* and the appearance of 'Southam'. In c.991AD the Bishop of Worcester, who since 889AD at the latest, held most of the estate based on Cleeve, which had been formed by combining the two earlier estates as explained above, leased out two hides of land at Southam. This is the earliest recording of that name. It was the settlement, i.e. 'ham', to the south of the main settlement of Cleeve and this was its main characteristic and so any earlier name was redundant. However, there does exist an alternative explanation for the formation of 'Southam', that it referred to the southern water meadow ('hamm'), later known as *Muckmead* ('big meadow'), for growing hay, to distinguish it from the northern water meadow, the name of which survives today as Northenham, the name given to the former allotments which lay in the Cleevelands alongside the Bishop's Cleeve bypass. We shall never know which one of these two meanings is correct.

The life of the minster as an independent church was short. Its takeover by the Bishop of Worcester was possibly to prevent the takeover of a failing venture by any one else. The bishop left a small estate to support the rector of the church, presumably the priest recorded in Domesday Book. In 1284 'Cleeve' became 'Bishop's Cleeve' to distinguish it from Cleeve Prior on the River Avon north of Evesham which belonged to the prior of Worcester Abbey. Being taken over by the bishop was a fortunate development for the historian because it ensured Bishop's Cleeve came into the hands of an institution which kept and preserved careful records. Without them our knowledge of Cleeve Hill and its common would be much the poorer.

The Boundaries attached to the Land Charter

It is important to understand that the charter dates from 777AD-779AD but the descriptions of the boundaries of the land are much later additions and describe the boundaries of the area formed by the two estates. The charter and boundary descriptions now exist in two copies in the Cotton manuscripts in the British Museum. The earlier is known as Birch's *Cartularium Saxonicum* Number 246 and probably dates from the early eleventh century. A second copy was made later in the same century at a difficult time for the church at Worcester for it had recently lost its manors at Sodbury, Tetbury and Woodchester. This could explain some of the differences between the two copies. There was a more detailed description of the boundary on the eastern edge of the territory, where it might have been under threat of encroachment from the adjacent lands of Winchcombe Abbey. The boundaries were first examined in print by Dr G.B. Grundy in 1935, and the introductory heading for this chapter is taken from his book. He mistakenly suggested *Timbingctun* was the name of the land unit and Cleeve the name of the minster church, making no distinction between the two estates.

The complete bounds provide a fascinating glimpse into the landscape and economy of Cleeve and its surrounding area during the late Saxon period, but here we are principally concerned with the evidence it provides for the hill and its common. The whole area included a variety of land use, arable, meadow, woodland and pasture. The careful definition of the boundaries around Cleeve Common indicate that it was now clearly attached to the territory associated with Cleeve in the vale and that it had already become a crucial part of the local economy which the church at Worcester sought to defend against other claimants.

The Boundaries

Both charters have the boundary clauses in Old English, which has been used on the first two maps in this chapter. The descriptions here in the text are in modern English, and to help identification, features which correspond in both descriptions have been given the same number. Where Birch's charter 246 gives boundary points on the hill, they can be translated as follows:

> From the gate of [Cocca's] camp (1) to Hengest's headland (2). So to the slade to Cyppa's enclosure (3) to a little stream. Along the little stream to the highway to hind's leap (4). Then to the clear spring. Along the combe to fern slade (5). Then to Pata's combe (6). Then to wolf clearing (7). Then to calf hollows (probably a copying error for calf hill) along the way to woodpecker meadows (8), and so to wheel hollow (9), and so to Anta's barrow (10), and so to Pippa's slade and to Herriht's barrow, and to wheelway to the roedeer fence to the hawk spring along the small stream to the Tirle (11).

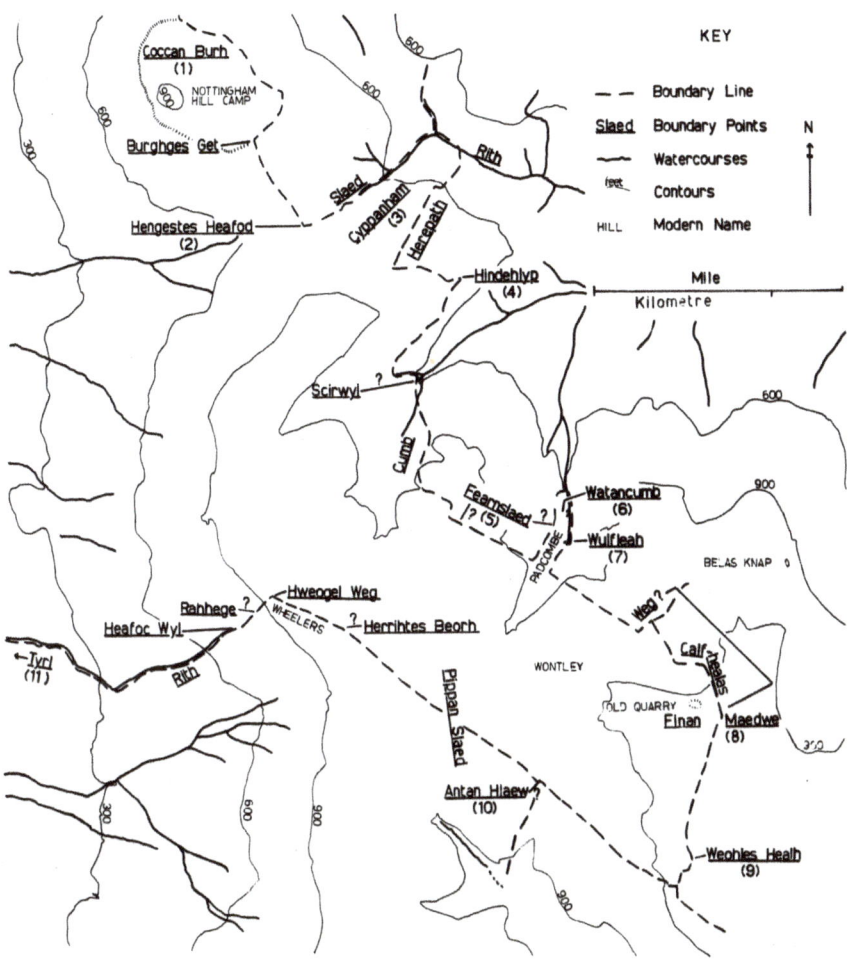

The boundary features defined in Birch's charter 246, recorded in the early eleventh century

The points correspond so closely with known points on the present parish boundary that a strong case can be made for the boundary having remained constant for a thousand years until the present. Where there is some uncertainty, the names have been given a question mark on the map. The details can be followed on any modern large scale Ordnance Survey map showing the parish boundary.

The camp is Nottingham Hill Iron Age hillfort. The boundary came up the prehistoric routeway of Granna Lane and ran round the north-eastern edge of the camp. This is precipitous in many places which made it an obvious boundary placing this area of open land firmly in Cleeve and not shared with Prescott, which belonged to Winchcombe Abbey until the Dissolution. It remained common land until the enclosure of Gotherington, part of the historic territory of Cleeve, in 1807. Hengest's headland was at the crossroads with B4632 although that obviously did not exist at this early date. The Saxon word *slaed*, our 'slade', meant a small valley with a wet bottom. The parish boundary still follows what becomes the valley of Langley Brook which runs round Cyppa's enclosure as it turns south east towards Winchcombe. Having followed a natural feature, the boundary next ran round the north west edge of the present Dryfield Farm before making two right-angled turns to run south south west along the field boundary to the northern boundary of the common. The sharp right angles could suggest this area was already cultivated and the boundary divided up the arable land. The

The fence dividing the common from Postlip Warren runs straight up the valley side, apart from skirting round the small quarry. Such straight boundaries indicate an artificially divided landscape, here between Cleeve and Winchcombe

highway might have linked the stream to the common as on the map, or it might have been the track, later the turnpike road, running parallel to the boundary of the common to Hind's leap, a man-made feature, at the very sharp turn the boundary makes at the gate on the track down to Postlip. The clear spring was located at the very end of Dry Bottom at the foot of Postlip Quarries from where the boundary climbed out of Watery Bottom above the Washpool along a 'cumb' – a steep-sided valley. The straight line of the boundary as it climbed out of the valley is an obvious artificial creation, dividing the open pasture which must have been inter-commoned between Cleeve and Postlip at an earlier date. It then ran along a slade with ferns to Padcombe Bottom; another steep-sided valley. The clearing where wolves could be found was another marker in Padcombe as the boundary turned on itself and ran across calf hill to reach the ancient way which still runs north to south through Wontley Farm. Woodpecker meadow must have been the name given to the shallow valley running south east from Wontley. Wheel Way was the name given to the track which leaves the common near the Wardens' Wood car park and the boundary then ran almost due south from the meadow to reach it. It clearly divided an important area of woodland into two between Cleeve and Winchcombe, artificially creating East Wood and West Wood. Historians believe that when King Coenwulf/Kenwulf founded a religious settlement at Winchcombe, possibly a re-founding of its earlier *monasterium*, in 798AD, he included Charlton Abbots in his grants. As at Postlip, the straight line running through the wood would suggest it had once been inter-commoned for its resources. This might be evidence that the boundaries had been fixed by 798AD, as here it shared a common boundary with Cleeve, but we might never be certain, as there is no clear evidence until this boundary was recorded in the eleventh century.

The possible site of Anta's barrow

The straight southern wall of West Down indicates the division of a shared common. In this case with Sevenhampton whose share of the common was enclosed in 1814 and became farmed land. This created the contrast in land use seen today

From the corner of the common to the wheelway the boundary ran in the straight line which still defines the southern boundary of the common. This was another artificial line dividing land that had previously been inter-commoned as its modern name 'West Down' indicates, because it lies to the east of Bishop's Cleeve. Anta's barrow gave its name to Wontley and was still visible on the boundary in 1830. The most likely place for its location is at or near the small kink in the boundary at present used to store animal pens for the Trust. The field here to the north of West Down was called Barrow Piece in 1830, providing further evidence for its location here. Pippa's slade is difficult to locate but could have been the very southern end of Padcombe Bottom. Herriht's barrow must have stood on the sky line beyond the pylons as here the boundary of the common deflects more to the west. The lidar aerial

Wheeler's Corner. This is where the road described by John Ogilby in 1675 entered the common (see Chapter 5)

view shows a very slight hump at this point but its interpretation at present remains inconclusive. Wheeler's Corner is still an entrance to the common. Few people who use it are aware it is a name in use a thousand years ago as the wheelway. The boundary here dropped down the scarp

The importance of water supply for animals on the upland is reinforced by references in the boundary clauses. This photograph of Hawk Spring is from the first edition as the intervening years have seen the growth of vegetation which has obscured the site

and off the hill into the vale, past a roedeer hedge and the spring where hawks drank to the small stream which became the Tirle, which we know as the Hyde Brook, skirting the southern edge of Queen's Wood and following once again the natural features in the landscape.

This second copy defined very few landmarks in the western part of the territory but it included much detail on the hill. The relevant part of the boundary is as follows:

> From Cocca's camp (1) to Hengest's headland (2) to Cyppa's enclosure (3) to Tocca's camp (here the scribe seems to have made an error and copied again the first landmark) to hind's leap (4) to mill spring to clear spring to fern slade (5) to four ways to Pata's combe (6) where stand an apple tree and a maple tree which have grown together. From the trees to wolf clearing (7) to the old ditch to the Welsh way to limestone hill to woodpecker's meadow (8) to wheelway (9) to Sprog's clearing to the old ditch to the single thorn tree to Honta's barrow (10) to the steep wooded slope with a spring in it (*Swelhongre*) to the grey (or boundary) stone to the South Tirle (11).

The church at Worcester was concerned to lay down a detailed description of the eastern boundary to cement its claim to valuable pasture on the hill from the surrounding communities. Charlton Abbots, Sevenhampton and Prestbury all abut Cleeve common around its south eastern extremity around Wontley and along West Down. The reference to two 'old ditches', reinforces artificial divisions in the landscape. From clearance in the Bronze Age to the present time, Cleeve seems to have been able to dominate this area of downland despite pressure from neighbouring communities and landlords, although this is now difficult to trace solely from the landscape; Sevenhampton's share of West Down

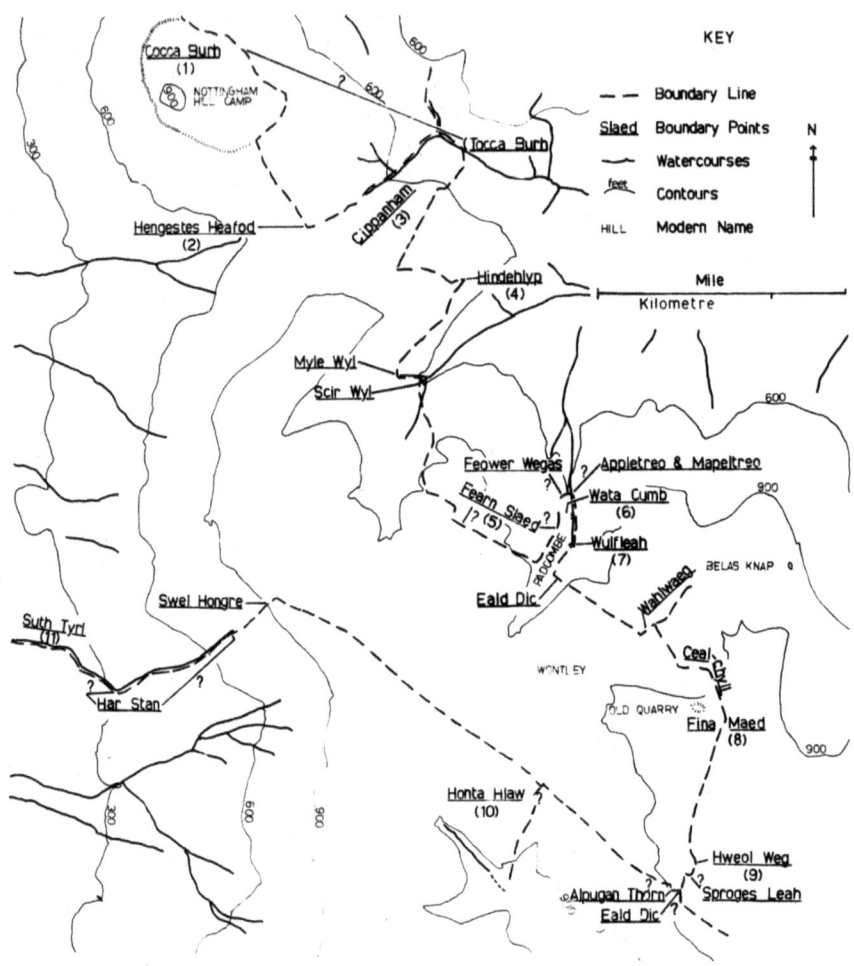

The boundary features defined in the late eleventh-century copy of the Timbingctun charter

was converted to arable after its enclosure in 1814. The names West Down and West Wood do remain to suggest conflicting claims to the land on this part of the hill. Cleeve's East Wood or Wontley Wood was cleared in the nineteenth century leaving today's straight line of the remaining woodland parallel to the Saxon boundary and hence this remaining woodland is known only as West Wood. It is possible that access to this important area of woodland was a main reason that the area of what is now Cleeve Common became attached to Cleeve, either by a Hwiccan king or by the Bishop of Worcester. The estate then contained arable and meadow in the vale, pasture and woodland on the hill; all essential components of a balanced land unit. Apart from the straight lines in the boundary, another strong piece of evidence of inter-commoning is the tongue of Cleeve territory which lies in Padcombe Bottom. On the Cotswolds this is called a 'chure', or more commonly a 'ture', which was designed to allow access to water for the grazing animals. A small stream flows along the bottom of this steep-sided valley and although it can dry up in summer, it provided water for Cleeve's livestock on the common in an area otherwise lacking this important resource and so it was important to create this boundary encroachment into Winchcombe Abbey's estate. The situation of an undivided upland pasture being shared by closely defined lowland territories has many parallels, such as the Dartmoor example quoted in the Introduction.

Having now defined the eastern boundaries of the common and having established that it continued to be an area under pressure of differing claims, what can the bounds tell us about the landscape on Cleeve Hill in the Saxon period?

The Saxon Landscape

The whole of the Cleeve estate was assessed at thirty hides in Domesday Book; this meant that by 1086 it paid tax at thirty units of assessment, but in the eighth century this would have meant literally that it could have supported thirty families. Two estate names, Cleeve and *Timbingctun*, have already been encountered, as have some personal names, Cocca, Cyppa, Pata, although whether these were legendary or real we do not know.

Pressure on the landscape pushed arable farming high up the scarp. Hengest's (a mythical name) headland, i.e. where the team of oxen was turned, reached up to Wickfield Lane near the route of the B4632, the parcel of land later farmed as Stony Cockbury estate was already in existence as Cyppa's enclosure and at the end of West Down Sprog had made a clearing. There is ample evidence for the use of the downs as pasture for the grazing of domestic and wild animals. Hindleap above Postlip, and Roedeer Fence above Southam probably indicated one-way jumps for wild animals on to the common, but not off it, which protected nearby arable crops and provided for easier hunting. The ture at Padcombe illustrates how water supply could be a problem for the stock grazing on the hill and the clearing used by wolves at this point also serves as a reminder of the dangers the stock faced from wild animals. The existence of a clearing also indicated the presence of woodland there, as can still be found today.

Woodland was an important resource in the local economy, providing timber for buildings and large items, coppiced wood for smaller items such as hurdles and handles, brushwood for lighting, and pannage for pigs. Wild bees provided honey and the woodland birds were killed for game. Timber grew in East and West Wood. It must have been the home of the woodpeckers which gave the neighbouring meadow its name. Solitary thorn trees still grow at the far end of West Down, as recorded in the second copy of the boundary. Woodland on the slopes of the scarp, probably coppiced wood, was indicated by *Swelhongre* above Southam. Although the woods on the western scarp face at Queen's, Stutfield and Thrift Woods are not on the boundary and so not named, the name 'Thrift' comes from an Old English word for wood, which is evidence it existed at the time the boundaries were described. Crucially this suggests that this part of the eastern boundary of the common was already in existence. Queen's Wood probably takes its name from Queen Catherine, the widow of King Henry V, who was granted a manor

The wood in the centre of the photograph is the descendant of that on Swelhongre

at Southam by her son King Henry VI in 1422. The origin of the name Stutfield is not known. All three today are classified as ancient woodland.

The wider economy is also indicated in the boundary landmarks. The mill spring above Postlip (which on topographical evidence must correspond to the clear spring in the earlier charter) recorded in the later eleventh century is evidence for at least one mill at Postlip and suggests it was built after the first copy of the charter boundary was drawn up. The reference to *Wendlesclif* in the introduction to the charter itself provides evidence for quarrying at Cleeve Cloud. Quarrying was also suggested by the description of 'limestone hill' near Wontley.

The bluebells growing in Thrift Wood are an indicator of ancient woodland

Cleeve Common was not only an important local resource but also an area crossed by many trackways. Charter references to them have been marked on the two maps. They must predate the boundary as it used them as identifiable landmarks. Granna or Grinnell Lane, described in Chapter One, was referred to as the old way or the green way leading through Cockbury Camp and on to the common and today known as White Way to fork and be picked up again in its eastern arm as wheel hollow, or way, leading from West Down and on to the Cotswolds through Roel Gate. The name Welsh Way, given to the track that runs north to south through the remains of Wontley Farm, indicated a long distance trackway used by strangers or foreigners. Its route from Winchcombe to Wycomb near Andoversford can still be traced on the present large scale Ordnance Survey map. Another track crossed the hill, coming up from Prestbury as a holloway past Queenwood settlement, and recorded as 'Wheleway' at Wheeler's Corner. It was by this track that John Ogilby recommended travellers between Gloucester and Coventry crossed the hill in 1675. From the hill the recommended way split, one route descended to Postlip directly and the other down

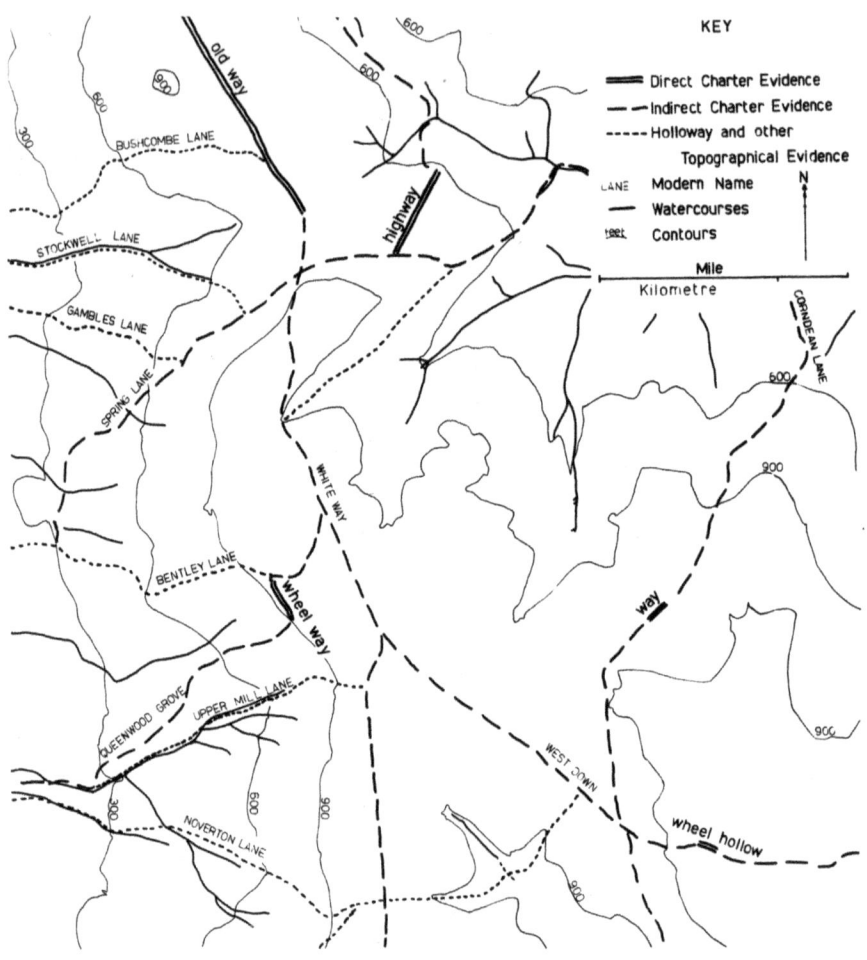

Cleeve Common and the scarp are criss-crossed by trackways. These are known to have been in existence by the early eleventh century; many are probably prehistoric (see Chapter One)

Dry Bottom. 'Four ways', recorded in the later copy of the boundaries, remains enigmatic. It was placed at the northern end of Padcombe yet there is little topographical or other documentary evidence to indicate a crossroads; this was perhaps another copying error. Dr Grundy searched in vain for it in 1935.

This discussion of the trackways across the hill, many of them originating in prehistory is a convenient place to consider the mysterious stone block made of peagrit and known as Huddleston's Table which lies between the hamlet of Nutterswood and the trees once known as

The White Way crosses the common from north-west to south-east

the Three Sisters, but now as The Twins because only two remain. Many local folk-tales are told about it. By tradition it is said to mark one of the rare occasions when Cleeve Hill featured in what might loosely be called national history. The legend recounts that when Coenwulf/Kenulf, king of Mercia, dedicated the great Benedictine Abbey in Winchcombe in 811AD, he took leave of several of his important guests at this spot, notable among them the king of Kent. However the evidence does not support this story. Firstly, the parting would not have taken place at this spot. Not only has the stone been moved at least once in living memory, but the present spot is not

The remains of Wontley Farm with the 'Welsh Way' running south towards Wycomb

on any trackway known to have been in use in 811AD according to the charter and topographical evidence. Secondly, the Huddleston family did not move to Southam until the 1520s, although it has been suggested that it is only a copy of an original.

Nevertheless the stone has continued to intrigue observers. In 1779 the *Gentleman's Magazine*

Huddleston's table with the Three Sisters on the sky line (T. Curr

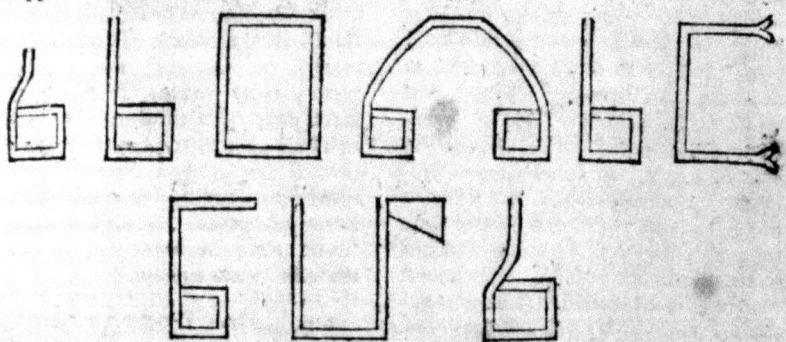

Inscription near Cheltenham.—*Anecdotes of Bishop* Hare.   441

Mr. URBAN,

I Laſt ſummer met with ſome traces of an irregular and not very extenſive encampment, upon the edge of the Glouceſterſhire Hills, near Cleve-Clouds, and juſt above Cheltenham. Upon ſome plain ground at a ſmall diſtance below the edge of the hill, which on this ſide forms a natural barrier to the encampment, is a large, nearly cubic, hewn ſtone, with the following inſcription upon its upper ſurface:

The characters ſtand in the above order, ſix in the firſt line, and three underneath; and are inſcribed nearly in the middle of the upper ſide of the ſtone. On the ſame ſide, and ſeemingly not long ſince, has been cut with a tool, in Roman characters, Huddleſton's Table. Whether this is to be conſidered as the information of tradition, or of ſome antiquarian who has inveſtigated this piece of antiquity, is uncertain. All the information that was obtained at a village a ſmall diſtance from hence, in the road to Cheltenham, relative to either the encampment or the ſtone, was, that the trenches were thrown up in the time of Oliver Cromwell. But if the civil war in the laſt century had been more conſiderable and extenſive than it was, it could hardly have been the occaſion of more works of this kind than report now attributes to it in theſe parts of the kingdom, notwithſtanding that, when the appeal was made to arms, the conteſt began, was chiefly continued, and terminated here. The ſtone's being hewn into a regular figure, the uniformity of the characters, together with its ſituation near an encampment, may be conſidered as ſome proofs of the authenticity of this inſcription.

As it is not noticed in Camden, and I have not been able to procure any information relative to it, ſhall be much obliged by your inſertion of it, and to any gentleman that will favour me with his ſentiments upon it.

Yours, &c.   H. M. W.

The Gentleman's Magazine article on Huddleston's table (Gloucester Library)

featured it in a short article which is more informative to the historian on eighteenth-century belief in Druids and mythology than about the stone itself. Likewise, the illustration taken from Emma Dent's *Annals of Winchcombe and Sudeley* informs us more about late-Victorian Romanticism than about the stone. Both pieces, however, illustrate the fascination with the unexplained, and although there is no evidence to

The origins of Huddleston's Table – a mid-Victorian fantasy

link the stone to the story, if there ever was such a parting it could very well have taken place somewhere on the hill because of the network of trackways which cross it.

The boundary clauses provided evidence of archaeological features which in some cases have subsequently been destroyed. Cocca's Camp referred to the hillfort on Nottingham Hill and has given its name to an area immediately to the east where can be found Rushy Cockbury, Cockbury Butts and Stony Cockbury (now Cockbury Court), although only the latter lies in the parish of Bishop's Cleeve. Today the hill is known as Nottingham Hill after William de Nottingham, who was the steward of the Bishop of Worcester between 1450 and 1470. Further round the bounds, Anta's Barrow (wrongly identified as Belas Knap by Dr Grundy) and Herriht's Barrow lie on the long straight southern boundary of West Down. They have already been discussed.

In this late Saxon period we know far more about the landscape and the boundaries on the hill than about the people who exploited the landscape, and this, in turn, is a result of the change in the type of evidence from archaeological to documentary. The picture that has emerged of the hill from the eleventh-century descriptions of the boundary attached to the eighth-century charter is of an area of upland plateau, extensively used for grazing by wild and domestic animals, essentially open as today with a wooded scarp. Even at this early date two recurring features are very apparent: one, people continuing to mould the landscape, with hindleaps, ditches, enclosures, clearings for arable, pasture and highways and, secondly, pressure on such a scarce resource, which led to the careful stating of the eastern limits in the eleventh century. This pressure helps to explain the jagged route of the boundary of the present common. One major difference with today is that long-distance travellers moved across the pasture and not across the face of the scarp as does the present B4632. Essentially, however, the upland pasture which became Cleeve Common with its boundaries had been created before the Norman conquest and possibly several centuries earlier.

Domesday Book

The successful Norman takeover of 1066 would seem to herald a new era in English history and provide an obvious starting point for the next chapter. Yet the great Domesday Book, which originated not very far away when King William visited Gloucester for Christmas in 1085, should be seen rather as a statement of the nature of the countryside at the end of the Saxon period than an early description of the area in the later Middle Ages.

There is no record of how the local peasants viewed William's commissioners, but his questions and their answers are not particularly helpful in throwing additional light on the development of the hill by the end of the eleventh century. The Conquest itself had made little impact. Bishop Wulfstan continued as Bishop of Worcester but he was an absentee landlord. Cleeve's church was not rebuilt, from Cleeve Hill stone, for almost another century, and no castle was ever built. Like most settlements in this area of Gloucestershire, the land belonging to the manor was mostly arable. The value of the manor had fallen from £36 immediately before the conquest to £26 in 1085. Presumably the bishop was having difficulty in administering his estate. The territory of Cleeve was recorded as the same thirty hides recorded in the land charter, but by 1085 Gotherington, Southam and the now lost *Sapletone*, which probably lay to the west of Southam, had been leased by the bishop to Durand, the

Sheriff of Gloucestershire, who had been one of William's many followers rewarded by positions of authority and land grants after the victory at Hastings.

The subdivision of large estates is well documented as a feature of economic and social change in the late Saxon period and Cleeve fits into this pattern, illustrated by the development of the separate sub-manor of Southam in 991AD, when two hides were leased out by Bishop Oswald to Ethelstan his brother; by mid eleventh century this sub-manor had increased to five hides; by Domesday it had expanded to six although its boundaries are not exactly known; their final form might be those of the later Medieval manor, which were first recorded in 1472 and which are discussed more fully in the next chapter. Cockbury might have been the extra sixth hide on this estate. Thus tenants of both Cleeve and Southam had rights to the hill and no doubt were already quarrelling over the assertion of those rights, as they were to continue to do so for nine hundred years. If we remember that the original land grant of the late eighth century referred to two separate areas of land which subsequently became one, it would seem that the thirty hide area entered in Domesday for Cleeve only survived under the direct control of the Bishop of Worcester for less than two centuries.

Conclusion

Cleeve Hill lay on the edge of a great estate and it is fortunate that the Saxon charter copyists were so interested in defining the edges of landholding units, since this allows a good understanding of a landscape not very different from that of today; pasture for grazing, woodland on the scarp with more arable on the scarp. This upland plateau was marginal not only to the forerunners of the communities of Bishop's Cleeve and Southam, but to those of the other communities which had claimed a part for themselves; Charlton Abbots, Postlip and Winchcombe, Prestbury and Sevenhampton. The boundaries described here clearly show that by the end of this period Cleeve had successfully claimed most of the hill as its territory. Into this landscape we can begin to place personal names, if not real people, Cocca, Hengest, Cyppa, Pata, Sprog, which implies that people were clearly responsible in their own small ways for developing the landscape. The hill was marginal to the main settlements but it had already emerged as a scarce resource. As the quantity of topographical and documentary evidence increases, we can also begin to distinguish sub-themes within the competition for land use; between manors, between pasture for grazing, woodland and settlement. It seems sensible to divide up the succeeding chapters into these sub-themes. The silent, majestic appearance of the hill today belies a cacophony of voices from the past each making their own claim.

FURTHER READING

This chapter has been based upon extensive fieldwalking following the boundaries of the land charter printed in G.B. Grundy, *Saxon Charters and Fieldnames of Gloucestershire, Volume 1* (Bristol and Gloucestershire Archaeological Society, Bristol, 1935) pages 71-90. They can now be found online at https://ia802706.us.archive.org/1/items/cartulariumsaxo02bircgoog/cartulariumsaxo02bircgoog.pdf. A.H. Smith, *The Place Names of Gloucestershire* (Cambridge University Press, Cambridge, 1965) has helped with the resolution of place-names, particularly in pages 86-95 in Volume 2. The interpretations have also been helped by careful study of lidar images available at https://www.lidarfinder.com from where the images in this book have been taken. This website is particularly useful as it allows for a seamless transition to modern aerial photographs of the same area. The historic twenty five inch Ordnance Survey maps of 1875, available online at the National Library of Scotland's website https://maps.nls.uk/os/6inch-england-and-wales/index.html, have also been used. John Moore's translation and commentary upon Domesday, published as *Gloucestershire Domesday Book* (Phillimore, Chichester, 1982), has helped the discussion on Domesday.

Several books have helped with the wider context. Carolyn Heighway's *Anglo-Saxon Gloucestershire* (Alan Sutton Publishing, Gloucester, 1987) is still a convenient summary of the period. Christopher Dyer's *Lords and Peasants in a Changing Society* (Cambridge University Press, Cambridge, 1981) and *Standards of Living in the Later Middle Ages* (Cambridge University Press, Cambridge, 1989) put the area into the context of the Bishop of Worcester's estates. They also have relevance for the next chapter. Della Hooke's *The Anglo-Saxon Landscape* (Manchester University Press, Manchester, 1985) recreates the landscape of the Hwicce by exploiting the potential of the West Midland Saxon land charters. The development of the territory of Hwicce is discussed by Steven Bassett in a collection of essays edited by him as *The Origins of the Anglo-Saxon Kingdoms* (Leicester University Press, Leicester, 1989). For his study of the Cleve charters in detail, see his chapter 'The Anglo-Saxon Minster at Bishop's Cleeve (Gloucestershire) and its Lands' in *Names, Texts and Landscapes in the Middle Ages. A Memorial Volume for Duncan Probert,* co-edited by himself and Alison J. Spedding, (Shaun Tyas, Stamford, 2022). Further discussion of boundaries appears in Margaret Gelling's book on place-names, *Signposts to the Past* (Dent, London, 1978). *The Landscape of Place-names* written by her and Ann Cole (Shaun Tyas, Stamford, 2000) explains the nuances of the different Old English words used for valleys and watercourses which have been used in this chapter.

3
SEARCHING FOR HIDDEN LANDSCAPES
(1086-c.1520)

The Lord Bishop of Worcester is lord of the manor and patron of the church.

> Survey of Bishop's Cleeve 1299
> in *The Red Book of Worcester, Vol. IV,* 1950

Sources and Contexts

During the later Middle Ages a wealth of evidence for the use of Cleeve Hill can be extracted from the records of the Bishop of Worcester, whose carefully administered estates gave rise to much documentation, not only for his manor of Bishop's Cleeve but also for his other manors scattered around the West Midlands. These have been carefully analysed by Professor Christopher Dyer in his book *Lords and Peasants in a Changing Society*, which provides the wider context for the material investigated in this chapter. The manorial court rolls for Cleeve recording the tenants, their obligations to the lord and their land transactions, and the detailed manorial surveys of *c.*1170 and 1299, form the backbone to this chapter and give the opportunity to re-people the later Medieval landscape and spy on the lives of its creators and users, especially the Medieval peasants for whom life was often hard and generally short.

The major development in this period for the historian is the increasing quantity of documentary evidence to complement that of the landscape. The first records of the upland pasture as common land come in c.1150; the first clear record of the names of people living on the hill in c.1170; the first reference to stinting in the thirteenth century; the first detailed records of quarrying from 1389; and by 1482 the first reference to a defined boundary across the common separating Bishop's Cleeve manor from Southam manor. We know much more about Bishop's Cleeve manor in the later Middle Ages than we do about Southam because the former lay under the direct control of the bishop, but the latter passed through the hands of sub-tenants and very few records have survived. All the records confirm the already established dominant theme of the hill's history, that of pressure on a scarce resource and conflict over its use, but the written record allows the historian to chart more precisely the changes affecting the hill and its landscape.

Before considering how the hill was used and moulded by the Medieval peasant, it should be considered in the wider context of the manor under the Bishop of Worcester's jurisdiction. It is essential to appreciate that it was but one part of a far more extensive landholding held by the bishop in order to understand its working. The bishop's manors stretched from Hartlebury and Alvechurch in the north to Westbury-on-Trym in the south; from Bredon and Fladbury in the vale to Blockley and Bibury on the high wold. No manor was totally self-sufficient and all were

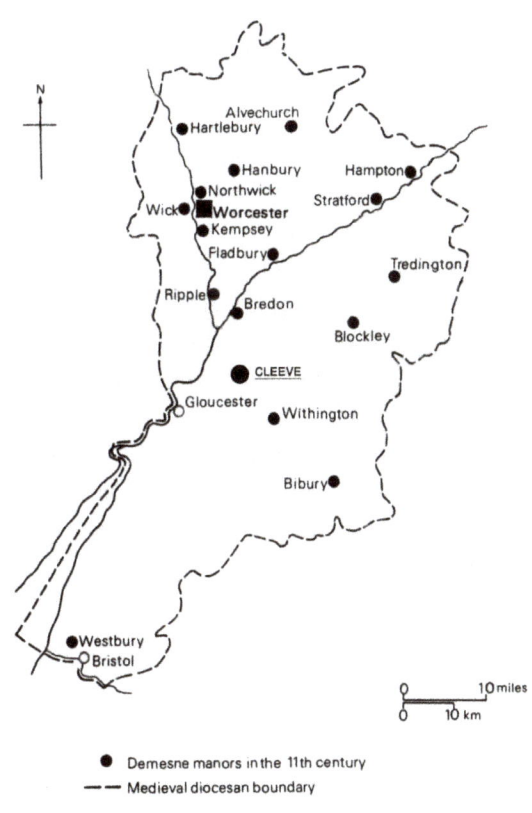

The main Domesday manors of the Bishop of Worcester. Based on C. Dyer's Lords and Peasants in a Changing Society

to some degree interdependent. Cleeve had over 1,000 acres of upland grazing and in summer could support sheep from the lowland manors as well as its own, but by 1246 Cleeve was itself subservient to Blockley manor which became the centre for sheep flocks before the wool clipping. In its turn Cleeve depended on other manors. Most of its hay came from the 50 acres of meadow land by the River Avon at Bredon, still known as Cleeve Meadow which is crossed by thousands of vehicles every day as they drive along the M5. Its pigs were pastured in the woods at Welland near Malvern and large timbers were brought down from Hartlebury when the bishop's great barn needed work done in 1465. They still survive in the Tithe Barn in the village. The timber came down the Severn to Tewkesbury, which was a favourite transport route. In 1396/7 the rector of Bishop's Cleeve bought firewood from Alveley in Shropshire, where he was also the rector. Not only was Tewkesbury an important market centre for Bishop's Cleeve, but we know the tenants also visited Gloucester and Winchcombe to trade. People continued to move around the landscape, as they have done at all periods.

During these centuries after Domesday the peasants of Cleeve who moulded the landscape lived in a world where they were subject to influences and controls from the wider world: influences which are in danger of being ignored in favour of a romantic vision of self-contained and self-sufficient local communities. This is the value of the documents as their increasing number enables a deeper understanding of the changes which can still be traced in the present landscape, if patient study allows the meaning of its hidden messages to be revealed.

Farming the Scarp

On the steep slopes of Cleeve Hill between the western wall of the common at the top and Woodmancote at the bottom lies a lost landscape created by increasing numbers of peasants scratching a living ever higher up the scarp from the thin shifting soil. Today, the best time to view this landscape is in winter when the melting snow, or long contrasting shadows cast by the low sun, pick out the ridge and furrow, dating from that period of Medieval agricultural expansion. Population growth probably halted in the second decade of the fourteenth century and contracted more rapidly after the Black Death of 1348-49. Although there is evidence that cultivation of these fields continued for at least

CLEEVE HILL

another century, when the Medieval ploughteam finally retreated to the more amenable lands in the vale, they left a pattern on the landscape which remains to this day.

The map is an attempt to recreate this hidden landscape between Southam and Bushcombe Lane using the evidence of lidar and other aerial photographs, field walking, eighteenth and nineteenth-century maps and field names, particularly those taken from the 1839 Tithe map. Bushcombe Lane is an arbitrary historical boundary, but its

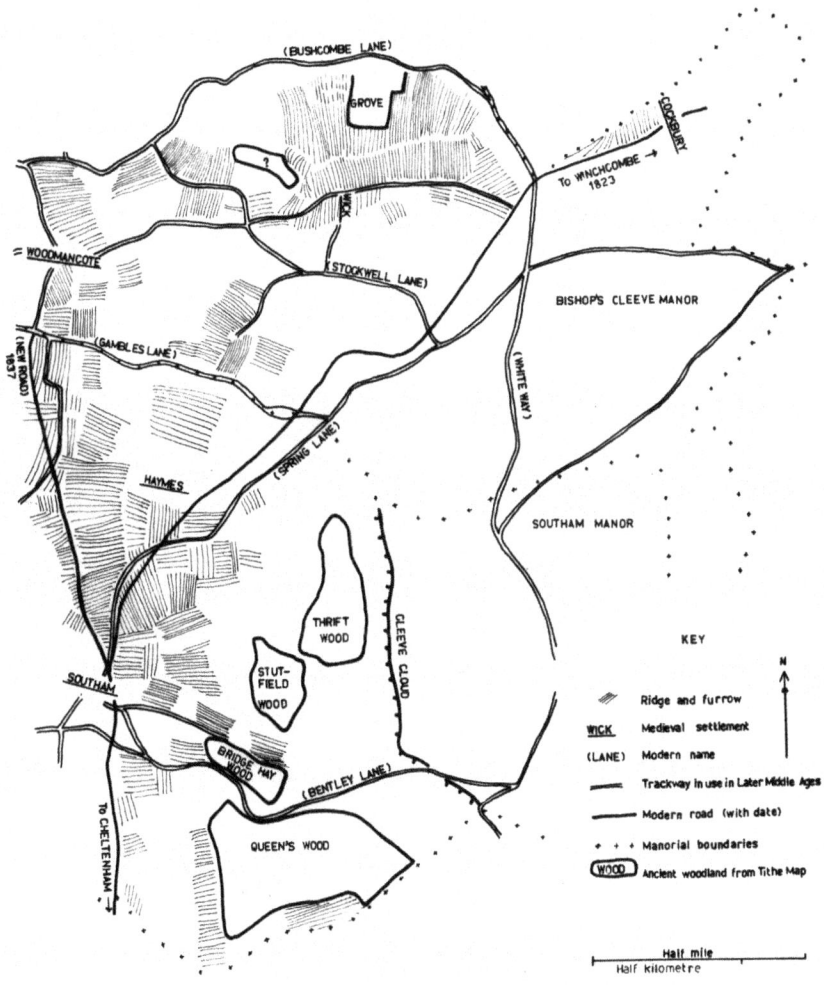

The surviving Medieval features referred to in this chapter

choice enables the area which is really a continuation of the Cleeve Hill landscape to be included. It cannot be claimed that the map is faultless. In some places the evidence is difficult to interpret and in other places soil slumping has destroyed Medieval features, whilst towards the top of the scarp the construction of the present B4632 in 1823 led to their destruction long before the modern requirement to record what was being destroyed. However, the main outline is quite clear. It is dominated by the corrugated, slightly curving ridge and furrow typical of Medieval arable cultivation. The current explanation is that it was created by the simple Medieval plough with its fixed mould board which started in the middle of the strip and cast the soil always to the same side, so that the soil was gradually moved towards the centre of each ridge from the edge. The curve allowed the ox ploughteams to begin their turn before reaching the end of the strip. Most of the ridges run with the slope, to improve drainage, and consequently the ploughing also led to a certain amount of soil creep which accounts for changes in levels either side of field boundaries, upslope being higher and downslope often much lower.

A low winter sun emphasises the ridge and furrow below the Rising Sun Hotel

Such a landscape is not, of course, particular to Cleeve, for the whole of the Cotswold scarp from Bath to Chipping Campden is covered with similar cord-like sinews gathered together into blocks or furlongs. Where such areas of land were added to existing areas, usually from woodland, they are known as 'assarts'. They reflect the work of the Medieval peasant desperate to increase cultivated land because of growing population and the low yields from the seed. Professor Dyer has calculated that c.1300 returns of the main crops of wheat and barley were fourfold in a good year and under threefold in a poor year. Expansion of arable land suggests population growth. The written records confirm this.

Domesday Book of 1086 recorded forty five people in the area, eight of whom were slaves without a claim to the land. The survey of c.1170 listed 83 tenants, and one taken in 1299 contained 102 names. We can assume that generally each recorded tenant represented one family but we know nothing of the unrecorded sub-tenants beyond that they existed. There is an indication from the evidence that this increase in population led to a halving in the size of the average family holding from about 50 acres in 1086 to 24 acres in 1299, and this in turn prompted demands to bring more land under the plough. The process of assarting is most clearly seen in the twelfth-century survey of Cleeve, Woodmancote and Wontley. Assarted land is recorded as follows: in Woodmancote, Robert Franceys 1 yardland (about 25 acres), John and Engelbalt 3 acres, Edric and Sefare 9 acres, and Gladwyn 4 acres; in Cleeve, Samson the priest (who had his own small manor separate from the bishop's manor) 3 acres, and Girold 170 acres; in Wontley 'a certain new land' paid 8d. The lidar aerial photograph shows a small area of ridge and furrow on the common adjoining Wontley's fields which is likely to have been this new land. All assarts, except Girold's, and probably Robert Franceys', were but a small proportion of the tenants' total holdings, suggesting perhaps, piecemeal enclosing of small areas of land at the margin of their existing holding. It is impossible to identify with certainty these small assarts today, although they could be the explanation for the small irregular shape of some of the fields on the hill slopes. Here the ridge and furrow stops at the field boundary indicating the field was reclaimed from the woodland before being ploughed. Contrast this with the longer established arable land of the vale where the modern field boundaries, which were a result of enclosure largely

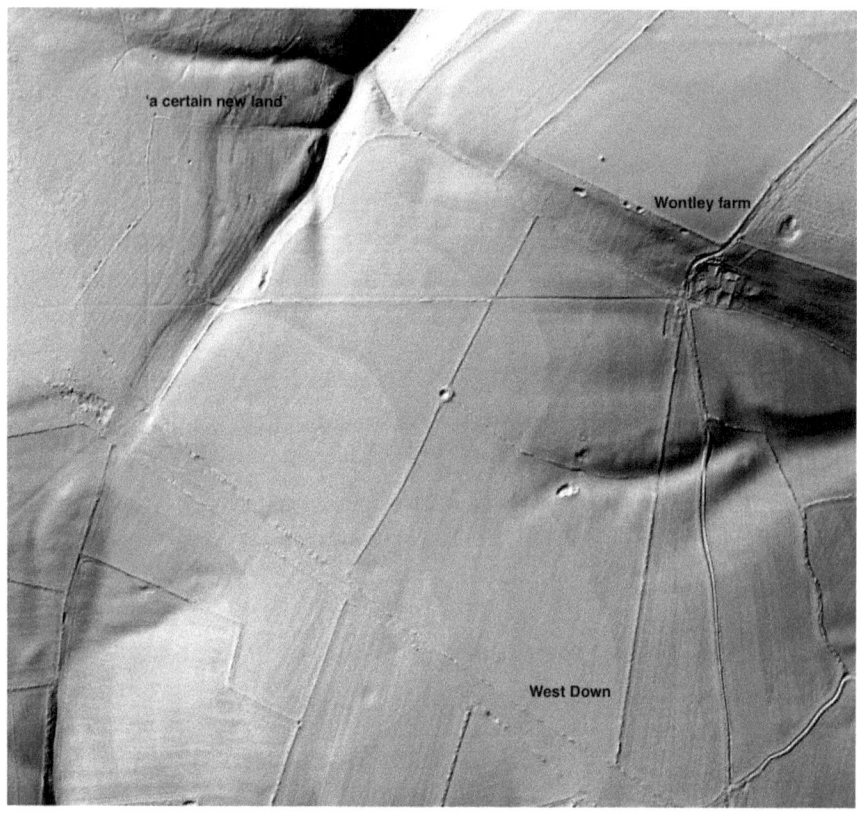

The 'new land' at Wontley taken out of the common, is picked out by the lidar image

of the nineteenth century, tend to run in straight lines ignoring the underlying ridge and furrow. Here the ridge and furrow came before the enclosing field boundaries.

The one notable exception to this small scale development is the assarting of a tenant who is known to us only as Girold. Both Professor H.P.R. Finberg and Professor Dyer have studied this shadowy figure and have been able to draw some general conclusions about the nature of assarting. It is a tale worth repeating here. The entry in the survey reads:

> Girold in Cleeve [holds] twelve acres which used to pay 3s. (as rent to the bishop) and another assart of four acres which paid 12d., and three acres which were Godfrey's which paid 4d. and four acres which were Richard's for 8d., and in addition to this one hundred and forty three and a half acres of assart with wood which remains to be assarted. The total of Girold's assart is one hundred and

seventy acres. And it is half in one field and half in the other, and for it he pays one mark, [13s.4d.] by [grant of] Bishop Roger and in addition to this he holds fifteen acres of assart for 3s.

It seems likely that Girold started off with the original twelve acres, or half a yardland, paying 3s. each year but then added to his holding by both acquisition and assarting. Quite how much of the 143½ acres was actually cleared from the woodland is unknown. The artificially straight south-east boundary of Bushcombe Wood is a sign of some woodland clearance. Most of Girold's assart was probably located on the lower slopes of Nottingham Hill where ridge and furrow can still be discerned.

This photograph taken in 1984 shows the small fields extending to Nottingham Hill where assarting was probably at its greatest extent. Bushcombe Wood can be seen on the sky line

The example of Girold can be further used to illustrate features of assarting which survive so clearly on the scarp today. His original holding was valued at 4d. per acre. Some of the smaller assarts, presumably on better arable land, also paid a similar sum. The large assart, however, paid only 1d. per acre rent, which was a clear sign that the poorer quality, less valuable land on the hill slopes was now being cultivated as a result of population pressure. Bishop Roger acquiesced in this assarting because he was grateful for any increase in his annual income from his manor of Cleeve, at that time worth 100s.8d. in total.

Girold was the first peasant on record who seemed to have control over labour and capital independent of his lord, Bishop Roger. He was the known precedent for a type of peasant who became increasingly typical of the population in Bishop's Cleeve, in contrast to the greater hold by their landlords over the villagers of Southam. However, even in this Girold did not possess complete freedom to use his assart as he liked. The clause 'And it is half in one field and half in the other' indicates it became part of the open fields used by the bishop's tenants and is also a reminder of the byelaws and traditions concerning cropping and fallowing, dates of ploughing, harvesting and opening of the stubble for animals to graze, the observation of which was integral to community well-being and cooperation. It also points to the inadequacies of relying solely on the landscape itself as evidence of how it was exploited and used in the past.

By 1299 assarting was coming to an end and the hidden landscape which can be detected on the scarp today represents the maximum extent of arable land by the first decade of the fourteenth century, growing crops of barley and wheat, with the odd patch of oats growing higher up the hillside. The retreat happened for a variety of reasons, of which fall in population was the most obvious. The soils were thin but the west and south-west aspects were favourable enough for vines to grow on Bushcombe in 1290. Perhaps The Wynyards along Butts Lane gives an indication of the site.

The number of tenants on the bishop's manor of Cleeve fell by thirty five per cent between 1299 and 1349, mostly as a result of the Black Death, and although tithe records show that ploughed land did not decrease by the same proportion, the population decline obviously took pressure off the upland slopes. Apart from occasional use for crops in the succeeding centuries, they have remained as pasture, thus presenting a clear impression of the Medieval landscape at its greatest extent.

This spread of arable land up the scarp ate into the pasture and woodland, both essential to the manorial economy. An indication of the continuing need for them is provided in the survey of 1299, when the value of pasture on Bushcombe, which had undoubtedly been eaten into by assarting, stood at 20s. per annum. The value of the underwood from Bushcombe Wood was 5s. and the pannage for pigs in the wood was valued at 12d. As noted above, the straight lines of the present south-east boundary of the wood are clear indications that the wood had been cut back to provide animal pasture. The best evidence that common pasture was a valuable resource comes from another of the bishop's manors, notably the heaths north of Alvechurch, where enclosures on them were thrown open by the men of King's Norton at some time before 1273. Two centuries later in 1462 John Sewell was ordered to remove a fence he had used to make a private enclosure on the pasture at Kerr's Hill on Bushcombe, land lying to the south of Bushcombe Lane just below its steepest part.

Assarting took place in many areas of marginal land during the later Middle Ages, not only here and along the whole Cotswold scarp but also on the bishop's other manors. Professor Dyer has estimated that over 2,000 acres were added to the arable land which, although a small proportion of the total of 30,000 to 40,000 acres, could be locally of greater significance, as here on the slopes of Cleeve Hill and especially Nottingham Hill.

The scarp itself is a major source of evidence because so much of the shape of the Medieval landscape remains visible today, which can allow a fuller interpretation of the pattern of fields and paths on the slopes of Cleeve Hill. However, arable expansion was not the only change to affect the later Medieval landscape of the hill, woodland too underwent changes during this period.

Woodland

The reference to Bushcombe Wood indicates that woodland was an important resource of the manor. Coppiced woodland was cut about every seven years to provide wood for furniture, tool handles, wattles, fences and hurdles. In 1302/3 and 1389/90 there were references to the cutting of hawthorn in Bushcombe Wood for the making of dead hedges and enclosures. In 1299 honey from wild bees and game also provided the villagers with further valuable resources. Timber came from high woodland, notably from Wontley and also from trees scattered around the landscape in the vale. Much of the evidence available from immediately after Domesday is indirect and fragmentary, although Domesday noted 'a little wood', probably Bushcombe Wood. The place-name 'Woodmancote' - the cottage or shed of the woodman i.e. someone cutting down trees, was first recorded in the *c.*1170 survey, but clearance of the lower slopes could have been taking place long before that date. Archaeologists and historians agree place-names are difficult to interpret. The continuing existence of woodland at this time, however, is evidenced by reference to a swineherd and two woodwards, or wood keepers, in that survey. Wontley or East Wood produced both timber and underwood; the woodland on the scarp slopes of Nottingham Hill, by now only small areas unsuited for arable or pasture, being used mostly as coppiced woodland; and the areas of woodland including the present Queen's, Thrift and Stutfield Woods being a mixture of timber trees, pollards and coppiced woodland. The reeve of the manor of the rector of Bishop's Cleeve took a cartload of wattles from these woods in 1391/2. They would have been intended for use with daub to fill the panels between the timbers in a timber-framed building, long since replaced by brick. In many places the Medieval boundary bank still survives, indicating the stable nature of the boundaries at least by the end of this period.

The view out of Queen's Wood confirms its existence in the later Middle Ages. The ridge and furrow respects its boundaries and constant ploughing down the slope has lowered the surface of the field

The wood at Wontley was a scarce resource of standing timber, so it is not surprising that both the Bishop of Worcester, and the Abbot of Winchcombe, who shared it, went to great lengths to protect its value and the use of its trees. Richard Cole and Henry Knight were the two woodwards recorded in 1299 at Wontley, for which service they were excused from paying half their rent. The timber was valued at £40 in c.1440, when the underwood was valued at 13s.4d., a figure unchanged since 1290. In 1474/5 the bishop's bailiff was paid a quarter (of a hundredweight) of wheat each year for looking after the wood. The importance of the timber from West Wood, on the Charlton Abbots side of the manorial boundary, to Winchcombe can be measured from a plea from the townspeople to Queen Mary some time between 1553 and 1558. She had replaced the abbot as landlord and they pleaded with her not to grant the wood away, for its 70 acres provided the only timber good enough to repair the queen's estimated 80 to 100 houses and five mills in Winchcombe, because the other two woods on the manor, Deepwood and Humleyhoo, were described as only coppiced woodland. This is a further indication that the problems of management of scarce resources were not peculiar to Cleeve in this, or any other period

The Common as Grazing Ground

It is the increasing documentation regarding the use of the common that reveals the conflicts created by demands on its natural resources; conflicts which have left some record in the landscape but which are closely identifiable only from the written record. These demands in this later Medieval period were those of sheep grazing, or overgrazing, and quarrying.

In *c*.1150 William de Solers established a chapel at Postlip and granted to the priest there a house, half a yardland and common rights for six cattle and one horse with his other domesticated animals, on the common pasture above Postlip. By inference we have here the earliest known written reference to the common on the hill. The reference could indicate continuation of inter-commoning, but it more likely confirms that what is now Postlip Warren lay outside the Cleeve territory. The grant attempted to lay down the number of animals the priest could put on the common pasture relative to the size of his holding, and gives an early example of stinting.

Postlip chapel before restoration in 1890. It is reputed to have been built by William de Solers

The landscape of Postlip Warren, rising above the trees, is indistinguishable from Cleeve Common

Professor Hoskins has shown how references to stinting became more frequent as manorial court records became more numerous throughout southern lowland England from the thirteenth century. At the same time a growing population increased the need for animals, especially to keep arable land fertile. This was recognized by parliament, which passed the Statute of Merton in 1236 forbidding lords to enclose common pastures in order to take them out of communal use unless they left adequate common for the freeholders. The problem of overgrazing was particularly acute from March to June every year, when both winter and spring sown crops were growing on the arable land and the meadow was closed to grazing before the hay harvest. In the vale, animals could graze only on the fallow field. This heightened the importance of the common pasture on the hill. The pasture on Nottingham Hill, now called Longwood Common, seems not to have been common pasture at this time as in 1290 the bishop was renting it out for 40s. per annum.

Stinting was first recorded in Bishop's Cleeve during the thirteenth century, when a freeholding of at least 20 acres provided grazing rights for two oxen, a cow and calf. However, frequent references to byelaws in the court rolls attempting to control stinting after 1400 suggest the stints were unenforceable, although overgrazing for the individual's profit was clearly seen as detrimental to the community. The problems increased after 1470 when the bishop no longer had his own sheep flock, as part of his movement out of direct management of his own lands using servants, and his tenants took advantage of the increased potential for grazing on the common. It seems that by 1400 at the latest the typical flock was the small peasant one, but added together they produced enormous numbers of animals grazing on Cleeve Common. If, as can be estimated, about 50 people with such rights lived in Bishop's Cleeve at that date, even if the stint was obeyed, 1,500 sheep could be put to graze on the common, in addition to unknown numbers belonging to Southam tenants who were, of course, no longer under the direct control of the Bishop of Worcester. The problem of overgrazing must have been worse in 1299 because we know that the bishop himself had kept 1,000 sheep on the hill in summer and 200 in winter, moving most off to winter in his vale manors. Professor Dyer has shown these were the wethers (castrated males) as the rams, ewes and lambs were kept at Kempsey, Fladbury and the other manors in the vale where the climate was gentler. The total number of the peasants' flocks is unknown, but at the end of the fourteenth century, the rector's tithes of newborn lambs indicated a combined total of tenants' flocks in the whole of the parish (Bishop's Cleeve and Southam manors) between 3,000 and 4,000. This is the only occasion in the later Middle Ages which allows an estimate of the total number of sheep likely to have been on the hill at any one time, without taking into account sheep from the rector's own manor nor the cattle or horses or donkeys and even geese, also grazing on the common. By 1538 a peasant with one yardland by law could, in theory, graze 30 sheep on the common.

Despite the importance of sheep to the manor, after 1246 Bishop's Cleeve became subservient to Blockley as the hub of the bishop's sheep farming business. There the sheep were driven for shearing or, if they had been clipped in Cleeve, just their wool was sent. A reference in 1450 to Helena Wollemonger, and a house called 'Wollemongers', gives some evidence that then, or in a previous generation, the peasants of the village had taken some control over the selling of the woolclip from their own sheep.

The written records offer information on the scale of sheep farming in Bishop's Cleeve in the later Middle Ages, but there are few clues to be found in the landscape, because the profits were taken out of the area. It is in the wool towns such as Chipping Campden and Northleach where the churches associated with the wealth of the wool trade are found. However, one feature in the landscape does give an indication of the pressure brought upon land: the division of the common between Bishop's Cleeve and Southam manors. In the absence of direct evidence it must be assumed that there was inter-commoning on the hill between the tenants of Bishop's Cleeve manor and the tenants of the manors of Southam which the bishop had granted out, initially in 991. However, with the enclosure of the fields of the deserted settlement at Wontley by 1482 amounting to over 300 acres, and consequent lack of inter-communal grazing there, the pressure created by the demand for grazing led to the recording of a boundary which can still be traced by boundary stones lined across the common and marked on large scale Ordnance Survey maps.

The earliest recording of the boundary running up and across the hill dividing the manors of Bishop's Cleeve and Southam lies in a document in the National Archives at Kew, and is concerned with a dispute of 1563 which is discussed in the next chapter. However, the description quoted here is from a slightly later from a similar document for 1591, but this contains much more detail and makes reference to the existence of the boundary clauses in 1482, the date that the fields of Wontley were enclosed. It reads:

> ...and so to a way call *Smale Way* which divides this manor (i.e. Southam) and the manor of Cleeve, following the same Way eastward as it leads to *Birkmore* to the Cross Way there, And there hence eastward as *steare waie* leads to *Chappmandeane* and so forward to *potteslipp* quarry, from there east and south to *hore* stone to the north corner of *Wontloe* pasture, and so following the east hedge thereof southwards as it leads to *Wontloe* south corner, therehence returning westward as *heath hedge* leads to certain stumps or hillocks towards *Whelewaies* corner and so by the utter southmost hedge of *Queene Woode* to Keane lease corner....'

This boundary has been marked on the map. Some of the boundary stones still survive. We do not know how many boundary

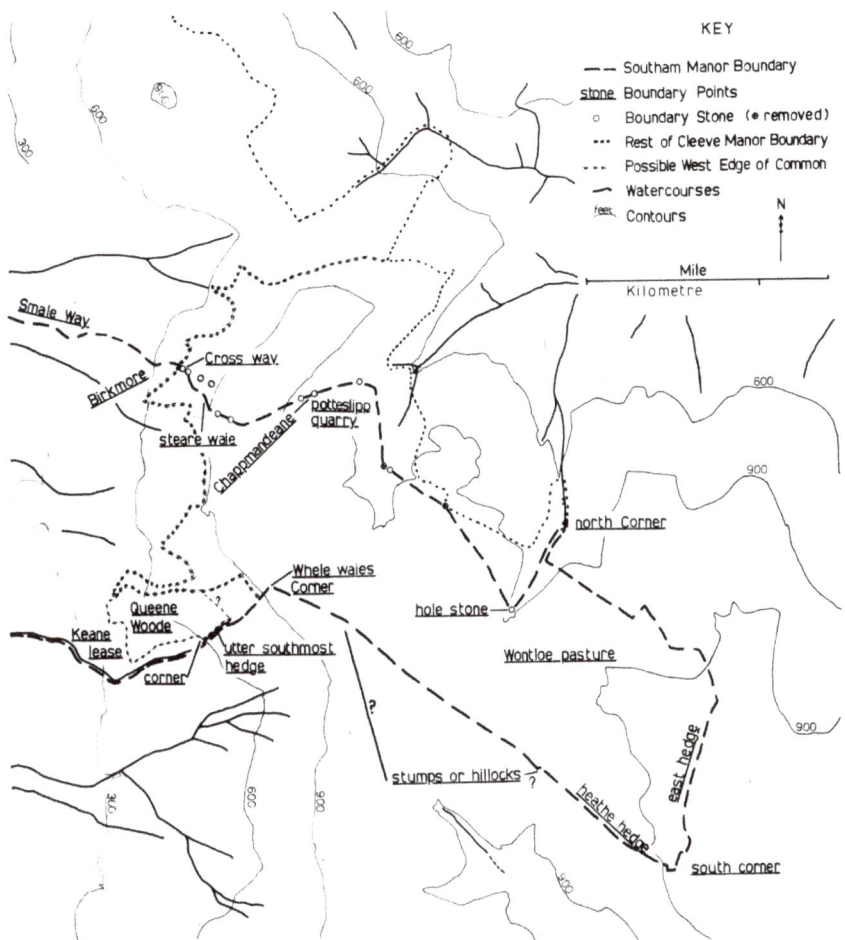

The boundary of Southam manor as recorded in a court case of 1591, in which the inclusion of Wontley was a claim. Without the inclusion of Wontley the boundary would probably have run from 'hole stone' to the southern boundary of West Down

stones there were originally across the common, for in 1882 when the Ordnance Survey commissioners surveyed the parish boundaries for inclusion on their large-scale maps, they noted that two stones were known to have been removed. One of the first acts of the newly formed Board of Conservators in April 1891 was to instruct Thomas Yiend to replace 'weather-worn' boundary stones. Were these the origin of the stones standing in a field lower down the hill off Ashleigh Lane, or were these the original stones which had been removed? One side of each legible stone on the common has a reversed 'S' which obviously represents the Southam side of the stone. How old are they? They probably date from shortly after the time that Lord Ellenborough bought the Southam estate in 1831, for he was very keen to re-establish local traditions and he re-introduced the beatings of the bounds of Southam, as explained in Chapter Six.

This boundary definition may just have reflected the prehistoric territories discussed in Chapter One, particularly in its use of the Cross Dyke across the common. However, the growth of Southam manor from two hides in 991AD to six hides by Domesday might indicate the area had not been the same. The claim to Wontley lying within Southam manor is puzzling because it formed part of Bishop's Cleeve manor until 1623. The best

One of the best preserved stones above the Rising Sun showing the reversed 'S' for Southam

Many of the stones have weathered badly. This stone lies in the side of the ditch of the Cross Dyke, called steare waie *in the boundary clauses*

possible explanation for this claim can be found in the nature of the document. It formed part of a court case in which Southam tenants were arguing their lack of grazing on Cleeve Common as a result of the common being shared with Bishop's Cleeve manor. Both had presumably previously enjoyed rights of inter-commoning at Wontley between its fourteenth-century desertion and its enclosure in 1482, and the best way, they felt, to have those rights restored was to claim Wontley lay in Southam manor.

Smale (or 'narrow') way ran up the hill and is now known as Gambles Lane; *Birkmore* is now Bittemoor and its recording here evidences that certainly by 1591 (and possibly by 1482) this area of rough grazing (i.e. moor) was no longer common land. Cross Way is where Spring Lane meets the Rising Sun Lane. The *steare waie* follows the line of the prehistoric Cross Dyke and is best seen from the vale looking exactly like a staircase as the view from the common is too close to appreciate the aptness of the description. The earlier definition of 1563 describes it then running across the side of an area called *Wylbyngton*, a name now lost but presumably referring to the slope down to Dry Bottom which was called *Chappmandeane*, i.e. the valley of the travelling merchant. The 'deane' element comes from an Old English word *denu* which means a long sloping valley between steep sides. It is a word in use from the eighth century and provides more evidence that people were travelling across the common linking to *Whelewaies*, identified in the eleventh-century boundary descriptions.

Potteslipp quarry identifies the actual quarry rented out by the Bishop of Worcester to the Abbot of Winchcombe in the later Middle Ages. From there the boundary ran almost straight to *hore* ('grey') stone. Here it met the parish boundary north of Wontley from where it ran around the former fields of Wontley and all the way back to the vale. Although the rights to the area enclosed by the boundary could be a cause for dispute, the topographical details were not. Three points on this final part are of significance, the most obvious being the recording again of *Whelewaies* (Wheelers) as a boundary feature. There is the reference to 'stumps or hillocks', one of which must have been the Wontley barrow, the *Hunta hlawe* of the Saxon charter bounds. Finally, the long West Down boundary was marked by a hedge, not a wall, which was similarly recorded in 1830. The Cotswold drystone field wall, which is such a feature of the modern Cotswold landscape, only appeared on this part of the common at least, after 1830. Maps of other Cotswold estates generally support the observation that such walls, stretching out across the wolds, have only been a feature of the last two and a half centuries. The Medieval Cotswold landscape was dominated by arable

open fields and would have appeared little different from the landscape in the vale. Even the peasants' houses were timber-framed. The 'traditional' Cotswold landscape is of comparatively recent origin.

The need to define this boundary was the result of increasing pressure on the common when its perimeter boundaries had been more or less defined and any change in the boundary was the result of encroachment, not expansion. The boundary defined the grazing areas for the animals of the tenants of Bishop's Cleeve and Southam manors, and the continuing conflict between the two sets of tenants is clearly documented in the post-medieval period, discussed in Chapter Four. However the need to define the boundary was also important in controlling quarrying, which was now increasingly documented and which, of course, not only destroyed animal pasture but also created

The closeness of the Postlip Quarries to Winchcombe is evident in this photograph

hazards for the animals. The lord held the right to quarry the stone, and by leasing out this right an income could be made. It was therefore important to know who possessed such rights over which parts of the common.

Quarrying

The two areas of quarrying which are recorded in the Bishop of Worcester's records are at Postlip and Cleeve Cloud, both of which produced good quality freestone for building. Unfortunately direct references to the processes of Medieval quarrying have not been found. Postlip Quarry was rented for 6d. per annum to the Abbot of Winchcombe from at least 1393 to the Dissolution in 1540. Practically all the stone used in Winchcombe came originally from this quarry. We can, however, glean from the record that the quarries were worked when required rather than continuously. Stone sold from a quarry at *Weryngewell*, now unidentifiable but probably above Nutterswood, was worth 9d. to the bishop in 1425/6 but nothing in the following year because nobody would rent it. We have references in 1392, 1394 and 1426/7 that the quarry at Cleeve Cloud was occupied by a tenant who refused to pay rent; another indication that in this period the bishop's direct influence in his manor was lessening. However, stone was needed for his manor house and farm buildings in Bishop's Cleeve. In 1426 Thomas Foxcote was paid 8d. for transporting a wagon-load of stone from Cleeve Cloud to the bishop's manor house, now Cleeve Hall. Stone was also needed for the building and upkeep of St Michael's church. In 1389/90 five hundred slates for the chancel cost 15d. and the carting of them from Ash Quarry (possibly near

Cleeve Hall, once the bishop's manor house shows three stages of building using good quality freestone from Cleeve Common. The far wing dates from c.1250, the nearer wing about 50 years later and the front wall between them with its porch is dated 1667

Most of St Michael's church dates from the end of the twelfth century. It was expanded in the fourteenth century when the wall between the porch and the transept under the tower was constructed

Cleeve Cloud above Thrift Wood) cost 10d. In 1396/7 the rector paid William Roch 10s. for 33 cart-loads of freestone brought 'from the hill to Woodmancote'. The rector was responsible for the building and upkeep of the chancel of the church whilst the villagers were responsible for the nave and aisles. Stone from the hill was also used to repair roads, for according to an entry in the court rolls for 1529, the bishop's tenants of Cleeve had to provide five wagon-loads of stone for every yardland they held. From later records some of this might also have been quarried on Nottingham Hill where the best road stone was found. Stone from the hill was used in a wide area. When archaeologists excavated the site of Holm Castle in 1974-75, before the construction of Tewkesbury Borough Council offices in the town, they recorded that the twelfth-century manor house had been built from stone from Cleeve Hill, which they also found had been used in the abbey opposite as well as in the building of Hailes Abbey in the following century.

The arches of the chapter house at Hailes Abbey were constructed of Cleeve Hill freestone but the hidden infill was of more local stone which was darker and of poorer quality

Settlement

The evidence clearly shows that more people lived on Cleeve Hill and its slopes in the later Middle Ages than either before or after, until the development of the 'Cotswold Health Resort' at the end of the nineteenth century. They were based in and around four clearly defined communities, which differ from the main areas of settlement at any other time in the hill's history: Wontley, Cockbury, Wick and Haymes, in addition to unknown numbers who had built their squatter homes on public land. The small cottages fronting onto Gambles Lane and Stockwell Lane, are the descendants of such developments. 'Birds Cottage' and 'Bentlies Cottage' in Gambles Lane are shown on the map of Haymes estate of 1731 shown on p.112.

Although documentary evidence does not survive until the sixteenth century, these houses in Gamble Lane photographed in 1972 reflect a pattern of roadside encroachments by squatters in the Middle Ages

The best documented settlement was Wontley, on the far side of the common. The settlement lay under the modern planation lying immediately to the west of the remains of Wontley Farm. Walkers following the Winchcombe Way pass by the site although there is nothing to see on the ground. Until 1623 it belonged to Bishop's Cleeve manor. We have no clear record of Wontley until the c.1170 survey which recorded six tenants with half a yardland each, and one vacant yardland, plus the 'new land' assart. Its position in relation to Cleeve's historic estate boundary and the common suggests two possibilities for its origins. It could have been a small early Saxon settlement which was attached to the land granted to the minster at Cleeve, thus explaining how it was enclosed by the boundary. However, and more likely, it originated as an outlying settlement creating its arable lands from the common and woodland, and so bringing additional revenue to the manor. The lack of any Romano-British or Anglo-Saxon artefacts found in the immediate area suggests a later settlement when the population was rising after Domesday. This latter explanation is also supported by a small area of the ture in Padcombe Bottom being recorded as belonging to the settlement, thus ensuring animals had access to water after the common had been defined. In 1299 there were eight tenants, six half-yardlanders plus two who farmed a half yardland and a smallholding between them; the settlement was worth 37s. per annum to the bishop. One of these tenants was Matilda Campion who held half a yardland, messuage and croft for 12d. annual rent and carrying out unnamed work for her lord.

The former openfields of Wontley stretching to the cleared Wontley Wood adjoining the truncated West Wood at the top of the photograph. The settlement of Wontley lay in the scrub ground between the ruined farm and wooded Padcombe Bottom. West Down runs along the edge of the former openfields

Yet behind the seemingly stable picture of this small settlement, there is evidence which points to structural difficulties within the community at a time when it seemed to have been thriving most. In c.1260 the *Landboc* of Winchcombe Abbey recorded the grant of a yardland at Postlip to John, son of Richard Faber (i.e. smith) of Wontley; the grant was witnessed by Richard himself, together with sons William, a clerk (in holy orders), and another Richard. The grant hinted at lack of opportunity in such a small settlement with clear limits to the expansion of its arable land, except onto the common. The Faber family reappeared in the 1299 survey. Also in this survey were the two woodwards mentioned earlier in this chapter.

It may be inferred from such reports that Wontley at no time had more than eight families, and so it is easy to understand how later desertion could have been a relatively simple choice based finally on the decision of just one or two family heads. Wontley was abandoned earlier than many other Cotswold deserted settlements. When the king's assessors visited the parish to collect a tax based on one-ninth of the value of the sheaves of corn, fleeces and lambs from the harvest of 1340, Wontley (and Cockbury) lay abandoned, 'destroyed by robbers', and their fields were said to have been uncultivated. The tax list also recorded a dearth of peas, barley and oats; a useful indication of the main crops grown by the villagers. The double reasons given for inability to pay should arouse suspicion that these were excuses designed to avoid payment because the village was in decline, rather than a statement of reality. Indeed, the Bishop of Worcester's records do not support abandonment then, for not until 1372/3 do they record that Wontley was unable to pay taxes and rents 'because of death'. Only then can it safely be assumed that its inhabitants had gone, because the fields were being rented out for pasture for 10s. per annum. In 1393/4 the rental had been reduced to 6s. per annum, but the continuing value of its wood is reflected in the sale of underwood for 32s.1d. in that year. Soon after 1394, when the bishop began leasing out his demesne lands in an attempt to increase his income, Wontley was at first included. But in 1437 the land was rented separately as pasture worth 13s.4d. Then, in 1482 there occurred a major change because the land was 'enclosed with ditches and hedges' to increase its value by taking it out of the common fields and renting it to two Winchcombe merchants, Walter Hicks and Robert Arch, for the exclusive grazing of their sheep, at the vastly increased sum of £6.13s.4d.; a rent which stayed stable for at least the next 50 years. Professor Dyer considers this was the action of the bishop's new steward, William Nottingham, who was intent on increasing the income from his manors. We then find the bishop spending 13s.4d. to put a fence around the wood at Wontley in 1505/6 to protect the underwood from animals straying off the pasture. The attempts by the bishops to increase income in general, and their profits from this small part of one estate in particular, was to the detriment of their tenants who lost common rights to this pasture. The consequences of the enclosing of Wontley will be followed up in the next chapter.

Today only the crumbling ruins of a single farmstead provide a reminder that people once lived here. The former arable lands can still be traced today in the landscape, although the Medieval ridge and furrow has been ploughed out. Its boundaries still form a distinctive eastern extension of the present Southam parish. Many landowners and tenants can be traced over the succeeding centuries, but they encountered repeated failures to exploit successfully this isolated upland farming area.

In 1327 Wontley was assessed with Cockbury in the Lay Subsidy (a national tax based on one-fifteenth of the value of moveable wealth) and between them they had five taxpayers paying a total of 6s.3d. From this we can roughly estimate Cockbury's population. Since it is usually accepted that only 40 per cent of households were recorded, and Wontley had eight in 1299, therefore Cockbury possessed four or five households. As discussed above, reference to abandonment in 1340 cannot be relied upon, and yet there is very little other evidence for the settlement. One reason for this is that Cockbury was held with Southam manor during this period and so its records have not survived. It is possible that it was added between 1038, or 1046, and 1086, when Southam's size grew from five to six hides. Certainly *c*.1170 it was held with Southam by William de Brause. Another reason for uncertainties about its history is that it is not always clear that references to Cockbury are to Cockbury in Southam. During the later Middle Ages it was known as Little Cockbury, to distinguish it from Great Cockbury attached to Winchcombe. Each was recorded as being one hide in extent. It seems likely that the reference to the conversion of 77 acres to pasture by Thomas Escort in 1512 related to Great Cockbury. This led to complaints to the king that two mills had become ruinous, six people had to leave and one plough had been given up. The site of Great Cockbury was probably at or near the present Cockbury Butts.

The geographical position of Cockbury, on the edge of the estate, mirrors that of Wontley and may indicate a similar origin. Its end was probably later than 1340 for reasons discussed over Wontley, but we do not know exactly when, nor by what process. The inquisition held in 1548 on the death of Sir John Huddleston of Southam recorded just one messuage with 175 acres of land. The messuage must have been the forerunner of Cockbury Court which dates back to that time and the

Cockbury Court dates back to the sixteenth century and probably stands on the site of the Medieval settlement

house with its surrounding farm buildings is likely to have been built on the site of the original village as at Wontley and a not unreasonable situation given the later history of many other Cotswold deserted settlements. The acreage of its land corresponded almost exactly to the area bounded by the manorial boundary along the Langley Brook, the boundary of the common and Wickfield Lane. Topographical evidence for its arable land still survives. In addition to the small area of ridge and furrow shown on the map on page 57, there is clear evidence that some arable land abutted the boundary of the common, for the change in ground level either side of the stone wall can be attributed only to ploughing down the slope which lowered the ground immediately next to the boundary.

There is a similar lack of documentary evidence for the small settlement at Haymes. It was always part of the Southam manor but its holders had considerable freedom. In 1299 Adam de *Haym*, knight, is recorded as holding three yardlands by military service together with his joint tenants. In the 1327 Lay Subsidy Adam le *Knyt* paid 2s. In 1462 Haymes was recorded with Stoke Orchard in the court rolls. More

The ridge and furrow associated with Haymes can be seen running under the modern hedge. The melting snow picks out the possible plots of the settlement's house

than that we do not know, except small house platforms lie either side of the present drive to Haymes and much late Medieval pottery was found when mushroom sheds were being built in 1965. Either or both areas could be the site of the Medieval settlement. The ridge and furrow plotted on the map on page 57 represent the arable lands of the village in addition to strips intermingling with those of Woodmancote and Southam as shown on the Haymes estate map of 1731 on page 112.

The smallest of the late Medieval settlements on the hill lay at Wick, where the landscape and documentary evidence combined to identify a small settlement of two dwellings on the hillside at the fold of Nottingham and Cleeve Hills. It was approached by two still clearly identifiable tracks off Stockwell Lane. In many ways it is the perfect example of how to locate a lost settlement from a modern Ordnance Survey map, for four footpaths (formerly tracks) meet at its northern end. The site has been destroyed by the building of a pond, but before this happened enough survived on the ground to identify the lay out of the buildings. The settlement first appeared in the survey of 1299. Walter and Matthew *ate Wyke* were living there, Walter having the larger holding, paying 8s.8d per annum in rental, Matthew paying 3s. In 1327 John *de Wyke* paid 20¾d. tax and Peter *ate Wyke* 6d. Both entries combined Wick with Woodmancote. The hamlet can therefore be considered as the final phase of the expansion of Woodmancote up the hill. 'Wick' here means an outlying farm.

Once population declined and pressure on land fell, Wick was affected by the retreat of settlement. In 1462 John Fowler was brought before the manorial court accused of possessing a messuage called *Wykens* 'which lies badly ruinous and wasted by neglect'. The building had been

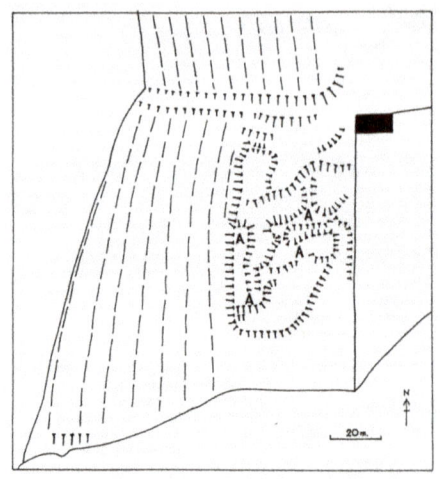

The plan of Wick shows at least four platforms (marked A) on which buildings stood. These are the remains of the two farms found in the documentary record. The trackway and ridge and furrow also stand out (C. Dyer)

This photograph of 1985 shows the remains of Dab's house with the earthworks of Wick to its right. The earthworks were destroyed by the modern pond

a small one with two pairs of crucks, but it had by then fallen down. Perhaps this marked the end of the settlement as such, although its attendant arable land, surviving today as ridge and furrow, possibly continued to be ploughed from Woodmancote for some time after that. The plan of the surviving features shows the remains of two farmsteads on marginal land on the scarp slope. The smallest and shortest lived of the four deserted settlements produced the best landscape evidence for its existence and its name continued in Wickfields, the vast expanse of its former open fields stretching up to the B4632.

The arable land associated with Wick is highlighted by the melting snow in 1976. The name Wickfields is still in use today as a reminder of the deserted settlement

It is clear that the Medieval inhabitants of the hill did not choose to live in these settlements for the view alone, for these were tiny settlements given a life by intense pressure of population. As the population fell, especially after the Black Death, the viability of such small communities was then in doubt, and simply because they had been small they had little resilience. In addition the arable land was not of the best quality and all were to a certain extent inconveniently sited for the main centres of community, particularly Wontley. And yet the sites were not totally deserted. The present houses at Cockbury and Haymes represent a continuous habitation on these two sites. Wontley Farm and its outbuildings still survive as ruins. Perhaps most interesting of all was the small house at Wick, shown on the plan as a black rectangle, a fraction of one wall of which still remains. This was last inhabited by an eccentric call Hab or Dab who was recorded in the 1839 Tithe Award. In his book on Woodmancote Hugh Denham recounted the story that he made his own coffin and kept his wife in a state of unease by the frequent rehearsal of his own funeral.

A convenient break in the history of the common comes early in the sixteenth century with the emergence into the written record of Thomas Yardington, a 'socially upwardly-mobile' peasant who took full advantage of the decline of the feudal system and the desire of the Bishop of Worcester to rent out his demesne lands, to become the lessee of the demesne in Cleeve from 1471 to 1525. The attempts by his descendants to control the grazing on the hill brought him into conflict with the tenants of Southam as everyone suffered from the decision to enclose Wontley in 1482, thereby reducing the common grazing area and a return to the well-established theme of conflict caused by overuse of the hill as a scarce land resource.

Conclusion

This chapter has demonstrated how the hidden landscapes which survive on the hill and its common can be brought to life by a careful study of these landscapes married to the written documents. In these years the people who lived near or on the hill brought great changes to the appearance of its slopes. Then, as the pressure on the arable land declined, the slopes took on their current appearance. In contrast, the common itself appeared unchanging apart from continuing quarrying and its main purpose continued to be providing grazing for the animals of the villagers and the bishop. The appearance of the landscape was now to change little until the end of the nineteenth century, but what does change is the nature of the evidence as the documentary evidence becomes much more important.

FURTHER READING

The essential context of this chapter is again provided by the two books by Professor Dyer. *Standards of Living in the Later Middle Ages* contains a valuable section on the peasant economy in Bishop's Cleeve. I am greatly indebted to him for allowing me to use his transcripts of the Bishop of Worcester's records held at The Hive in Worcester, reference 009:1. The *c.*1170 and 1299 surveys are printed in full in *The Red Book of Worcester*, edited by M. Hollings (Worcester Historical Society, Worcester, 1950). The *Victoria County History Volume VIII* again provided background detail. Professor H.P.R. Finberg's *The Gloucestershire Landscape* (Hodder and Stoughton, London, 1975) has also proved useful.

The 1327 Lay Subsidy is published in Peter Franklin's *The Taxpayers of Medieval Gloucestershire* (Alan Sutton, Stroud, 1993). The manorial boundary was abstracted from the Southam manorial records in the Duchy of Lancaster collection DL42 in the National Archives at Kew. The register of Winchcombe Abbey edited by Reverend D. Royce in 1892 as *Landboc, sive Registrum Monasterii ... de Winchelcumba Volume 1* (W. Pollard, Exeter) has provided some material on Postlip and Cockbury, but much of the chapter has been based upon fieldwalking, studying Ordnance Survey and lidar aerial photographs, and by back projection from the 1731 Haymes estate, 1839 Tithe and 1847 Enclosure maps held at Gloucestershire Archives. The National Library of Scotland website has extensive collections of historical Ordnance Survey maps. Lidar images have again been taken from https://www.lidarfinder.com. The report on the excavations at Holm Castle can be found in the *Transactions of the Bristol and Gloucestershire Archaeological Society,* Volume 115 (1997).

4
CONFLICT IN THE COMMUNITY
(c.1520-1818)

> The hills towards Winchcombe are at present mere downs, lifeless and unamusing, though the country below is agreeable!
> Thomas Dudley Fosbroke,
> *History of the County of Gloucester*, 1807

Sources and Contexts

For the next three centuries the face of Cleeve Hill changed little. The common was established; quarrying cut into the exposed limestone beds; the scarp slopes had developed into small irregular fields with areas of woodland; animals grazed the grasslands, and human habitation remained unobtrusive to the observer in the vale. During these years the landscape itself provided the essential continuity, as background to the turmoil and strife recorded in the written word. The period's unity is based upon the importance of the common to the local economies of Bishop's Cleeve, Woodmancote and Southam; a period ended by the arrival of Cheltenham races in August 1818.

During this period the manors of Bishop's Cleeve and Southam passed from the Bishop of Worcester and the king respectively into more local hands. In 1561 Bishop's Cleeve manor passed to Queen Elizabeth. After her death, it was granted away again in 1604 and it changed hands quite frequently and in doing so, its lands were sold off, so that by 1735 only 173 acres were attached to it and by 1885 only the manorial rights, which largely meant the right to the minerals on the common.

Unfortunately these factors prevented the accumulation of a body of manorial records for the historian to use. Consequently the story of the common has to be pieced together from fragmentary references in other sources. Chief of these are the Southam manor records.

After the division of the latter manor, first clearly recorded in 1165, the larger part, represented today by the Pigeon House complex of buildings with its large barn, came to the future Henry IV by his marriage in 1380/81 to Mary de Bohun. From his succession to the throne in 1399 until 1604 the manor remained Crown property. It was sold in 1609 to Richard Delabere and again in 1831 to Lord Ellenborough. Such continuity of ownership led to a substantial collection of manorial records, now held in the Archives in Gloucester. When Lord Ellenborough was negotiating to purchase the smaller part of Southam manor, represented by Manor Farm, from the Coxwell-Rogers family, in order to possess the whole of Southam manor by 1833, he insisted on a search of all the known records to establish their right to title and therefore the right to sell. Copies were made of many of the records and these, too, are kept in the Archives although some of the originals are now lost.

From these manorial records it is possible to gain an impression of the hill and its common in the local context, but it is also necessary to look at the events of these three centuries with reference to the wider world which, in the period covered by this chapter, brings with it a new development encapsulated by Thomas Dudley Fosbroke, whose words at the head of the chapter represent comments of visitors travelling over the hill and its common. By 1807 the growing number of visitors to take the spa waters in Cheltenham demanded a variety of attractions. One of these was a tour of the surrounding countryside. Southam, Winchcombe and Sudeley lay on one tourist route. The visitor could not avoid Cleeve Hill, travelling on the old turnpike road across the common, but theirs was a superficial interest based on the hill as an obstacle to travellers; it was the view to the vale which was appreciated. As will be discovered, 'lifeless and unamusing' were particularly inappropriate descriptions of the common during these years. However, they are a reminder of the importance of the perception of the hill and its common. The possible Bronze Age perception of the hill as seen from the vale as a landscape for the dead was discussed in Chapter One. Chapter Seven focuses on the perception that it was a health resort which then led to its present perception as a pleasant place to live as well as a place for recreation and freedom from daily cares and worries. It has always served as the backdrop to the lives of the generations who have lived at its foot but its appearance has been changed by them over the centuries.

A major impact on the hill in this period came from the general growth in the country's population. From approximately two million in 1500, the population of England grew to five million in 1700 and to eight million by 1801. Although outbreaks of famine, disease and depression meant rates of growth were not consistent, particularly in the sixteenth and seventeenth centuries, the underlying upward trend led to increased demand for food. Livestock rearing became very profitable, to provide meat for the markets and manure to feed the soils in areas of mixed or arable farming. Communal grazing on the open fields and particularly on the commons and wastes came under pressure. The problems this created in the Early Modern period were summed up in 1976 by the late Joan Thirsk, a leading historian of the countryside, in the following words:

> Complaints from villagers all over the country against John Brown and Henry Smith who overcharged the commons with their herds and flocks ... kept more stock on the commons in summer than they could support in winter on their home grounds. The complaints were all of one kind, recording the resentment of the many at the selfish ambitions of the few.

The Common as Grazing Ground

For John Brown and Henry Smith we must substitute the names of Sir John Huddleston of Southam House and Richard Southall, who had a house and land in Woodmancote. In October 1539 Sir John accused Richard of trespassing on the common open fields of Woodmancote and Southam, by grazing there over 200 sheep and an unknown number of cattle. He had already sent his sons to impound the animals, and they used such force that Richard Southall complained that many had had to be destroyed. However, that Richard's motive was for personal commercial profit was strongly suggested when he denied the existence of a two sheep per acre stint, and he blamed the action on a personal grudge held by Sir John. The case could not be resolved at Southam Manor court, and so it was taken to the Duchy of Lancaster court, where

The Old Farm in Bishop's Cleeve was Thomas Yardington's statement he had moved up in the world

the finding went against Richard Southall, declaring he had no rights of common and was therefore a trespasser.

What effect the ruling had we do not know and we do not know on whose behalf Sir John Huddleston acted. We might suspect it was to protect his own interests in grazing animals on one of the open arable fields when it was left fallow to regain its goodness as animals grazed on its weeds and dropped manure, but the case set the tone for a long series of court cases over grazing rights on the common itself between the tenants of Bishop's Cleeve and Woodmancote against those of Southam. To these cases we now turn.

Professor Dyer has traced the upward mobility of the Yardington family in Bishop's Cleeve during the late fifteenth and early sixteenth centuries. In addition to Thomas leasing the bishop's demesne, he also held various official posts in the manor, including reeve, bailiff and juror at the manor court. After his death his namesake son took on the demesne lands calling himself a yeoman, a term of status, so the family had moved up in the world, building for themselves what is now Old Farm at the bottom of Station Road. At Easter 1563, when both Bishop's Cleeve and Southam manors lay in Queen Elizabeth's hands, we find a Richard Yerrington, whom it is reasonable to suppose was of the same family, accused in the Duchy of Lancaster court of preventing Southam tenants from commoning on *Cleeves* Hill by impounding cattle grazing at Barnard's Cross (where the White Way crosses the top end of Dry Bottom). Yerrington rested his case on the whole of the common belonging to the manor of Bishop's Cleeve. Although the tenants of Southam inter-commoned freely with their animals, it appears that Richard sought to have their rights removed by playing with definitions. He insisted he knew the hill only by the name of Cleeve Hill, not *Cloude*

Cleeve Cloud was the name given to the quarried area above Thrift Wood

nor *Covere Clowde*. This was only half the truth, for the latter names referred exclusively to the Southam portion of the manor, to the south of the manorial boundary running across the common. He must have known this but was relying on the ignorance of the Duchy's officers of the local situation, in order to gain a ruling to deny Southam tenants rights to any part of the hill.

The case smacks of an attempt to claim exclusive rights for the profit of one set of Her Majesty's tenants against those of the neighbouring manor. But the Southam tenants were well prepared. They produced a plan showing the boundaries of the common (which was last known to be hanging on a wall in Southam House early in the nineteenth century) and the two articles of 1482 and 1483 by which the Bishop of Worcester enclosed Wontley for sheep pasture. The court accepted the evidence of these documents and found that Southam cattle had been wrongly impounded and that Southam tenants should enjoy exclusive rights to their part of the common. An order was also made to throw open Wontley for Southam tenants' animals and, once that had been done, Bishop's Cleeve and Woodmancote tenants would be able to inter-common upon the *Clowde*, i.e. the Southam part of the common.

But that was by no means the end of the case. Wontley, of course, still remains enclosed to this day. Its subsequent history is traced later in this chapter. The decision, although technically correct, reaffirmed that the few wealthier and more businesslike freeholders and copyholders in Southam enjoyed grazing rights to two-thirds of the common, confining the much larger number of Bishop's Cleeve tenants to the northern third. What had been won in law had not been won in practice. Before the end of the year Bishop's Cleeve tenants were back in the Duchy court. The record of these proceedings throws much light on attitudes towards this precious land resource of lowland England, and provides a classic example of Joan Thirsk's general observation.

Richard Yerrington renewed the attack on behalf of the Bishop's Cleeve tenants. Their anger and sense of injustice can be gauged from their language, carefully recorded by the courtroom clerk. Richard argued that the Southam tenants had won the judgement by being better organized and better informed. The three leading freeholders, Edward Wallwyn, the farmer (i.e. lessee) of the manor, Kynnard Delabere, father of Richard who bought the manor in c.1609, and William Lorenge of

Haymes, who were speaking, it was claimed, on behalf of themselves and no more than a further two freeholders and nine copyholders, had 'of their covetous mind' claimed exclusive rights to the common for their own profit and for those of their heirs and tenants. They had produced records, court rolls and evidence to support their case, which the 'poor plain men and only copyholders' of Bishop's Cleeve had not been able to counter, their counsel being 'not suitably learned'. Thus at a stroke the traditional common rights 'for the time being time whereof no remembrance of man is to the contrary' were granted exclusively to the Southam profiteers 'to the utter undoing of fifty of the queen's majesty's tenants of the said manor of Cleeve and their wives and children without your pitiful consideration thereof'. These latter had now, however, themselves found an old court roll book of account and other documents dating back to Edward IV (1461-83) proving the freehold of the common was part of Bishop's Cleeve manor, and they wished the case to be re-opened.

Underlying the case we can perceive the search for economic profit by the few in Southam conflicting with the greater economic necessity of the many from Bishop's Cleeve and Woodmancote. Richard argued that they relied on the common to graze sufficient animals to keep their arable fields fertile, but leadership of the community lay in their own hands, being a village of many smaller farms, and they thus lacked the ability to put forward a good case in law. However for their part, they were only intent on using the law to their own advantage for they had just ignored the 1563 judgement. We know this from questions put to John Garne, of Bishop's Cleeve, when the case re-opened the following summer. His replies, even as written down, were a mastery of evasion. He started convincingly enough but then became more hesitant. He knew Cover Cloud and Nutter Wood and Bentley belonged to Southam but the rest of the common he knew belonged to Bishop's Cleeve. He had heard the 1563 judgement only through his neighbours. He had no idea by whom and upon whom the decree was issued. He did not know the names of Bishop's Cleeve tenants who had interrupted Southam tenants, but he did know Southam tenants had been fined at Bishop's Cleeve manor court for trespassing on the common. When first asked whether he knew the Bishop's Cleeve tenants were taking out a writ against Southam tenants in the Duchy court he only admitted to the possibility and claimed ignorance of its cost. On being pressed further by the Duchy's sergeant at law, William Fleetwood, he changed his answer and we discover he had himself already contributed 5s. to the estimated £50 - £60 bill for the case. This was all too much and he then refused to answer any more questions. Silence was the best defence in portraying Bishop's Cleeve tenants as the injured, but not innocent, party, and no further witnesses were called. Whatever the outcome of the case (and this is not known), the tenants of Bishop's Cleeve and Southam continued to graze their animals exactly as they had been doing for centuries.

The records of this case, still carefully preserved in The National Archives, provided a point of precedent for further similar disputes as the conflict between Bishop's Cleeve and Southam tenants periodically spilled into the courts during the next 200 years. Significantly none ever again questioned the existence of the boundary, but rather the rights over the two separate parcels.

The Duchy court rolls recorded another complaint by Southam tenants in November 1591, before the 1563 case was repeated almost exactly in May 1593 and January 1594. Both cases were pressed by Southam tenants against Bishop's Cleeve and Woodmancote tenants overstocking the common and trespassing with their animals on the Southam part of the common. In January 1594 the complaint was not only against the overstocking of the Bishop's Cleeve tenants but also against the appearance of fourteen or fifteen hundred 'strangers' cattle on the common. These were animals of people living outside the manor in places lacking adequate pasture, who had made some sort of agreement with the Bishop's Cleeve tenants who did have rights to graze their animals on the common. This private economic gain was once again perceived to be to the ultimate detriment of the whole community. The continuing enclosure of Wontley made the problem of overgrazing worse.

The scrabble to claim grazing rights over commons at this time was not confined locally to the villages of Bishop's Cleeve, Woodmancote and Southam. We only need to look over the wall of West Down into Sevenhampton. Before enclosure in 1814 the people of Sevenhampton possessed grazing rights on their part of West Down. In 1581 the lord and tenants disputed their respective rights to their narrow strip of common. Theirs was resolved by dividing the length of their common into two even narrower strips by the digging of a line of holes parallel to the existing wall to act as a dividing line: to the north of the line the tenants had their rights of common; to the south, the lord.

One major cause of the continuing conflict over pasture rights on Cleeve Common lay in the inability to fix and enforce any stinting of animals based upon an agreed ratio of animals to acreage of tenants' land in the vale. As mentioned in the previous chapter, in Bishop's Cleeve in the thirteenth century 20 acres gave grazing rights for two oxen, a cow and calf, and in 1538 one yardland gave rights to graze 30 sheep. Such arrangements were recognized only in their breaking, for during the period of these disputes no stinting seems to have been enforced. Surveys of the manors in 1620 and 1631 explicitly stated that stinting did not exist. Not until May 1695 do we possess further evidence of attempts to stint the common. Eighty five freeholders of Bishop's Cleeve (79 male and six female) agreed to contribute to a High Court action to introduce stinting on the common and in the common arable fields because 'foreigners' were buying an acre or two of land in the parish in order to put cattle on the common, to the prejudice of the locals. Now not only was the community suffering at the hands of the individuals intent on personal gain, but these individuals were outsiders whose only interest seems to have been their own personal economic gain. We are not surprised to learn that Southam tenants then agreed to meet the costs of another case in order to establish their rights to the common. The Bishop's Cleeve v. Southam feud continued just below the surface. It last boiled over in 1666, but, as before, it continued to be impossible to prevent intermingling of animals on the common.

Although no reference to the outcome of this High Court case has been found, the case was important because it revolved around that development first recorded (but no doubt of much older origin) in 1594. This concerned the overgrazing of the common by the animals of 'strangers' or 'foreigners'. It is here in this traditional world of pre-industrial agriculture that we can discern the seeds of a conflict of interest which became all important in the later nineteenth century and which still finds echoes today. This is a conflict between those who wished to continue their traditional use of the common and who were opposed to outsiders, particularly in the nineteenth century from

Cheltenham, whose demands ran totally counter to the commoners' interests and rights.

Overstocking continued to be a problem. Another clear indication of the difficulties of enforcing stinting can be found in 1749 when some of the Southam landowners complained that overstocking meant the common had little value for them. Counsel could not give any opinion for the reason that there was no way of being able to enforce any judgement. The tenants were being ordered to act against their own interest and in the continuing absence of any enforcement, not unsurprisingly carried on as before. Just how valuable were such rights to the common can be measured from two other examples. Firstly in the mid-seventeenth century there was a dispute whether occupation of Cockbury brought rights to the common. In the mid-eighteenth century it seems to have brought rights to the common on Nottingham Hill, and the mention of the right to graze 200 sheep there suggests some form of stinting. When Lord Coventry gained Great Cockbury in Winchcombe and made an attempt to claim rights over Cleeve Common in 1749 the freeholders of Bishop's Cleeve, gathering together in a vestry meeting, prevented him from doing so. Rights to the common were purchased for Huddleston's Cockbury at about this time. They must have lapsed at some time since the Middle Ages when Cockbury was part of Southam manor, as explained in Chapter Two. Secondly, in November 1770 Henry Harvey from Winchcombe was accused in Southam manor court of stocking the common without any right. How many others went unrecorded or even unnoticed? Surviving records show it is possible to identify this use of the common as pasture as its most important function at this time. Indeed, when the Reverend Thomas Rudge published his county history in 1803, his first reference to the hill was to its excellent sheep pasture.

The themes running through this period, litigation, stinting and over-exploitation, are symbolic of the main theme that runs throughout this later history of Cleeve Common: the conflict arising from the interests of inhabitants who defended their own rights and attacked the rights of others, which gives some coherence to the attempt to understand the development of the landscape. Until 1818 these interests were almost exclusively based on the common's value to the local community and society.

Quarrying

The rights to pasture were enjoyed by the tenants but the rights to exploit the minerals remained with the lord. Partly as a result of the lack of manorial records, and partly because in this period the quarries seem always to have been worked by individuals, there exist very few records of them until later into the nineteenth century. Consequently it is necessary to fill in the gaps between the isolated references with assumptions that workings continued across the hill. The lack of any references to the damaging of the pasture by the spread of quarrying suggests that even at Cleeve Cloud the actual workings seem to have been on a small scale. In 1620, when Southam tenants were allowed to take away freestone for building, it was worth only £1 to the Delaberes. In 1714 Abel Wantner referred to the 'great quarry of freestone' at Cleeve Cloud in the notes for a history of the county which he never published. By 'great' he was presumably referring to its appearance rather than meaning the scale of exploitation. Freestone was the best quality stone, as explained in Chapter Three.

This sketch of St Michael's church dates from c.1770. The upkeep of the church provides us with some of the most detailed records of quarrying in the eighteenth century. The Priory behind dates from a century earlier and is also constructed from Cleeve Hill stone (E. Powell)

The fullest continuous record of the exploitation of these quarries during this period can be found in the church wardens' accounts for Bishop's Cleeve. From the early eighteenth century periodic payments were made for the purchase and hauling of stone, lime, slates and gravel from the hill for use in the church and churchyard. These confirm the lack of a regular demand for the minerals, and highlight one major problem. The cost of hauling almost always exceeded the cost of the stone itself.

In 1705 stone costing 2s. cost 8s. to haul from the hill. In 1719 1500 slates were bought at a cost of 13s.9d., but it cost 10s. to bring them to the church. In 1840 a load of gravel cost 19s.6d. at the hill, but £4.11s.0d. to haul it, again to the church. Lime burning was expensive. In 1723 it cost 19s.2d. to buy coal and haul it from Tewkesbury. In the same year 3s. was spent on two barrels of Bristol lime, presumably because Cleeve Hill lime was unsuitable for some purpose. We can readily imagine the difficulties not only of loading and carrying the minerals along the steep, narrow tracks of the common itself, but also the severe problems of braking horse-drawn carts as they slithered and slipped down Stockwell Lane and Gambles Lane or down to Southam along the old route along Spring Lane and Lye Lane. Such references do not provide a comprehensive history of quarrying but they indicate its general nature and confirms that in this period exploitation of the minerals coexisted with the demands of animal grazing and were not the source of conflict they were to become later.

Fortunately, we do have clear reference to quarrying at Postlip Quarries in the *Valor Ecclesiasticus*, the great survey of the lands of the Church, made in 1535 just before the Dissolution of the Monasteries. It states that Winchcombe Abbey was still paying 6d. each year to the Bishop of Worcester for the stone from these quarries. The need for Cotswold stone in Winchcombe from such convenient quarries meant a continuing demand. Even after the abbey's dissolution in 1540 the demand continued. Some uses are instantly recognisable, such as the cluster of buildings at Postlip itself, dating back to the twelfth century; and in Winchcombe St Peter's church dating back to the fifteenth century, the early seventeenth-century Jacobean House, and the multitude of humbler cottages lining the main streets, which received a cladding of Cleeve stone from the dissolved monastery over their original timber framing. This stone from Postlip from the demolished abbey and

Not only was St Peter's church in Winchcombe built from Postlip stone, but many of the houses received a cladding of stone from the demolished monastery

its surrounding buildings was recycled on a huge scale at Sudeley Castle. Sir Thomas Seymour, the brother of King Henry VIII's third wife, Jane Seymour, was granted Sudeley Castle and the site of the abbey in 1547, the same year he married Henry's last queen Catherine Parr, who came to live at Sudeley. Examples of the decorative worked stone which was not used in building work are on display at the castle. Postlip Quarries continued to be worked after the Dissolution. There is a reference in 1749 to the fact that the quarryman, a James Tarren, was renting the quarries from Isaac

This shows how the front ground floor wall of timber-framed houses was extended under the jetty to provide a flat surface for the stone cladding (Sheldon Bosley Knight)

Sudeley Castle has been built and re-built over centuries. Sir Thomas Seymour used stone from the abbey to build a home suitable for Henry VIII's widow Catherine Parr. This engraving of 1789 shows the castle before the Victorian additions

Since 2019 DigVentures has been conducting annual archaeological digs at Sudeley Castle on former gardens lying to the east of the existing gardens. The carved stones from the abbey which could not be used in the castle were dumped in the garden

Bailiss who in turn leased them from a Mr Bruges, described as Lord of Cleeve Manor. So three people felt they could profit from them.

Cotswold quarries are notoriously badly documented. As David Bick showed in his study of Leckhampton Hill, which provided Cheltenham with its major source of building stone, there is little that can be written with certainty of the period before the nineteenth century. This will be followed through in Chapter Six.

Woodland

Between c.1520 and 1818 the physical appearance of the hill from the vale changed little. The feature which can change the appearance of the landscape the most obviously is woodland and its clearance. By the end of the Middle Ages a balance had been reached between continued clearance for increased arable, and the need to maintain supplies of timber and wood for their many uses. During these three centuries the only significant change in the woodland coverage took place off the hill scarp, in the vale just to the north of Southam village, with the clearance of eight acres for pasture of *Muckmead* coppice in the 1620s. This was the 'big meadow' which could have given its name to Southam as discussed in Chapter Two. How many people walking their dogs in the fields near Southam realize that this accounts for the oval area completely devoid of ridge and furrow just one field away from Ratcliff Lawns? The other woods remained, little changing now that their banks had become established features of the landscape. In 1620 Thrift Wood (then also called Nutt Wood) was described as coppiced but Stutfield and Queen's Woods had areas not only of coppiced woodland, largely hazel, but also of timber trees, particularly oak, ash and beech.

Lower down the slopes towards Southam lay areas of wood pasture, while Wontley Wood grew mostly timber trees. In addition more trees for timber grew around the manor, mostly in hedges. These numbered 2,500 in the smaller part of Southam manor in 1620. Their value as a manorial asset is indicated by the £1,000 value placed on them. The present landscape confirms the importance of woodland as a valuable resource at that time. The pollarded trees, now overgrown, in the field above the B4632 as it skirts Southam village provide evidence of the wood pasture. This was an attempt to balance woodland and animal grazing where there was pressure on land, for it allowed coppiced wood to grow above the heads of the animals. Significantly the trees grow on the ridge and furrow of Medieval arable farmland, abandoned as population declined from the fourteenth century.

These landscape indications that woodland was a precious resource are confirmed by the documentary record. In 1537 George Wallwyn, the lessee of the larger (royal) part of Southam manor was accused of taking timber to repair his house and farming implements, and for firewood, to the detriment of the rest of the villagers. In 1591 Reynold Nicholas was

The browned grass lying on top of the ridges betrays the Medieval ploughland later used as wood pasture at Southam

accused of allowing his cattle to spoil 100 young oaks in Queen's Wood. The wood at that time extended to 40 acres and the young oaks had been planted 'thin set' amongst the coppiced wood. This accusation was repeated in 1599/1600, and again in the following year when he, in turn, accused widow Elizabeth Cocks of illegally cutting timber in Queen's Wood. Reynold Nicholas was the lessee of Queen's Wood for we find in 1613 Richard Delabere exchanged a house and smithy in Prestbury for Reynold's lease of Queen's Wood in order to consolidate the Delaberes' holding in Southam. Fortunately there still survives a survey of Queen's Wood made in 1604, when the manor was originally sold by the Crown. It listed rights to the trees (for timber), to the wood and underwood (for tools, stakes and firewood), to herbage (for cattle and sheep) and to pannage (for pigs). The lopping (cutting the top) and shredding (cutting the side branches but leaving the top) of great trees also enabled the trees destined to provide timber to produce coppiced wood in the years before they were felled.

The complex of internal banks and ditches, now much decayed, reflects the divisions of the wood into its different parts. All the woodland was susceptible to the damage caused by intruding animals, but especially coppiced woodland with its many young, tender shoots. Such damage was a constant feature of complaints. In c.1800 the value of Stutfield Wood was said to have been reduced by two-thirds because cattle had broken in and damaged the growth.

The most important area for timber lay over the common at Wontley or East Wood. In 1604 this extended to 40 acres and we can measure the importance of the timber. In a survey of 1620 the 2,500 oaks and elms were valued at £1,000, the value of 100 acres of coppiced woodland was valued at £25 per annum. Even over a complete seven year cycle the value would only be £175, a sixth of the value of the timber, and a measure of the relative economic importance of the two types of woodland. However, the total area of this woodland was much larger; the rest of it belonged to Winchcombe. Its importance can be inferred from the plea by the townspeople to monarchs Philip and Mary in 1554 not to grant it out with the rest of the manor, which was successful.

There is little more that can be said about the woodland in this period. Physically it remained a stable feature in the landscape; economically it remained an important resource for the tenants. Significantly there are no records of any conflict between the much larger number of villagers in Bishop's Cleeve with their much smaller area of woodland, notably Bushcombe Wood, and the smaller number of Southam villagers with their more extensive woodland. The manorial claims to woodland were much clearer than to grazing.

Settlement

The post-desertion history of Wontley is characterized by attempts to make a profit out of an isolated estate of over 300 acres. Until 1623, Wontley descended with Bishop's Cleeve manor which was sold by the Crown in 1604 to Peter Vanlore (merchant) and William Blake (gentleman), both of London. Their purchase included the land at Wontley and the adjoining woodland. We know the land was still used as pasture and was producing the same annual rental as in 1482, i.e. £6.13s.4d. In 1620 the manor was sold again, to Giles Broadway of Postlip, producing a profit to its owners of £400 on a £2,700 sale. In December 1623 Giles Broadway sold off Wontley to Ralph Cotton of Whittington for only £920. The latter rented it to Thomas Nicholas, who might just have been the same person, or his son, who had exchanged the lease of Queen's Wood for a house and smithy in Prestbury with Richard Delabere in 1613.

The failure of any owner to make any real profit from the estate is confirmed by a rapid succession of seventeenth-century owners including one John Jenner, described as of Hawling and Wirdhill in Wiltshire. This episode sheds some light on the complicated financial arrangements people were prepared to enter into in order to gain some personal profit. In the case of Wontley hope and ambition always outran realisation. John Jenner paid only £1,000 for Wontley in 1674, holding a mortgage from Sir Henry Pollexton, the Lord Chief Justice. However, John Jenner 'soon after broke, and ran away beyond sea so that he could not be foreclosed'. Sir Henry reclaimed the estate and let it to Carew Williams for £40 per annum, which meant Sir Henry received just £29 profit after taxes, a return of 2.9 per cent. In June 1691 Sir Henry died, leaving debts of £1,400 on the property. The next year his executors were approached by Carew Williams who offered to rent it with a £10 reduction. They refused and then let it at the original £40 to a Thomas Carter. His motives are not known, but it is difficult to imagine they were solely financial for he knew that during the previous sixteen months Wontley had produced only £13.15s.11d. profit.

On Lady Day 1701 the estate again changed hands, being sold to William Dodwell of Brockhampton Park, which belonged to the Sandywell estate at Dowdeswell, for £1,000. The annual profit at that date was £20, but there was none for the next 26 years because the lands were said to have been without a tenant. However, we do know that in July 1706 a William Maull, described as being of Wontley, supplied William Dodwell with 130 ewes for £40, William Dodwell then paying Maull 3s. a week for looking after them on the common until Michaelmas. Here, perhaps, is the clue to the continuing interest in a land holding which always ended as a liability for both its owners and tenants. It gave them rights of access to Cleeve Common for free grazing in the hope of making good profits from the sale of the animals. This emphasises the importance of the narrow tongue of land stretching northwards along Padcombe Bottom, as noted in the previous chapter. Its incorporation into the Wontley estate was carefully established in deeds which go back to 1623. Wontley was still part of the Sandywell estate in 1777, when it was being rented with neighbouring Whitehall, built *c.*1720 by William Dodwell, to William Cox for £350 per annum. In the light of its recent history of economic failure this combination seemed a much more sensible arrangement.

How far did the developments at Cockbury parallel those at Wontley? Although it possessed a similarity with Wontley in being a remote location, it remained a much more valuable and valued estate. The present, largely sixteenth-century, house is one indicator of this. It contrasts starkly with the ruins at Wontley. Another similarity was that it passed through a succession of absentee landowners who bought the property, partly, at least, for the rights attached to it on both Nottingham Hill and, later, Cleeve Common.

Our first picture of Cockbury is provided by the inquisition, or enquiry into his possessions, taken at the death of Sir John Huddleston of Southam at the end of 1548. He held Cockbury from the king, who at

Cockbury as it appeared c.1803. The house itself is the building nearest the centre of this pencil sketch which shows the area before the building of the present road in 1823. Also in the sketch is the barn next to the house and to their left, Dryfield (Gloucestershire Archives P368/1/MI/3/7)

that time was young Edward VI, and it was worth 26s. 8d. per annum. The description of the estate provided a reason for its continuing value, for it possessed a mixed economy unlike the great dependence at Wontley upon pastoral farming and woodland. The inquisition listed a messuage, 60 acres of arable, 40 acres of meadow, 60 acres of pasture, twelve acres of wood and three acres of moor and heath. It was a microcosm of a balanced estate. The total acreage fits the area between Langley Brook and the old turnpike road along the common and as such probably reflected the land attached the Medieval settlement at Cockbury. Its potential value attracted continuing interest which led to its subsequent descent becoming even more complicated than that of Wontley. It seems likely that the present house originated during the time of the Huddlestons who also built the neighbouring large barn, now converted into a residence.

In 1609 the Huddleston family sold it and their estates at Guiting for £1,800 to John Stratford, described as salter of the City of London. John Stratford was the youngest of five sons of the Stratford family of Farmcote. Following countless younger sons he had left home as a teenager to seek his fortune in the City of London at some time during the 1580s. He entered the salt trade as an apprentice, then became a member of the London Salters' Company. Always with an eye open to develop his business, John dabbled with importing flax from the Baltic companies in c.1601 with such success that in two years his initial capital of £200 had increased to £1,200. In addition, he developed businesses in tallow, potash, soap ashes and oil; all part of a salter's business. In danger of over-stretching himself, he began to sink some of his capital into more secure investments, and his Cockbury purchase was made at a time when he had begun to buy land not too distant from the family home in Farmcote. In 1621 he was joined in this venture by another salter and a lawyer, both from London. The next year they sold out to another London salter and a merchant, who were then joined in 1627 by two more salters, a lawyer, a merchant and a gentleman, all from London. Ten years later they all sold out to William Rogers of Dowdeswell for £1,119.6s.8d. The importance of such 'foreign' capital for the area at this and in subsequent years provided a powerful stimulus for change, and its presence warns against taking too parochial a view of the evolving landscape.

It is clear that part of the interest in Cockbury in this Early Modern period lay in its rights to common pasture. By 1630 the 60 acres of arable recorded in 1548 had shrunk to sixteen acres, tilled in two lots, one for wheat and the other for barley. In that year Timothy Gates, rector of Bishop's Cleeve, took a lease of Cockbury for seven years, paying £55 per annum. Timothy was a rich man having married Catherine, the granddaughter of Sir John Bridges, first Lord Chandos of Sudeley. He had bought the manor of Bishop's Cleeve with its manor house (the former bishop's manor house) in 1624 for £3,000, when farm labourers were earning £5 per year. The land at Cockbury was valued for its pasture: it could support sheep, and conversion to arable was prohibited on pain of a £5 per acre fine. Timothy's purchase had included 46 acres in Wickfields. Cockbury adjoined Wickfields so it made sense to add it to his holding to have a continuous block of land on the hill. Then in 1641 Gates sold Wickfields to William Rogers of Dowdeswell for £330. As Rogers had bought Cockbury four years earlier at the end of Gates' seven year lease, he now had the continuous block of land. Wickfields at that date was described as pasture but recently arable. A century later it was described as 'poor soil and uneasy for tillage'. These are the only fragmentary references to the lands of the deserted settlement of Wick in this period.

Cockbury then descended with the main part of the Rogers' Southam estates until purchased by Lord Ellenborough in 1833. It was an investment for the absentee Rogers family and tenanted by a succession of local farmers. It is fortunate that the survival of many relevant records in the County Archives gives a fairly detailed picture of Cockbury during these years. In 1680 William Rogers leased the farm to John Ballinger. When the latter's widow died in 1724 she owed £550 in arrears in rent. As compensation Rogers took her moveable wealth which was listed in an inventory or list taken of her possessions. It is printed opposite. Here is the transcription, because the information it contains provides us with a rare insight into an early eighteenth-century farm. The list was drawn up and valued by her sons and the landlord, so we can have confidence in its accuracy.

Opposite page - Jane Ballinger's inventory of 1724 (Gloucestershire Archives D627/8): transcript on page 108 overleaf

An Inventory of ye Cattle Goods & Chattels of ye Widow Jane
Ballinger as appraised ye seventh day of Novr 1724
                                                              £ s d
Imprimis Money in Purse & wearing Apparell   —   5- 0-0
         320 Sheep   — 125- 0-0
         035 Cows Heifers & Yearlings   — 100- 0-0
         13 Horses & Colts   — 080- 0-0
         Eight Piggs   — 009-10-0
         Six Stocks of Bees   — 001-10-0
In Sawcombs Barne one Oat Rick one Barly Rick & one Bay } 30- 0-0
                                       of Oats   }
In ye Grounds six Hay Ricks   —   50- 0-0
In ye Upper Barn at ye House two bays of Barly one } 80- 0-0
Barly Rick and one wheat Rick   }
In ye Lower Barn a Lyte house two bays of Barge & Rye } 40- 0-0
Grass and three Loads of Wheat   }
Wool 36 Tod   —   25- 0-0
Two Waggons two Carts two Ploughs 10 pair of Gears } 26- 0-0
seven Harrows 7 Horses body 5 Ox Yews & Yoaks   }
In ye Kitchen eight Kettles 3 Brass Pans   }
3 Brass Pots 17 dishes of Pewter 4 plates a Bason   }
5 Porringers 12 Spoons two pair of Tongues &   }   7- 0-0
a fire Shovel a Cleaver & Pothooks & Links &c   }
In ye Brew house 12 Barrells a Cheese press and   }   3- 0-0
Brewing Tubbs & Stools &c   }
In ye Room above stairs nine Beds & Bedsteads   }
Tables 13 pair & one Sheet 12 Napkins ten   }
Towells 5 Tables & Feathers five Coffers a Clock   } 20- 0-0
Clock case 12 Chairs &c   }
12 Baggs   —   0-16-0
23 Blanketts & Ruggs   —   5- 0-0
Eight hundred of Cheese   —   8- 0-0
                                         Tot   614-16-0
                               as appraised by us
                    The mark of Wm W Ballinger
                                Theo: Ballenger
                                John Rogers Junr

An Inventory of ye Cattle Goods & Chattells of ye Widow Jane Ballinger as appraised ye seventh day of Nov(embe)r 1724

	£	s	d
Imprimis Money in Purse and wearing Apparell	5	0	0
320 Sheep	128	0	0
035 Cows Heifers & Yarlings	100	0	0
13 Horses & Colts	080	0	0
Eight Piggs	005	10	0
Six Stocks of Bees	001	10	0
In Sawcomb's Barne One Oat Rick One Barley Rick) & One Bay of Oats)	30	0	0
In ye Grounds Six Hey Ricks	50	0	0
In ye Upper Barn at ye House two bay of Barly one) Barly Rick and One Wheat Rick)	80	0	0
In ye Lower Barn at ye house two bays of Pease &) Rye Grass and three Loads of Wheat)	40	0	0
Wool 36 Tod	25	0	0
Two Waggons two Carts two Ploughs 10 pair of Gears) Seven Harrows 7 Horse Pads 5 Ox Tows & Yoaks)	26	0	0
In ye Kitchen eight Kettles 3 Brass Pans) 3 Brass Pots 17 dishes of Pewter 4 plates a Bason) 5 Porringers 12 Spoons two pair of Tongues &) a Fire Shovel a Cliver & Pot hooks & Links et(c))	7	0	0
In ye Brew house 12 Barrells a Cheese Press and) Brewing Tubbs & Skeels et(c))	3	0	0
In ye Rooms above stairs nine Beds & Bedsteads) 4 Tables 13 pair & one sheet 12 Napkins ten) Towells 5 Table Cloathes five Coffers a Clocke &) Clocke case 12 Chairs et(c))	20	0	0
12 Baggs)	0	16	0
23 Blanketts & Ruggs	5	0	0
Eight hundred of Cheese	8	0	0
Tot(al)	614	16	0

as appraised by us
The mark of W(illia)m **W** Ballinger
Tho[mas] Ballinger
John Rogers Jun(io)r

The picture that obviously emerges is of a prosperous tenanted farm producing wealth for both the tenants (the Ballingers) and, through the rental, to the landlord (the Rogers family). The farm was sufficiently large to need three barns. The inventory was drawn up after harvest but before much of the produce of the land was consumed, so that we see the farm at almost the richest time of the year. The greatest wealth lay with the animals, with a total value of £314, and the importance of the rights to common grazing emphasized by the possession of 320 sheep. They had created further wealth in the 36 tod (i.e. 72 stones or almost half a ton) of wool valued at £25. The cattle were obviously largely for rearing, although they provided milk for the cheeses recorded in their usual storage place, upstairs. The pigs and bees provided meat and honey for the home. Although the gear for oxen was recorded, the only beasts of burden were horses, which is perhaps surprising and represents either an early move to horses or the fact that the oxen on the farm did not belong to Jane Ballinger.

The value of the stored crops came to £233 if the wool and cheese are included, £200 if not. Oats, wheat, peas and barley (for brewing) were grown in quantity; hay and rye grass had been cut for animal feed. Earlier, in 1630, only wheat and barley were recorded; later in 1774 only wheat and rye, but we do not know how complete these records were, except that the lease taken out in 1774 makes reference to wheat grown on 21 acres. It is clear from a valuation carried out in 1775 that the farm had by then lands in Bishop's Cleeve and Winchcombe as well as Cockbury. By that date it extended to just over 200 acres with only 43 acres of arable, growing wheat, turnips and seed corn.

The implements and tools are those necessary to run a large farm, but there is a surprising absence of detailed lists of furniture. The total value was £32.16s., which included £7 for the kitchen utensils, Why such absence? It could have been, of course, that the furniture had already been nominally passed on to the family. The lack of any furniture recorded in downstairs rooms might support this. However a more likely explanation could be that some of the furniture came with the house. This is indicated in the original lease taken out by Jane Ballinger's late husband John in 1680. It included a list of furniture: a cupboard and table board (i.e. just the table top) in the inner chamber (bedroom); a bedstead and a wainscot (an oak chair with arm supports) in the outer chamber; a table, bench, form and side cupboard in the hall (main room). If we assume these, or their replacements, were still in the house in 1724, we have a not untypical quantity of furniture for a farm like Cockbury. Even so, to modern minds it appears to have been unbelievably spartan, but tenant farmers were only just entering the world of conspicuous consumption based on continuing demand for food as the Industrial Revolution gained pace in the second half of the eighteenth century. Perhaps this can help explain why the annual rental increased modestly from £150 in 1774 to £163.3s.8d. in 1801.

The farm continued to be a mixed economy. When William Arkell of Postlip took on the lease in 1774 he was granted permission to extend the arable land by only six acres at *Sestons*, the area abutting Wickfield Lane on its way up to the golf club house. He was only allowed to plant wheat or rye and had to follow a rotation of three years' plough and two years' grass. He would have to pay £10 to plough any other area. By 1801 the figure had risen to £30 per acre. This was presumably an attempt by the Rogers to maintain an emphasis towards pasture to keep the holding attractive to future tenants. Thus Cockbury succeeded where Wontley failed, in providing landlord and tenant with a profitable income.

But what was happening to that other deserted Medieval settlement, at Haymes? For over two centuries it was the home to the Lorenge family, who were first recorded when John died in 1500, but he had inherited it from his father. They held the estate indirectly from the crown which held Southam manor. In 1610 Thomas Lorenge acknowledged the over-lordship of Richard Delabere for 120 acres by the token payment of 11s.5d. per year and the traditional pound of pepper. Thomas was actively adding to his estate, having recently purchased the enclosure at the top of Gambles Lane called Bittemoor which had belonged to John Stratford. The Lorenge family continued to add to their estate, purchasing valuable meadow land in Prescott by 1631 and coming into possession of the Town Meadow along the Dean Brook in Bishop's Cleeve by 1671. In 1675 Thomas settled his lands on his son Charles. By 1679 the estate had grown to 150 acres of arable with 50 more acres added shortly afterwards; 100 acres of pasture, with rights to the common; and 50 acres of meadow together with two gardens and two orchards. It also included six messuages and five cottages. The latter probably lined Gambles Lane but actual locations are uncertain as the Medieval settlement near the house had long since disappeared. By then, however, Charles Lorenge had overstretched his finances. He had mortgaged his estate to provide capital and debts had mounted to £3,860 by 1685. In 1688 his father Thomas was killed at Cirencester fighting for James II in the unsuccessful attempt to prevent William of Orange taking the throne in what is known as the Glorious Revolution. Four years later Charles sold Haymes to Thomas Gooding, a lawyer of Grays Inn, London, for £3,300, thus ending over 200 years of its association with the Lorenge family by the introduction of yet more 'foreign' capital into the area.

Gooding continued to develop the estate, enclosing 50 acres from the open fields by 1717, when he settled the estate on his daughter Margaret for her marriage to William Strahan, living at that time in London, but described by Samuel Rudder in his county history of 1779 as 'a baronet of Nova Scotia'. Strahan took up residence in Haymes, spreading his local influence by purchasing the residual manor of Bishop's Cleeve in 1735, and trying, but failing, to re-establish himself as lord of the manor in the village. As part of that attempt he completely remodelled the house which stands in Station Road, almost opposite School Road, into his manor house. Haymes was too far out and the Cleeve farmers by now too independent to bow to an outside lord, even

William Strahan's house in Bishop's Cleeve

though William built himself a private pew in the centre of St Michael's church in 1746. He was, however, more successful in extending his influence around Haymes where he was active in exchanging land to consolidate his estate.

The accompanying map of 1731 provides an invaluable source for the extent of the Haymes estate at this date and the appearance of this part of the hill. The comparison with the modern aerial photograph gives some indication of the continuities and changes in the landscape over nearly 300 years. It can be inferred from the map that the common once extended below Lye Lane and the position of Bickmoor supports a conclusion that it had been taken out of the common. Unfortunately the map does not show anything on its northern, or left, side. The enclosed pasture fields surrounded by hedges and ditches with clumps of trees dotted around them, as at Bickmoor, Bush Hay and Long Croft, contrast starkly with the ridge and furrow of the lower slopes and into the vale. Here neither the Lorenges, Thomas Gooding nor William Strahan had been able to consolidate all the Haymes land into separate fields, for the gaps in the map between the fields and strips indicate land in the ownership of others, and therefore of no interest to the maker of a map of the Haymes estate. Even on the slopes around Haymes House, consolidation was not complete. It seemed self-

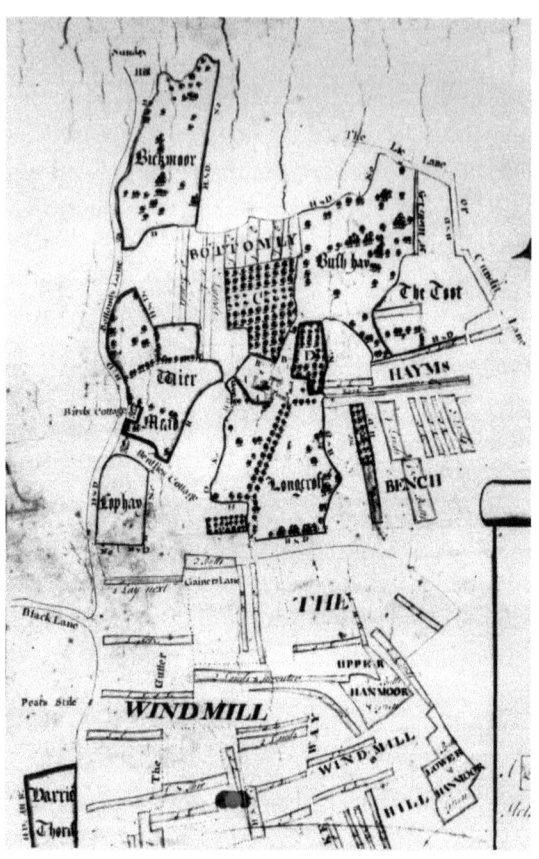

Haymes estate in 1731
(Gloucestershire Archives D309/P2)

An aerial view of the same area

evident to landowners in the eighteenth century that by consolidating land to form blocks which could be enclosed, they could be taken out of the communal system of agriculture and become the place for private experiments. Private gain, to the possible detriment of the community, seemed more acceptable in the arable fields than on Cleeve Common. This can be seen at Bottomley where part of an area of former ridge and furrow was already planted as an orchard.

The detailed view of the house in 1731 provides an image of the earlier building before it was swept away to be replaced by William Strahan's red brick, rather than stone, mansion two years later. It looks a typical seventeenth-century Cotswold farmhouse surrounded by its barns. A dairymaid brings in the apples from the orchard and through the doors of one of the barns, a labourer can be glimpsed as he threshes the grain with a flail. These interesting details remind us that without the countless ordinary people, whose names are never found in the documentary record, but who moulded the landscape, the story of Cleeve Hill would be incomplete.

Much of the 1731 landscape pattern remains today, but there have been changes. New Road of c.1844 now cuts across, as a continuation of Black Lane; the main Cleeve Hill road cuts through Bickmoor and across

Haymes farm and buildings in 1731 (Gloucestershire Archives D309/P2)

Lie Lane, and more houses now line Bottomley or Gambles Lane. More importantly, as far as the changing landscape is concerned, the strips of the open fields have been hedged over to create the modern enclosures we call fields.

William Strahan continued to add to the Haymes estate. In 1754 he bought up Bottomley Cottage in Gambles Lane, first recorded in 1718, for ten guineas, but the estate was a source of income rather than a holding to be farmed directly, and William got into difficulties when his expenditure, chief of which must have been on the remodelling of Haymes House, outran his income. In 1772 he was declared bankrupt and was forced to sell all his interests in Bishop's Cleeve. Two Worcester gentlemen, John Thorneloe and William Lily, bought the whole in 1773 for £11,000. The following year Lily sold his share, which included the Haymes estate, to Joseph Cocks, yet another London lawyer, for £3,738. The owners were absentees and the land seems to have been leased to local people to farm. However the fact that the features mapped in 1731 still remain largely identifiable today, indicates little change to the landscape took place then on this part of the hill.

During the Middle Ages the settlement on Cleeve Hill formed small, clearly defined hamlets at Cockbury, Haymes, Wick and Wontley. However, in the Early Modern period we find the first documentary references to another type of settlement, the squatter settlement. Families took advantage of encroachments on the common and wide grass verges alongside roads, such as at Bird's Cottage and Bentlies Cottage seen on the Haymes map. The earliest clearly documented example dates from 1582 and describes a cottage on the plot now occupied by Gambles Cottage. When Thomas Lorenge bought Bittemoor from John Stratford in 1607 it contained a cottage on part of it. It cannot have been a very substantial building for it does not appear on the 1731 map. In 1693 the bailiffs were sent by John Delabere, lord of the manor at Southam, to evict a man named King who had built a cottage on the common at Nutterswood. They took swords and pistols, and razed his house to the ground, but the foundations of the small community at Nutterswood had been laid. Once squatters' rights had been established they tended to remain. The folk tradition that rights could be established if a house could be built overnight and have smoke coming out of the chimney by morning had no legal basis, but squatting on common land was tolerated. For example, in 1812 Charles and George Hawker were presented at the manor court in Southam for their encroachment at Nutterswood. Their defence was that they worked the quarries and so they were able to establish their right to remain by paying an annual rental of 1s.6d to the Delaberes in 1816, although they were not reliable payers for in 1830 they were accused of being behind with their rent. By 1716 the piece of land at the top of Stockwell Lane, where Sheep Way and Emblem Cottage stand, had

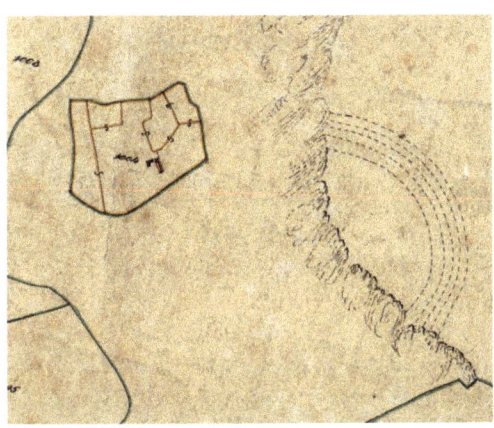

Even in 1839 when the Tithe map of Bishop's Cleeve was produced, there was only one building at Nutterswood shown as a dwelling by its pink colour (Gloucestershire Archives GDR/T1/26; Rector and Parochial Church Council)

Nutterswood today

been taken from the common, which was not then divided by the main road. In that year it changed hands for £26. By 1837 the forerunner of Emblem Cottage had been built there. It is known that by c.1783 an encroachment had been made along Spring Lane by William Kitchen. By 1866 two cottages had been built where Spring Cottage stands now

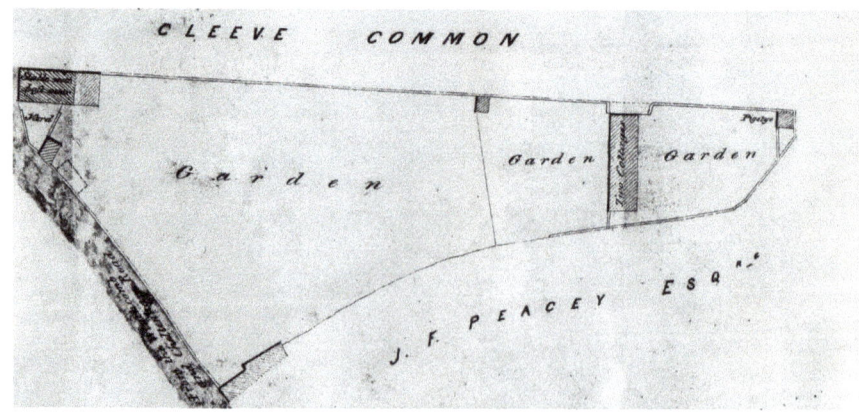

Plan of 1866 showing William Kitchen's encroachment (R. Salter)

and William Kitchen or his son, also William, had built a stable with a loft over, the forerunner of Sunnyside, because they were hauliers of the stone. These seem to be the oldest surviving houses on the hill, the traditional appearance of Spring Cottage reflecting its close links with the hill and standing in stark contrast to the later mansions and villas reflecting the wealth of the Cheltenham traders a century or more later.

Not every encroachment led to building. When Timothy Gates bought Wickfields in 1624 he also bought Oat Piece, that field crossed by the old road across the common to Postlip and Winchcombe. Presumably it took its name from the high elevation which meant it was best suited for growing oats. This provides a documented example of a very early encroachment which has remained as a field taken out of the common until the present day. This subject of encroachment will be considered in more detail in Chapter Six.

Tobacco and Flax

The later history of the deserted Medieval sites has been characterised by the interest shown in them by London merchants and lawyers seeking a return for their investments. At a time of rising population and prices, lands at Cockbury and Wontley and the estate at Haymes presented attractive propositions for the purchase of real estate. The present landscape helps us visualize the location of their endeavours, but we would learn very little without the written record. Due partly to the over-ambitious, acquisitive nature of the owners, and partly to the nature of the ground and situation, especially at Wontley, long-term financial success eluded Vanlore, Blake, Lorenge and Strahan. But for one short period some of their investments seemed to have paid off. In the early seventeenth century Cockbury and Haymes saw experimentation in tobacco and flax growing, in a variety of ventures which provided jobs for the poor and income for the entrepreneurs, in the words of Joan Thirsk, 'mutual aid in the Vale of Tewkesbury'.

The mastermind behind such schemes was John Stratford, the Farmcote lad who had made good in salt, flax and a variety of other trades in the City of London. His purchase of Cockbury in 1609, and the subsequent interest taken in it by fellow merchants from London, can be explained as attempts to experiment with new crops. It was truly mutual aid, as they sought to make a profit while giving employment to the many hundreds of poor of the area. In 1619 John Stratford had 100 acres in Bishop's Cleeve, Winchcombe and Cheltenham. He involved some of the local gentry. We have already met Giles Broadway of Postlip whose daughter he married, Timothy Gates the rector of Bishop's Cleeve, and Thomas Lorenge of Haymes. John Ligon of Arle Court in Cheltenham and Sir John Tracy of Toddington were also involved, but the capital to set it up came largely from London.

The one year of full tobacco production on the estate was 1619, when good weather and careful cultivation gave work to upwards of 200 local people between May and November, growing, harvesting and curing the crop. Joan Thirsk has calculated the net profit per acre in 1619 was £26.9s., compared with £2 per acre for old pasture or meadow. However, at the end of the season the government banned the crop to protect interests in the colony of Virginia. The summers of 1620 to 1622 were cold and wet, and the gentry withdrew, leaving the poor to continue the tobacco growing illegally until it was ended forcibly in 1690. No records have survived which reveal the scale of this later operation. We know that attempts were made to stop it in 1634 and again in 1636, but they must have been hampered by the fact that the local Justice of the Peace was Timothy Gates.

John Stratford had taken land at high rents on the basis of the likely good profits. He desperately needed another venture and so turned to flax, growing 40 acres at Cockbury and Winchcombe. From tending the plant to weaving the linen, he argued 800 jobs should be created. It was certainly sensible, for between 1623 and 1627 he claimed the profits had enabled him to pay the £8,000 debts incurred in his tobacco growing venture.

Although such ventures did not, apparently, change the landscape, it is relevant to this landscape study to ask where such cultivation took place. Unfortunately the answer is very difficult to find. The tobacco growing area identified with the Haymes estate amounted to eight acres. It is known from a dispute between Thomas Lorenge and John Stratford, recorded in the Court of Requests in London in May 1621, that only two acres belonged to Thomas Lorenge; the rest was owned by his brother, John. The land was referred to as *Conygree Layes* which lay in the manor of Bishop's Cleeve as part of the ridge and furrow in the common fields, and was cut by the common path to Gotherington. Other references to parts of the land as 'Butts' and 'Short Butts' would reinforce the theory that tobacco was grown off Butts Lane on the lower slopes of Nottingham Hill, quite a distance from Haymes itself. At Cockbury land transactions enable us to be reasonably certain that some of the growing of flax took place in the Wickfields. It is known that John Stratford was growing 40 acres of flax at Winchcombe and Cockbury from 1623, and Wickfields itself was 46 acres, so it is unlikely that the whole of the area was used. It belonged to Giles Broadway of Postlip from 1620 to 1624, when it was sold to Timothy Gates, a time at which John Stratford was struggling financially after the failure of his tobacco venture. In 1622/23 John had paid Giles Broadway 300 sheep, worth £10 each, to cover his rent. In the following year he paid with twenty hundredweight (i.e. a ton) of flax. It is just possible that by selling off large parts of the manor of Bishop's Cleeve, including the manor house, to Timothy Gates in order to raise £3,000, Giles Broadway added Wickfields because Timothy Gates was already heavily involved in these ventures.

It is unclear how long this flax growing venture lasted. When Timothy Gates took on the lease of Cockbury in 1630, only sixteen acres were described as arable, with only wheat and barley growing on the estate, which would suggest flax growing no longer took place there. A possible further clue that the site of the flax growing was at Wickfields can be found in the agreement drawn up when Gates sold it to William Rogers in 1641. The ground was described as being pasture but had previously been arable, which might have been a reference to the recent flax growing.

Also included in the sale was a 'recently built barn in the close'. Was this the 'Tobacco Barn' of local folklore, lying just off Stockwell Lane and standing in a field called Sheephouse on the 1839 Tithe map? Certainly the doorway and the coursed rubble stonework at its eastern end look seventeenth century, but the building appears to have been much altered. The roof has been lowered and the long walls could be nineteenth century. It is most unusual for a barn to have a doorway in the end wall. In 1990 Dr J.T. Smith of the RCHM passed judgement that it is impossible to base any historical conclusions on the standing building. Even if it is accepted that this is Timothy Gates' barn, documentary evidence suggests it was much more likely to have been built for drying and storing flax than tobacco, although it is interesting that a folk memory of the venture is still alive.

Tobacco Barn off Stockwell Lane in Woodmancote

Early Travellers and Visitors

This chapter has focused on the fact that the appearance of Cleeve Hill changed little over three centuries, and that to understand more fully its life it is necessary to investigate the written record. Although this life can be viewed superficially in an entirely local context, in reality much of the economy of Cleeve Hill during this period depended upon outside influences, chief of these being the demand for food, and capital made in London seeking investment opportunities in the provinces. Hence the continuing interest in Cockbury and Wontley and the experiments in tobacco and flax growing.

However another interest began to develop which was to become increasingly important. Cleeve Hill was viewed by outsiders, such as Thomas Dudley Fosbroke, as a piece of scenery, with little or no awareness on their part of the conflicts and tribulations arising from the varied attempts to exploit its soils and minerals to provide community well-being and/or private profit. The earliest travellers regarded the hill, not unnaturally, as a barrier to progress. John Leland, antiquary to Henry

CLEEVE HILL

VIII, travelled from Winchcombe to Southam in 1543 and was the first to leave a permanent record of his journey 'by good Corne Pasture and Wood but somewhat Hilly', he wrote in his itinerary. In John Ogilby's *Britannia*, a road book of 1675, the hill was 'a Mile in Height' and the way across it 'irregular'. His accompanying road map showed the continuation of the Medieval route along Dry Bottom as part of a long distance way, described in

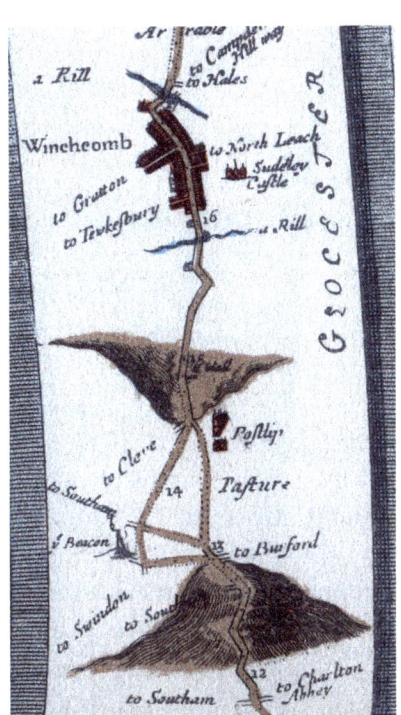

right - The route across Cleeve Common from John Ogilby's roadbook Britannia. *The western route was along Dry Bottom; the eastern route has been destroyed by later quarrying at Postlip*
below - The upper reaches of Ogilby's road are much overgrown today

the book as the road from Gloucester to Coventry. It entered the common at Wheeler's Corner and it was probably down this track, past Queenwood Grove and down into Prestbury, that 5,000 Roundheads had slipped and slithered on their way to relieve the siege of Gloucester some 30 years earlier in September 1643. The night was wet and windy, 'the wind blew a hurricane, the storm descended in torrents'. Most of the soldiers found shelter in Prestbury but the artillery remained on the hill protected by the rearguard. Around midnight the Royalists gave them two alarms, and in the confusion a Roundhead was shot by his fellows. Local folklore has nicknamed the trees known as the Three Sisters (now, of course, The Twins) as 'Cromwell's Umbrella'. This, however, is another good story unfortunately unsupported by the written evidence. The Earl of Essex, not Oliver Cromwell, commanded these soldiers, and the trees themselves are nowhere near as old.

One traveller who might have used Ogilby's atlas was Thomas Baskerville, who kept a diary of ten journeys he made in England from the early 1660s to the early 1680s. The manuscript is kept in the British Library and only now has it been published (see Further Reading). On one of his journeys into Gloucestershire he passed over Cleeve Hill. The original spelling has been kept as it captures the local pronunciation of place names.

> On St. James's day 1682 wee went from Winchcombe to Cheltnum to see a fair there and soe wee began to ascend the hills again till we came to a famous Beacon above a small house of my Lord Coventrees in a warrin with a little chapel by it, which Lord as a countryman told us is a kinsman of Sir William Coventrees who now lives at Byberry. From the top of this high and aery becon hill the prospects are soe alluring and intermingled with soe much variety, that as a man may say it may be like that with which the devill did tempt Christ, a shew of the glory of the world and its riches. (viz:) great cities and Towns, and a plentifull country under you, for as you travell this ridg country way, here you see Glocester there Worcester, here Teuxbury and there Easome with many more eminent places. (but to proceed) As to Cheltnum, 4 miles from Winchcombe, 'tis seated in a plain encompassed with the hills like an amphitheatre, with these rich parrish towns about it. Cleve, Pressbury, Charlton Kings, and Lackington.

Lord Coventry's 'small house' was Postlip Hall. Both it and 'a famous Beacon' were recorded on Ogilby's atlas and so it can be assumed Baskerville was following the western route across the hill whether or not he was actually using the atlas. It was this western route which enabled him to look down on the vale and make his vivid comparison with the devil tempting Christ as recorded in the bible. At this time in the past, any attractiveness Cleeve Hill might have possessed for the traveller was the view from it, not the open spaces of its common which attract the modern visitor.

Two famous people visited the hill before the end of the period under study in this chapter. When King George III made his visit to the embryonic spa town of Cheltenham in 1788 a favourite ride was from The Hewletts on to the common, from where it was reported he enjoyed the views and showed a great interest in 'the vestiges of a Roman Camp' (i.e. the hillfort), spending over an hour there on one occasion. Dr Edward Jenner made several visits to a summer house he is said to have built in a wood on the slopes of Cleeve Hill in c.1800, where he collected cowpox matter in his experiments to conquer smallpox. Queen's Wood was probably the most likely choice as it was reasonably accessible and near pasture ground for the cattle.

Such incidents give local history much of its fascination but they are not central to the main theme of change as a result of outside influences. In the years between the visits of these two gentlemen of distinction there occurred a development of much greater importance to the local population. The old routeway across the hill, recorded by Ogilby, was replaced by a turnpike road running across the face of the scarp and traceable today as a bridleway across the common and down Spring Lane and Lye Lanes.

On 1 June 1792 a meeting was held in Winchcombe at the White Hart Inn for the purpose of improving the road system centring on that ancient town. The usual complaints about the inadequacies of the roads for trade were made. As a result the existing way along the western edge of the common coming up as Spring Lane and on down to Postlip was turnpiked as part of a Cheltenham to Evesham road. Bars were set up at the Corndean Lane turning near Winchcombe and on the Cleeve Hill side of Southam village just above the present junction with New Road. The list of tolls reflected the usual charges on traffic, draught animals (horses, mares, geldings, mules, asses, oxen or bullocks) were charged 6d. when in harness, but 2d. when not. Exemptions from tolls not only included the more obvious mail coaches and soldiers but also empty wagons, wagons with loads of stone for roads, dung, ploughs and people going to church on Sunday.

Thirty one years later the road was lowered to its present line, at a cost of £248.10s.6d.; a move thoroughly approved by the county magistrate, Francis Witts, rector of the Slaughters, who recorded 'a much improved journey' along the new road in an entry in his diary in late

The milestone is clearly visible on the left of this view taken c.1900. Tom East was the road man

December 1823. The trustees had to set up new milestones. The present milestone which gives its name to Milestone Quarry dates from this time. It has lost its plate but represents four miles out of Cheltenham and three miles to Winchcombe. Despite the lowering of the route, Cleeve Hill still presented a major obstacle to travellers.

Two years after this turnpike act was passed, a second act was passed to turnpike the road from Andoversford, through Syreford and along West Down to Wickfield and Granna Lanes and thus down Nottingham Hill to meet the Gotherington to Gretton road. Anybody who has walked up or down Granna Lane will wonder how anyone, even in the age of enthusiasm for building turnpike roads, could ever have considered this a suitable route. So it was no surprise that the act was never put into practice. However in 1803 this route was described as being used to drive cattle to fairs and markets. This supports the explanation given by the Cleeve Common Trust's archaeological adviser, Tim Copeland, that the enigmatic lines shown on lidar images at the eastern end of West Down represent the last traces of cattle holding pens where the animals could rest on their journey to market. The route is shown as footpaths on the 1883 Ordnance Survey map and part runs along the White Way. As the need to reach and cross the hill increased in the nineteenth century the problems intensified. They will be discussed in the next chapter.

Finally, the Early Modern period provides the first visual record of what Cleeve Hill looked like. Southam Delabere was depicted in an

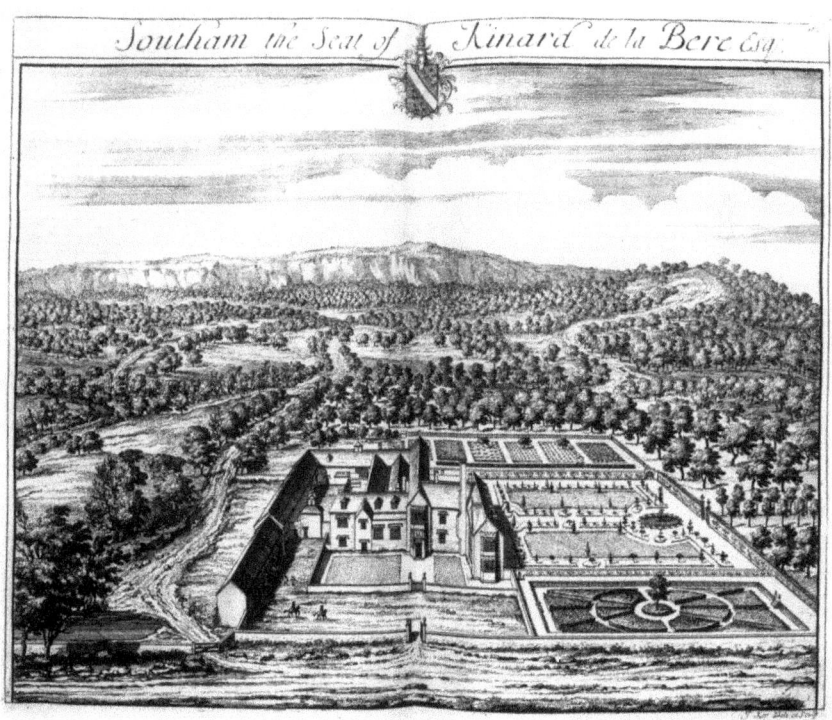

Kip's engraving of Southam House provides the first representation of Cleeve Hill. Although stylized, many feature can be recognised (Birmingham University)

engraving by Kip for Sir Robert Atkyn's county history of 1712. The hill is shown as a stylized backcloth, yet it is instantly recognizable, Cleeve Cloud with the woodland below, is easily identifiable. So too is the representation of wood pasture and the tracks leading to the summit, even the driftway between Sunset and Bentley Lanes in the left of the print. The road depicted in the immediate foreground is evidence of an early route, to the west of the house, which was replaced by the present route behind the house a century later. Kip's engraving is confirmed on many points by Thomas Robins' pencil sketch of 1760 showing the windmill which stood between Southam and Woodmancote. Robins'

Thomas Robins' pencil sketch contains much visual evidence for the hill in the second half of the eighteenth century

print is full of fascinating detail; the hunt chasing across the unenclosed ridge and furrow and the heavily laden horse. Again Cleeve Hill in the background is clearly recognizable, while to the right are Cleeve Cloud and Thrift Wood, the hedges dividing off the pasture fields and a lane twisting up to the common. On the common itself two clumps of trees have been drawn with a representation of a wall below each on the right. The trees have gone but the remains of the walls can just be discerned when the grass is short on the footpath along the top of the scarp which cuts through the hill fort, in which one of them is located. There is a third ring where The Twins grow and the best explanation for their existence is that they improved or 'tamed' the view of the hill from the vale. They must have been created some time before Thomas Robins drew his sketch as the trees had grown quite tall, perhaps planted by the Delaberes. The representation of Haymes after rebuilding by William Strahan is particularly interesting. Nicholas Kingsley, the foremost historian of the county's country houses, describes it as being built on an 'improbably grand scale' and suggests that it was never completely finished because William was living in a rented cottage in Hucclecote by the 1770s. It is possible this was after he had been declared bankrupt in 1772, no doubt partly caused by the building of the house. In 1778 Haymes was described only as a farm and what is without doubt is that all but the pavilions had been demolished by 1792 when the county historian Ralph Bigland wrote, 'Sir William's elegant mansion house… in a few years was levelled to the ground, and the materials sold'. This view from the vale is no longer possible, not only by the growth of vegetation but by the building of a mushroom farm in 1965.

Pictures can be notoriously misleading as accurate representations of past landscapes, but the visions given by Kip and Robins do seem to agree with the topographical and written evidence that by the eighteenth century the appearance of Cleeve Hill had stabilised into that which is recognizable today.

Conclusion

This chapter began with a contemporary quotation on the landscape; it ends with another. This comes from Samuel Griffiths' *New Historical Description of Cheltenham,* published in 1826, aimed at the large number of visitors to the spa. In common with many guide books, he published a series of rides from Cheltenham, one of which went over Cleeve Hill. The resultant eulogy to the vale contrasts with the travellers' attitude to the hill, reflected in Griffiths' text; it is ignored. Apart from the perception that it protected the vale, nothing more is written. This perception of the hill would not have been shared by the local inhabitants for whom it had existed as an important economic resource during the three centuries discussed in this chapter.

> The boundless beauties of the vale - the ascent of the protecting upland - the appearance of steeples and church towers, uprising like so many landscapes, and the multiplied and countless dwellings that give variety to the wooded plain, through which

the Severn, joined by its tributary streams and rivers, runs its impervious course - all the vast tract of country, extending on the one side far into Herefordshire and Worcestershire, and on the other to the bold and formative heights of the Welsh mountains - all combine to form one grand and glowing picture, all life and light, all splendour, immensity and magnificence!

FURTHER READING

Many of the sources have been referred to in the text. Details of Joan Thirsk's articles are as follows: 'Projects for Gentlemen, Jobs for the Poor; Mutual Aid in the Vale of Tewkesbury 1600-1630' in P. McGrath and J. Cannon (ed.), *Essays in Bristol and Gloucestershire History*, (Bristol and Gloucestershire Archaeological Society, Bristol, 1976) and 'New Crops and their Diffusion: Tobacco Growing in 17th-Century England' in her own *The Rural Economy of England* (Hambledon, London, 1984). An updated account of the tobacco growing can be found in Jean Bray, 'The Golden Leaf' in *Winchcombe History Journal* (Gloucester Street History Group, 2020). Joan Thirsk was also editor of *The Agrarian History of England and Wales, Volume IV* (Cambridge University Press, Cambridge, 1976), which has provided a general background to this chapter. David Bick's *Old Leckhampton* (privately published, Cheltenham, 1971) details the quarrying on Leckhampton Hill. The *Victoria County History of Gloucestershire, Volume VIII*, carries the descent of the manors; and the *Transactions of the Bristol and Gloucestershire Archaeological Society, Volume 50* (1928) carries an article by Canon Dowdeswell on Southam House and its deeds. The history of Haymes was taken from Nicholas Kingsley, *The Country Houses of Gloucestershire, Volume 2, 1660-1830* (Phillimore, Bognor Regis, 1991). Thomas Baskerville's diaries are published in Anthea Jones, *Travels in Industrious England* (Hobnob Press, Gloucester, 2023) with an introduction by John Chandler. I am grateful to Anthea for allowing me access before publication.

Surviving Southam deeds and manorial records are deposited in Gloucestershire Archives, particularly collections D1637, D2025 (especially boxes 30,31,69,70) and D2957. The descent of Haymes has been traced from D127; Wontley from D444 and Cockbury from D627. Disputes in the Court of the Duchy of Lancaster can be found at The National Archives in collections prefixed DL1/3/4/6/42, where the Court of Requests case can also be found (Req. 2, Bundle 30/44). I owe this reference to Joan Thirsk. There is a long account of the Civil War episode in *Bibliotheca Gloucestriensis, Volume I*, in Gloucestershire Archives.

5
CHELTENHAM MOVES OUT OF TOWN
(1818-1859)

WEEP Kingscote, weep, thy raining glory's o'er;
Let Bibury boast her matchless sport no more:
Thro' Gloucester's vale let Cheltenham's fame resound,
And prince of courses Cheltenham's course be crown'd!
Cheltenham Races: A Poetical Description, Anon, 1820

The Context

The year 1818 marked a turning point in the history of Cleeve Hill and its common. In that year Cheltenham races were first held on the western approaches to West Down. They signified the arrival of a new and increasingly important influence on life on the hill - Cheltenham moving out of town. From this point onwards our story becomes dominated by the spa town's spreading influence on to this great area of upland common. It was now increasingly seen as an empty open space for the recreational use of the leisured classes and masses, who viewed the sheep and cattle as an irrelevance and intrusion. Recreation now became a major new use of the common. Thus in this period the local farmers and freeholders, whose jealously guarded rights provided the driving force of the hill's story over the past thousand years, became marginalized in their own territory, bought off for a few pounds by the fashionable *beau monde* attracted to the growing spa town of Cheltenham with its multitude of amusements and distractions.

Cheltenham certainly did grow, from approximately 3,000 people in 1801 to 35,000 in 1851 and 45,000 in 1891. During the 'season' from April to November many thousands more visitors swelled the town, demanding, and receiving, all manner of entertainments and pastimes to while away the dreary periods between bouts of taking the spa waters. Balls, card parties, dinners, plays and concerts attracted the English (and Irish) nobility, the county gentry, and manufacturers and traders who, having made their money in the Industrial Revolution, escaped to Cheltenham to aspire to gentility. They were followed by their servants, hangers-on, and an immeasurable underclass of petty criminals, pickpockets, confidence tricksters and swindlers. Not without cause was Cheltenham described as 'The Merriest Sick Resort on Earth', and when a few local traders decided to add a race meeting to the attractions, choosing Cleeve Hill on account of its open space and good racing turf, the local commoners were submerged by a new influence against which their existing methods of social control were to prove no defence at all. The self-governing vestry meeting in Bishop's Cleeve and the continuing manor courts in Southam had always tried to balance the existing uses of the common for the benefit of the community against the private gain of the individual. They were unable to adequately protect the commoners' right to grazing against the hoofs of racehorses. They did insist on, and receive, although invariably after a struggle, £30 annual rental from the racecourse Turf Club. This was later increased to £60, but it only really served as a token of their powerlessness and irrelevance in the face of the new modernity flooding in from outside. Their impotence is well illustrated by a further passage taken from the ballad quoted at the head of the chapter:

> With sluggish step departs the surly clown,
> And drives his flock from Cleeve's deserted down;
> The dog's loud bark, the sheep's quick tinkling bell
> Are heard to sound amid the neighbouring dell.

Cheltenham races on Cleeve Hill not only formed an important episode in the history of the hill, but also form part of the history of Cheltenham and the prehistory of its present famous course.

Cheltenham Races on Cleeve Hill

From the radio masts at the west end of West Down it is difficult to visualize the hustle and bustle of an early nineteenth-century race meeting. It is well-known that such meetings were held here, but written accounts of them usually form little more than a footnote to the history of the present course at Prestbury Park. However, they are entitled to more than a footnote. They stand important in their own right, not only in the history of horse racing but also because they represent the first major threat to the traditional life of the common.

The races formed part of the social whirl of the spa. Their rise and fall mirrored the rise and fall of the varied attractions of the spa, unlike the contemporary meetings at places like Ascot and Newmarket, where the races themselves were the sole focus of the social whirl. A tale much repeated throughout the nineteenth century was that they originated in the occasional sweepstake run for a plate by the horses of the local gentry on the top of Nottingham Hill. Ruff's *Beauties of Cheltenham*, published in 1806, seems to have been the earliest guide to carry the story, 'Here but a few years hence, a plate or two used to be run for, annually, by horses belonging to the neighbouring gentlemen well-attended by visitors from Cheltenham'. It has been impossible to be more precise than this. Until the enclosure of Gotherington in 1807, the top of Nottingham Hill lay as unenclosed common land which was a favourite place to hold races. From at least 1721 to 1813 races were held on Tewkesbury Ham and until 1827 races were held on Minchinhampton Common. In 1818 they started on Cleeve.

In July of that year the *Cheltenham Chronicle* announced the intention to revive the races as an added attraction in the spa, should enough subscribers be enlisted for a sweepstake. By the middle of August ten five-guinea subscribers had been found to run a mile race on Cleeve Common, which took place on Tuesday 25 August. The whole meeting was a rather local, rustic affair. It was open only to hacks living within three miles of Cheltenham. The arrangements were organized by Mr E. Jones of the Shakespeare Inn, now the Shamrock, in the West End of the High Street. Fittingly, it was his five-year-old brown mare 'Miss Tidmarsh' which 'won easily' to become the first winner of the Cheltenham races and claim the 50 guineas prize money. Three further races followed, and the meeting was declared a success.

Two months later steps were taken to make the meeting permanent and much grander. A public meeting was called at the Town Hall, then in Regent Street, to open a subscription to lay out a race course and build a stand on Cleeve Common. Alex Fotheringham, Master of Ceremonies at the spa, headed the committee. Baynham Jones, owner of Cambray Spa, John Cossens, the Postmaster, John Gardner, owner of the town's largest brewery, Theodore Gwinnett, solicitor and clerk to the Town Commissioners, and J.D. Kelly, owner of the new Assembly Rooms, all added their support. Colonel Berkeley of Cheltenham's leading family

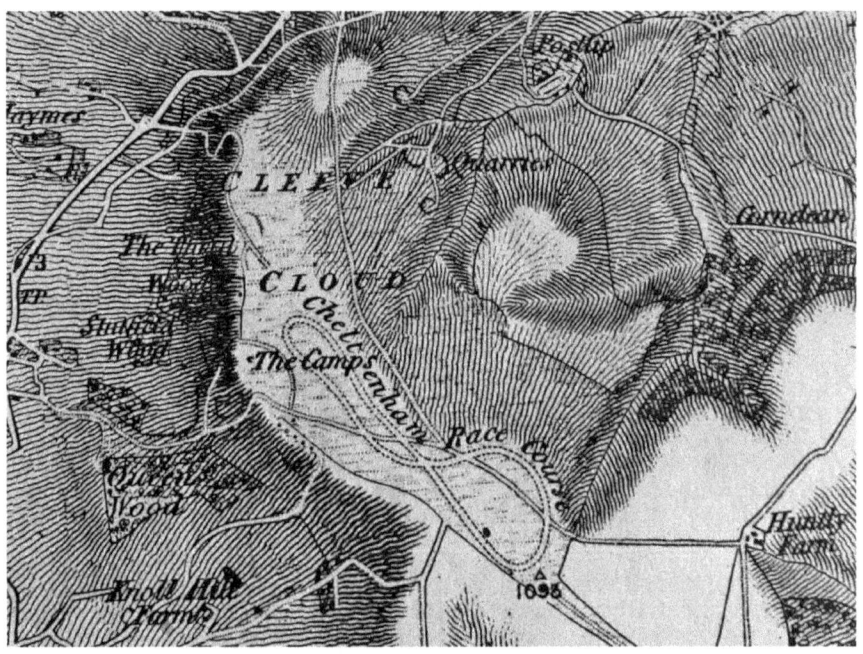

Cheltenham race course, showing the figure-of-eight course and the original grandstand. (Reproduced from the 1828 Ordnance Survey map)

subscribed 1,000 guineas to open the list. Thomas Morhall, the town surveyor, was appointed secretary with the task of finding subscribers, not only painting an image of 'the finest turf' in England, but also emphasising the employment it would bring to both the rich and poor of the town. The Duke of Gloucester agreed to become the necessary prestigious patron and subscribed 100 guineas. Sufficient funds were raised to support annual races until 1824. This was necessary as the other main income from the races was the rentals taken from the stall holders, spectators paying nothing to attend.

Who were the poor commoners of Bishop's Cleeve and Southam to stand up to this onslaught of foreign money and men of weighty provision in order to defend their ancient common rights against the *beau monde* who were intent on turning their precious resource into an open-air extension of the spa's many amusements? In vestry assembled in Bishop's Cleeve church, the freeholders demanded some recompense. As noted, they were granted £30 a year for the intrusion by the stewards of the racing club. To the latter this must have been a minor matter in their accounting; they spent in the first year over £400 on improving access to the course and setting it out. Yet they were bad payers. By 1822 they were two years in arrears and the villagers threatened to deal directly with the stall-holders at the races if the money was not paid into parish funds. £60 was paid and used to subsidise the local ratepayers in Bishop's Cleeve and Woodmancote, Brockhampton, Southam and Stoke Orchard. Thus the tradition and traditional rights were bought for a small price and their upholders thereby cast as people of little importance in this new and exciting world in which the people who mattered most were those with the largest purses.

A figure-of-eight course was set out approximately from where the trig point on West Down now stands to the hillfort. Plots for booths were rented out for five guineas each, balls and dinners were arranged for the evening entertainments and posters were printed to spread the good news. Racing then took place over three days from 23 August 1819. The big race was the Gloucestershire Stakes over two miles, run on the first day. It was worth 125 guineas and was won by Mr Calley's three-year-old, 'Champignon', after a good race. It was always the main race on Cleeve Hill; the Cheltenham Gold Cup was only the second big race of the meeting, run on the second day. Run over three miles the first ever winner of that cup was a Mr Bodenham's four year old horse 'Spectre'. Unfortunately, Thursday was left without a major race, which continued to be a problem for several years. The meeting, however, was hailed to have been a great success, despite the difficulties of access, either along the route described by John Ogilby or via The Hewletts, but its turf made for good sport, particularly in that hot, dry summer which had cracked many other courses and spoilt many races.

A poster advertising the first fashionable meeting of Cheltenham races (J. Tester)

Yet the venture was not without its critics. Even before the first race, and over eight years before the Reverend Francis Close published his well-known pamphlets on the evils of race-going, a lively debate was being conducted in the *Cheltenham Chronicle*. The protagonists argued the races would stimulate better breeding and increase local demands for hay, straw and oats. The antagonists claimed they would encourage 'bad company and profligacy', and pointed out that Waterloo had been won by horses fit for steeplechasing, not thoroughbred flat racers. The economic versus moral argument is a familiar one, whilst steeplechasing was considered fit only for heavy cavalry horses, not the true racehorses of England.

What was it like to attend these early races? The ballad already quoted above paints a picture of the racegoers struggling up the hill and contains an interesting comparison between the rustics coming up from Postlip (and Winchcombe) and the *beau monde* from Prestbury:

> Up Postlip bank winds slow the rustic throng,
> And clouds of dust attend their march along;
> But not such clouds as Southam's hill can boast,
> Where Cheltenham's varied, gay, unnumbered host
> Roll, like the stormy waves on Brighton's shore.

For many the day started at The Plough Hotel in Cheltenham, demolished in 1984 for the building of the Regent Arcade. From Winchcombe Street a variety of carriages made their way up out of Prestbury, covering their occupants with white dust as they toiled up the hill. On the downs an amazing sight met the eyes. There was a grandstand overlooking the course, which was staked out and clearly marked by the carriages bordering its length. Behind them stood booths, sideshows and other attractions. In 1825, and possibly other years, Mr Wombwell's famous 'Exhibition of Wild Beasts' kept people amused between the races, but there were always stalls with toys, dolls and gingerbread, gambling booths, pea and thimble tables, all designed:

> With thousand other idle schemes to drain
> The hard-earn'd savings of each rustic swain!

Pickpockets thrived. In 1825 they roamed in gangs estimated to be up to 200 in number, but none were caught and in crowds estimated to be 50,000 strong the pickings were easy. Thirty two carriages are said to have been stripped in one race alone. The local press complained that no arrests had been made, which was not surprising as law and order was still the responsibility of the unpaid parish constable, elected annually by the parish vestry. Just another example of how the traditional way of life of the villagers was swamped by this new development on their common. The festivities continued after the day's racing. The Turf Club held its dinner on the eve of the meeting; the stewards held their dinners on each day; there were balls on three nights in race week and plays on two nights. Cleeve Common just happened to be a very convenient place for visitors in Cheltenham to amuse themselves watching horse racing during three days in high summer.

Yet there were always problems associated with holding the races on Cleeve. Reaching it was one of them, even after the present road across the face of the hill lowered the approach in time for the 1823 races. Three years later the new road from Cheltenham to London was constructed (now the A40) and patrons were advised to use that and approach the course via Whittington. In addition the weather could be bleak when the wind blew and the rain slanted in, as happened in 1823. There was little shelter and attendances fell. In that year the first rumblings to move to Prestbury Park were heard, but they came to nothing for another eight years.

However, towards the end of the 1820s Cheltenham was becoming a more sober

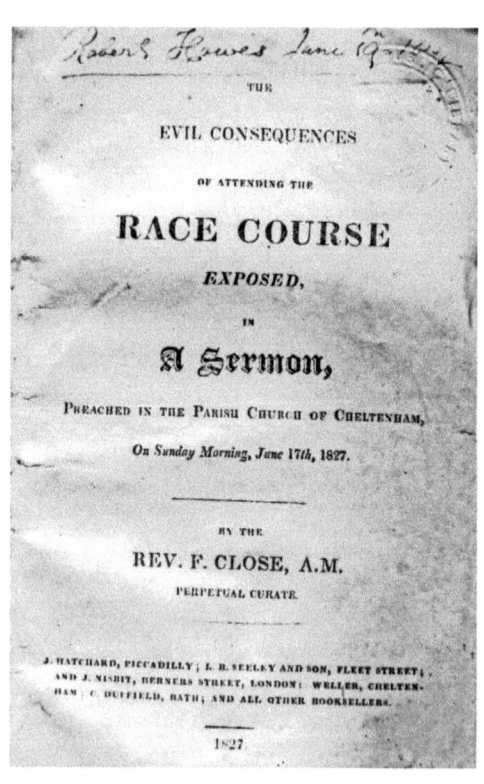

The sermon which started the lively controversy over the races and which subsequently split Cheltenham in two (Cheltenham Library)

place, as 'The Merriest Sick Resort on Earth' became a hotbed of evangelicalism after the arrival of Francis Close in 1824. He arrived from London to be the curate at the newly-built Holy Trinity church in Portland Street. Two years later he moved to be perpetual curate at St Mary's, now Cheltenham Minster, where he served for 30 years before moving to be the dean of Carlisle Cathedral. His campaigns against horse racing, the theatre and political Radicals are well known: "And this I know, that the roads, and fields and pathways leading to the emporium of vice and folly, are strewed with the victims of vice and vicious excess", he thundered from the pulpit in June 1827, just before the race meeting of that year. The sermon was printed as a pamphlet, sold 4,500 copies within the month and led to a lively controversy splitting the town into opposing camps. His opponents claimed that such religious 'enthusiasts' created nothing but civil wars and feud and, anyway, horse racing was necessary to improve the breed of thoroughbreds. Despite such criticisms and the fading of the spa's attractions, the races continued.

The 1823 Cheltenham Gold Cup. The horse 'Angelica' won 120 guineas for its owner, Mr West (E. Gillespie)

In the same year that Francis Close preached his sermon, Martin's the jewellers, whose shop still exists at the end of The Colonnade at the bottom of the Promenade, produced a gold cup 'of most chaste and elegant design' modelled on a Roman urn. The first winner of the Gold Cup and the £100 prize money, was Mr J. Sadler's 'Jocko' from a field of only four horses. Also in the same year it was decided to incorporate the races from the former prestigious meeting at Bibury which had folded in 1827, a move, according to the *Cheltenham Journal*, which would enable Cheltenham to rival the great flat meetings of Doncaster and Newmarket. In 1828 the meeting was brought forward to June to be nearer the start of the spa season, but despite all the hopeful changes, the newspapers reported that the fashionable people were not in attendance, and the crowds were smaller than in previous years. Things improved the next year when 20,000 or so people watched the Gold Cup on 23 July, but the controversies continued. Francis Close continued to rail against them and he continued to be attacked. In a satirical account of Cheltenham spa life and the races by the fictitious Dolly Dubbins, which first appeared in the national *Morning Post* newspaper, her servant Boxiana expressed her opinion, having attended St Mary's on 19 July:

> You must not to the Races go,
> At least, your Pastor tells you so,
> Who's fraught with proper notions;
> And if you to the Playhouse get
> Old Nick will know it, for he'll set
> One CLOSE to watch your motions.

Later in the year disaster struck when the grandstand burnt down, aided, whispered some, by the followers of Francis Close. The races could well have folded completely after 1830 if Lord Ellenborough of Southam House had not offered his newly purchased Prestbury Park to the Turf Club. The park had been the hunting ground attached to the Bishop of Hereford's Medieval moated manor site in Prestbury and had remained mostly intact being used as farmland after 1600

There was renewed enthusiasm, not least because the problem of accessibility had been solved. The Jearrad brothers, architects from London who were responsible for the design of the Queen's Hotel and Lansdown Parade and Terrace, were commissioned to build a 'handsome and substantial' grandstand for 700 spectators in the hope of attracting more ladies to the course. Paganini, the famous musician, gave two concerts in the Assembly Rooms during race week in order to boost funds. The meeting was cut to two days and while the crowd of 10,000 was said to be satisfactory, the sport was said to be poor. Nevertheless many wondered how Cleeve Hill had ever survived for so long.

Four years later racing was back on Cleeve. From today's perspective this seems an odd decision. Although the races at Prestbury Park were well-attended, concern was expressed at the race dinner on 15

The 'new' road to the race course through Whittington which still serves as an entry to the common. In 1897 it was still being referred to as 'the race road'

July that a new course was needed, either in the park or back to the old course, for the quality of the races at the park had been far below that of races on the hill. A subscription list was opened and by the following April it had collected 60 names, compared to the 36 names in the list to finance the 1834 races; a demand for the return to the hill obviously existed amongst the racing fraternity. The hill's superior turf won the day. In preparation the road through Whittington was improved and a new three-storied grandstand was constructed. The stewards chose a local builder, William Haselton, to design and build it and he quoted £800, having been knocked down from £840. It was modelled on the one built at Warwick in 1809. His proposals don't quite match the descriptions in the local papers but the original features are clear. The grandstand was built of stone from the common. It was a substantial structure with walls twenty inches thick. On the ground floor were the vestibule, weighing room, bar, restaurant and two water closets. The first floor comprised a saloon with windows looking out over the course, two of which were Venetian windows to allow the ladies to their seats on the roof of a projecting portico. The men sat in the open air on seats

William Powell Frith's famous painting of Derby Day at Epsom races is dated 1858 but shows many of the features of the races on Cleeve common: carriages lining the course, the booths, the varied nature of the spectators. The centre of the grandstand was not dissimilar to the grandstand on the common (Public Domain: File: William Powell Frith - The Derby Day - Google Art Project)

fixed to the roof of the saloon, as many as four hundred according to reports. It was said it could be seen on the sky line from the centre of Cheltenham, another statement that the town was making a claim to the common. Hopes for a successful return to the common were high as the grandstand had been financed by the sale of £25 shares with investors expecting to make a profit in the third year. From a modern perspective considering the grandstand was to be used for just three days each year and all the supplies, food and drink for the spectators, water for the water closets and coal for the fires, had to be brought in along difficult roads, this was an optimistic endeavour.

The accounts for 1835 and 1836 survive in the archives and they give glimpses into the high hopes and the careful preparations for the return to the common. From the former we learn that Mr Wolseley was paid two guineas for laying out a new course and that Mr Pettifer was paid £37 for bringing assets from the course in the vale, including removing the old posts, whilst £10.13s.4d. was spent on 30 new posts and 160 yards of rope, no doubt helping to mark out the new course. The rent to the vestry of Bishop's Cleeve was £60 and £23 was paid for constables to try to keep order. The £2.8s. paid to three men to guard Lord Ellenborough's wood i.e. Queen's Wood, was a further indication that the stewards were taking anti-social behaviour seriously, although not always successfully. The race-goers still did not pay to attend the races although carriages might have paid one shilling, but such payments did not appear in these accounts. Most of the money came from subscriptions from the Turf Club and the worthies of Cheltenham, totalling nearly £213 (out of a total turnover of £381). In addition, renting space out for booths amounted to £128. The account for the following year recorded sixteen booths paying £64 and so the sum for 1835 probably reflected 32 booths. There is nothing in the accounts to indicate why the numbers halved in 1836. Much of the other income and expenditure remained constant but obviously some of the assets brought from Prestbury Park were on their last legs. A new judge's chair had to be bought, for £6.4s., a new bell and remounting the old one cost £5.11s.9d. and a new winning post cost 7s. Placing advertisements in the local newspapers cost nearly £24.

If the financial backers had taken notice of what was happening in the local racing world, they might have hung back. 1834 had not only been the last flat meeting in Prestbury Park but it had seen the first steeplechase meeting, primarily designed for the horses of the Berkeley Hunt. The next year, on 1 April, barely three months before the meeting in July on Cleve Hill, Cheltenham's Grand Steeple Chase took place in Andoversford. According to the *Gloucester Chronicle* thousands of well-dressed spectators enjoyed watching eleven hunters race across streams and fields, fences and walls, 'Bobadil jumped the highest wall leading into the turnip field without touching a stone'. The finish was equally exciting with the winning margin just half a neck. The newspaper enthused as steeple chasing attracted bigger crowds than racing on the flat. It was obviously much more exciting. Possibly as a consequence, some of the early races on the hill were designed for the hunters which had been ridden in the steeplechases.

Nevertheless, back on Cleeve Hill the *Gloucester Journal* declared they were the best attended races since 1819, although the sport was disappointing. Only ten ran in the Gloucestershire Stakes and only two in the Cheltenham Gold Cup. Despite the best intentions of the stewards the great days of Cheltenham flat races were fading into the past along with the spa which had given them their birth. Two years later the *Cheltenham Chronicle* recorded the fashionable world still attended but in smaller numbers than before. The next year an interesting episode took place provoked by the small number of 44 people who attended the Stewards' Ordinaries (a dinner) instead of the expected 200. The blame was laid at the local Tories who were holding their annual dinner the following evening so they could buy up the unused food to provide 'a secondhand dinner' according to their opponents. This was strenuously denied.

However, four years after returning to the hill with such high hopes, the races were again in difficulties. On 7 July 1839 the Turf Club held a public meeting to raise funds. The secretary was owed £100 from the previous year and the total cost of £450 for the next meeting had to be met. £200 was raised and the races were able to go ahead, but a securer financial footing was desperately needed. A solution came from opening a three year subscription list to the county gentry, and renaming the races 'The County of Gloucester Races on Cleeve Hill Course'. Strictly speaking Cheltenham races had ceased to exist and the Gold Cup disappeared from the calendar. Despite raising enough to guarantee racing for the next three years, interest was not reawakened. The first county meeting took place on 21 and 22 July 1840 over a changed course to try to increase the excitement of the races. There were two races on the first day, and three on the second. Only six ran in the Gloucestershire Stakes, although four of them crossed the line together after an exciting competition. The grandstand was full but there was little other life around the course, not even, according to the *Cheltenham Free Press*, any thimble tables. The following year only nine races were run over the three days. The *Cheltenham Chronicle* commented, 'The County of Gloucester races appear to have lost all traces of bustle and activity which used formerly to attend when designated the Cheltenham races.'

In 1842 subscriptions and enthusiasm finally ran out. The nation was gripped in an economic depression. Cheltenham had metamorphosed into a sober, pious centre for education. There was little future for an activity which belonged to the merriest sick resort. The *Gloucester Journal* commented, 'They were viewed quite as a local amusement in which few but the good folk of Cheltenham took any interest'. Only 40 couples attended the race ball; the meeting itself was 'stale, flat and unprofitable' according to the *Cheltenham Free Press*. The weather on the last day was 'wretched' and the report of the last race in the *Cheltenham Examiner* provided a fitting epitaph,

> In consequence of the fog, the whole went the wrong side of the post, and were forced to pull up. They then groped their way in the dark the best manner they were able, and the race was won by Delusion by a head.

The last rental was paid to the Bishop's Cleeve vestry; once again it was late. When a Mr Herbert offered the parish vestry £20 a year to take over the racecourse after the last race had been run, their refusal reinforced the opinion that the horse races on Cleeve Common had had their day. On 1 September the grandstand was sold by auction at the same Plough Hotel from where many had set out for the races in former days. It had cost £800; it was sold for £155 after the furnishings and fittings had been removed. The *Cheltenham Chronicle* had a final word, 'This looks as if Cheltenham races had become a dead letter'. Two years later only 40 people turned up to a meeting in The Plough Hotel to consider revival. Racing on Cleeve Hill had ceased to exist, the victim of changing fashions and times. It could not outlive the decline of the spa which had given it its birth.

Away from the genteelness of the flat, the same years which saw the decline of the summer race meeting brought the rise of a spring meeting for the less polished horses of the Berkeley Hunt, as a way of rounding off the hunting season. It was in these rustic cross-country races, not the sophisticated races of the thoroughbreds, that the present Cheltenham meeting had its origins and the increasing popularity of steeplechasing was undoubtedly a factor in the decline of the races on Cleeve Hill. By 1840 the Cheltenham Grand Annual Steeplechase had earned the reputation of being second only to the Liverpool Grand National. Three races had been held in the March before the final meeting on the hill in 1842. The first had been based at Sandywell Park near Andoversford and the second two at Prestbury Park. For several years they were run around the lower slopes of Cleeve Hill. The 1847 race has passed into literary history as the subject of the poem *How We Beat the Favourite*, written 22 years later by Adam Lindsay Gordon, who became Australia's national poet. He had watched the race as a fourteen year old lad. In the poem he described how he beat the favourite ridden by the famous local steeplechase jockey George Stevens, after a hard race. The reality was even harder. The course ran from Knoll Hill to The Hewletts, and it was a hard ride; one of the horses was ridden into a tree and killed. Not surprisingly this route was never ridden again. Yet the memory of the races on the hill lingered on. In April 1854 three races were run over the old course as a 'sort of supplement' to the existing steeplechases. The first was a two horse race for £100, then followed a two pony race for £10 and a sweepstake for seven horses. A hundred people then sat down for a picnic.

The Grand Annual stayed around Prestbury Park until 1855 when Prestbury Park was bought by Mr Dodson of Rose Hill, which stood where the UCAS building now stands by the racecourse roundabout, for £19,600 in January of that year. He was determined to bring the racing to an end and so the steeplechase moved to Bibury. At this point the idea of resurrecting the flat racing on Cleeve Hill grew in the minds of the racing fraternity. Thus developed a little-known episode in the history of

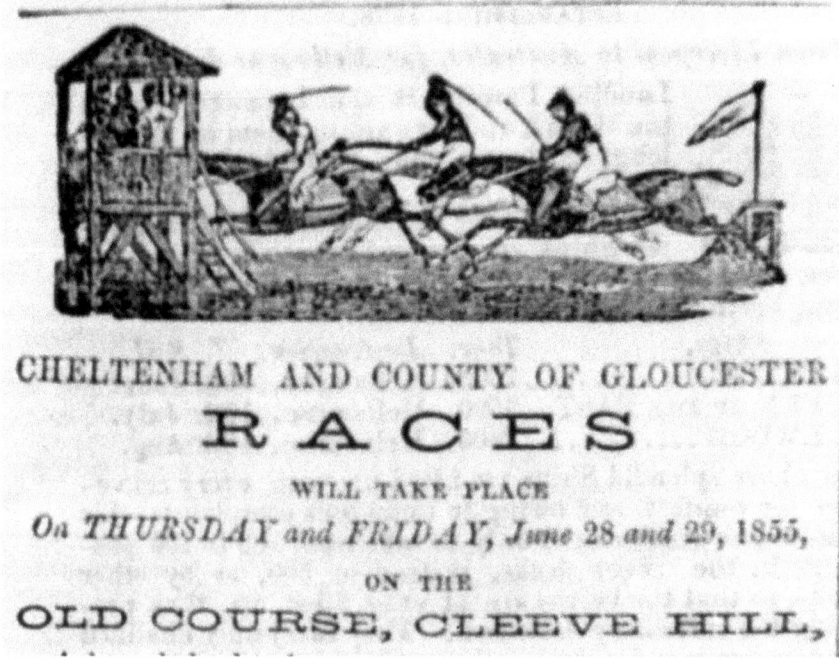

An advertisement for the revived race meeting of 1855. The race representation is stylized rather then realistic (Cheltenham Library)

racing in Cheltenham; the 1855 Cheltenham and County of Gloucester races run over two days in June on Cleeve Hill. They were a conscious attempt to revive an old tradition.

A race committee was established in May. It persuaded the Duke of Beaufort and Captain Francis Berkeley to agree to become the prestigious stewards necessary to attract the finance and entries. An agreement was reached with the commoners to set out the course on payment of a rent of £20. A temporary grandstand was built; booths and refreshment stalls erected on the course; the Great Western Railway ran the first recorded race special to Cheltenham. Carriages came via Whittington and those on horse or foot via Prestbury. Thursday 28 June proved a warm, pleasant day. Five races ran, the sport was good and the grandstand full. A further five races were run on the Friday and they, too, provided good sport, but attendance was poorer and the grandstand was described as nearly empty. This only seemed to confirm that the races belonged to the faded spa years. They had been replaced by the excitement of steeplechasing and the problems of reaching the common had never really been solved. In 1856 the Grand Annual Steeplechase returned to Cheltenham and was run along the (old) Gloucester Road and in 1857 it was run around Andoversford. In 1859 there was no steeplechase, so guess what? Members of the Imperial, Cheltenham and Gloucestershire clubs organised races on the hill solely for hunters 'having been regularly hunted with a Pack of Foxhounds' and 'not in a training stable', to replace the annual steeplechase. A one mile circular course was set out with its starting point from 'the spot which was supposed to be the stand'. Horses ran round twice. There was a good attendance but they were never repeated. Never again would organised horse racing take place on the hill. For a period in the 1860s the steeplechase was run around Kayte Farm on Southam Lane; and since 1902 at its present home at Prestbury Park.

The story of Cheltenham races and its close association with Cleeve Hill is worth telling because it forms a prelude to the history of the present course. But its context was wider than that of the hill itself and the story could not be told if it were confined solely to that small area of the common between the radio masts and the hillfort. At the simplest level this is because there is nothing left in the landscape, except for the new road from Whittington and an archaeological site

In 2022 members of Gloucestershire Archaeology carried out a geophysical survey of the plot on which the grandstand stood, now an area of slightly raised ground to the east of the pylons. The white lines indicate hidden walls and although the layout is rather confusing, the measurement across the width is 53 feet; exactly the same length as in the builder's specifications. An internal division can also be discerned (GlosArch)

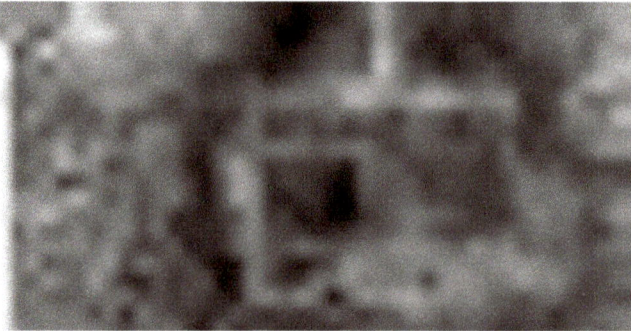

near the car park at the entrance to the common from The Hewletts. At a deeper level we have to seek out the Cheltenham newspapers and pamphlets to provide us with the evidence upon which to build the story. At the deepest level we have to recognize that the conflict of interest over this use of the common was the result of the development in the wider world of a leisured class intent on its own pleasures, riding roughshod over the interests of the inhabitants of Bishop's Cleeve, Woodmancote and Southam who were forced by such outside influences into a position in which they were portrayed as country yokels potentially getting in the way of the county society and their hangers-on.

Nowhere is this better exemplified than over the annual payment due from the Turf Club to the vestry meeting of Bishop's Cleeve for the right to hold the races. A minor item in the budget of the Turf Club, it was a major source of income to subsidise the local ratepayers. It was used to contribute to the poor fund, for repairs to the church and local roads, and to defray the expenses of the haywarden appointed from 1821 to look after the animals on the common. The feeling of impotence among the parishioners faced with the alien might of the Turf Club can be gauged from the minutes of the parish vestry meetings. The request to the Turf Club to pay its arrears was an almost annual feature of the minutes, right to the last meeting. The commoners had to fight hard to retain their traditional rights to the soil in a widening world in which, increasingly, money had the loudest voice. They, consequently, had none. Cheltenham races were important in changing the wider perception of the common from its being a vital local resource to being an open-air playground for Cheltenham moving out of town. But they were not the only manifestation of this change. The uses of the common were changing.

The Common as a Training Ground

Thus the races vanished, but horse training continued until the early years of the twenty-first century, for the superior qualities of the turf which first attracted attention to the common provided excellent training ground and it is the training rather than the racing which has left its mark on the landscape with the finer turf and flatter ground extending over much of the former race course.

The most obvious legacy of the horse training on the common is the former Cleeve Lodge stables in the quarry opposite the top of Stockwell Lane. They were built in c.1850, by Captain Barnett of Bayshill Lawn who converted an existing property and they were home to William Holman and his five racing sons for over 40 years. William Holman won

Captain Barnett's stables which were added to a house built in a disused quarry on the common in c.1850

The caption is mistaken: Emblem won the Grand National in 1863 (P. Jones)

the Cheltenham Grand Annual five times and trained three Liverpool Grand National winners. His first Grand National success was with a horse called 'Free Trader' which won the 1856 race as a 25-1 outsider. The jockey was George Stevens, once a local hairdresser, who had been trained to ride at the stables.

George Stevens still enjoys a modest fame as the only jockey ever to have won the Grand National five times. It is not a feat which is often included in the history books because steeplechasing including the Grand National was not, in the middle years of the nineteenth century, regarded very highly by the true sons of the sport on the flat. In 1863, when George won for a second time, he was riding for Lord Coventry. His horse 'Emblem' won by an unprecedented twenty lengths. When

Emblem Cottage at the top of Stockwell Lane with inset of the house name

he repeated his success the following year on her sister 'Emblematic', Lord Coventry's reward enabled him to buy that small cottage on a piece of land long stolen from the edge of the common, which he renamed Emblem Cottage. There he set up a small racing stables of his own in 1866 at the top of Stockwell Lane in sight of Cleeve Lodge. Further success for George in the Grand National followed on 'The Colonel' in

1869 and 1870. In 1871 he rode the same horse into fourth place. He then went on to win the Licensed Victuallers' Plate at the Cheltenham Steeplechase meeting. This was his last success, for in June he was dead, thrown from his cob 'The Clown' in Southam after it had bolted down the hill when returning from a day at Cheltenham market. A stone marks the spot today. George was 37 years old; each time he had won the Grand National a bonfire was lit on the hill. From the Spanish Armada in 1588 to Queen Elizabeth II's platinum jubilee in 2022 the elevation of Cleeve Common has made it the logical place from which local people send messages to the wider world.

George Steven's roadside memorial in Southam

George Stevens learnt to ride with William Holman but he learnt his tricks from Black Tom Olliver, a larger-than-life character who trained on the hill from his Prestbury stables. "The post is the place to win at, lie away from the horses" was the advice which won George the Nationals but lost him his job with Lord Coventry who thought he had lost his nerve. Black Tom was always in arrears with his payments to the vestry meeting in Bishop's Cleeve for using the common as training ground. In 1855 he promised to pay the £20 still owing only if the race meeting on the hill was a success for him. It was not enough to keep him out of the courts, however, and the following year we find him sued for bankruptcy in Bristol and Ipswich.

The problem presented to the commoners by trainers using the common was a constant source of friction during the nineteenth century. This new usage of the common had no legal precedent as a guide. In 1834 the vestry served the trainers with an order that they were trespassers on the common. Some freeholders entered into private arrangements with individual trainers under the threat of court action for following an activity which, in theory, could be considered as causing damage to

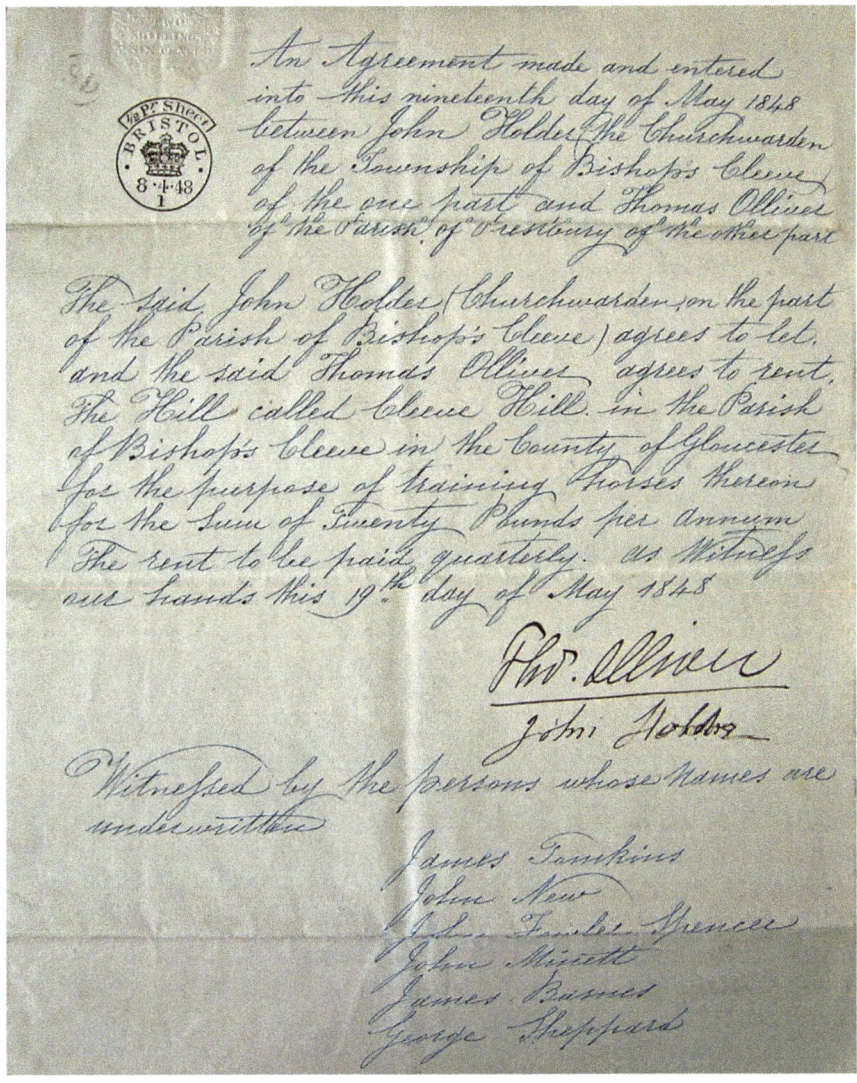

An 1848 agreement between Tom Olliver and the churchwarden of Bishop's Cleeve, representing the freeholders, to train on the common (Gloucestershire Archives D2216/Box36)

the grazing. However, the main method seems to have been based on Bishop's Cleeve's village worthies, meeting as a vestry, entering into arrangements with individual trainers such as the three discussed above. In 1868 William Holman agreed to pay 'a fair and reasonable sum' but as already indicated above, payments were not always readily forthcoming.

However, they did provide the parish with some income, part of which went towards the upkeep of the common.

Conclusion

This story of the races on Cleeve Hill has been expanded from the first edition of this book, because it has become better known. Not only is it an interesting episode in the history of the common, but it also bears a wider significance for it marks the entry on to the hill of the influence of a wider, developing world in which wealth, leisure and recreation were playing an increasingly large part. It was a world in which the inhabitants of small villages like Bishop's Cleeve, Southam and Woodmancote could not, for the most part, hope to enter. It threatened their way of life, made them feel inferior and reinforced their need to knit together as a community in order to survive. The old division of Cleeve Common into its Bishop's Cleeve and Southam parcels ceased to have any meaning as past conflicts were forgotten in the face of the greater threat from outside. And yet the old continuities of grazing, quarrying and living on the hill remained.

FURTHER READING

Gwen Hart's classic *A History of Cheltenham* (Leicester University Press, Leicester, 1965, reprinted Alan Sutton Publishing, Gloucester, 1981) remains essential reading for the history of the town. Anthea Jones' *Cheltenham: a new history* (Carnegie Publishing, Lancaster, 2010) is more wide-ranging with copious illustrations. *The Victoria County History Volume 15* covering Cheltenham and its neighbouring parishes is in progress at the time of writing. Owen Ashton, 'Clerical Control and Radical Responses in Cheltenham Spa 1838-1848', *Midland History, Volume 8,* (1983), sets the controversies over the races into a wider Cheltenham context.

This story of the races has been pieced together principally from the collection of local papers in Cheltenham Library: *Cheltenham Chronicle, Cheltenham Journal* (from 1824), *Cheltenham Free Press* (from 1834) and *Cheltenham Examiner* (from 1839). The first two and the latter are now available online at the British Newspaper Archive, by subscription or free access at the county's libraries. The main source for the career of George Stevens was *The Sporting Life*, copies of which were consulted in the British Newspaper Library at Colindale, North London, but which are now also online. *A Poetical Description*, the Close controversy pamphlets and other miscellaneous ephemera related to the races are in Cheltenham Library.

The vestry minutes of Bishop's Cleeve which have provided the freeholders' perspective on the races are in the County Archives, indexed under P46. D2216/Box36 contains correspondence over the rights to train horses on the common.

6
THE COMMON UNDER THREAT
(1818-1890)

> Such a large space of common land, at such an elevation, and within easy reach of the town, is a very great advantage.
> S.S. Buckman, *Cheltenham as a Holiday Resort*, 1897

Sources and Contexts

We know so much about the commoners' reactions to Cheltenham races because of the survival of such a good collection of parish records held in the County Archives in Gloucester. From these records it is also possible to trace the more traditional uses of the common during the nineteenth century, to learn more about the continuing demands of grazing, quarrying and settlement which continued to make changes to the appearance of the hill in this period, leaving many traces for the careful observer to seek out and identify.

The Industrial Revolution and the rapid growth of population, particularly in the developing industrial centres of the north and the midlands, had the effect of making traditional rural societies like Bishop's Cleeve, Woodmancote and Southam increasingly part of a pre-industrial past, despite their own modest population growth. Evidence for this growth lies not in the fields on the scarp slopes as in the Middle Ages, but in the growing number of houses appearing on the hill at this time.

The Common as Grazing Ground

The consequence of Cheltenham races on the commoners was that for two or three days a year over twenty years, their rights to grazing were literally overridden by outsiders from the town and further afield. But what was happening during the rest of the year?

The enjoyment of grazing rights continued to be the greatest contribution the common made to the local community, but the nature of the conflict of interests over such rights now changed somewhat. The struggles between the commoners of Bishop's Cleeve, Woodmancote and Southam to protect their respective rights to common gave way to an informal system of management by the vestry meeting in Bishop's Cleeve and so squabbles over boundary infringements became an activity of the past. The manorial boundary ceased to have any real significance. Although Lord Ellenborough had a new description of the boundary drawn up when he re-instituted beating the bounds of Southam manor after 1830, this archaic practice was only repeated six times until 1855 by which time the manor was ceasing to have any real significance. Lord Ellenborough's interest remains the best explanation for the boundary stones with their reversed 'S' on the common, as explained in Chapter 3. The decay of the importance of the manorial boundary was confirmed by the Ordnance Survey commissioners who had been given the task of drawing parish boundaries on their maps. As a result of their visits in 1880 and 1882 the whole of the common became part of Southam parish. By the deletion of a few lines on a map a link with the past and a source of much litigation and argument was ended by 'foreigners'. Once again, the local inhabitants were subject to a decision taken elsewhere, a trend which would increase during the next century.

The major development of the common as grazing land during the nineteenth century concerned the first real attempts to control its over-use. In June 1821 the vestry meeting in Bishop's Cleeve took the important step of appointing a haywarden, John Agg, to enforce stinting, check that the boundaries were in good repair and impound all animals not marked as belonging to those local people who possessed rights to the common. The haywarden was then hired each subsequent year from May to September at a wage variously fixed at 5s. per week, or 16s. to £1 per month. John Agg continued until 1838 when William Stanton took over, but the office had disappeared by 1868 when a public meeting was held to re-establish a haywarden and insist stockholders marked their stock. Why had it taken until 1821 to introduce the first measures to attempt to control grazing over the whole common? An answer can be partly found rooted in the contemporary attitudes which regarded all regulation with scepticism, even if the community's best interests were not being served by existing practices. Funding did not come until the Turf Club paid to hold the races on the common.

Even when it existed, the post had varied success. Stinting still proved an elusive goal. In 1839 the Tithe Commissioners, who were responsible for converting a tenth of the produce of the land which went to the church into a money payment, reported, 'There has in practice been no limit of common exercised over the common lands by the inhabitants', and ten years later Magdalen College, Oxford, which had an estate in Brockhampton near Swindon Village, repeated the assertion. More was accomplished in the securing of the boundaries. In 1826 the commoners paid to put all the walls and gates in good order, in 1835 part of the newly-revived race fund was used to repair two gates and in 1836 and 1837 further repairs to gates and fences were authorised out of the same fund. Acting through the haywarden the vestry attempted to force quarrymen to fence the quarries and claimed compensation for encroachments on to the common. In 1834 Thomas and James Simons were fined £2 to pay for a wall around their quarry, and a Mr Hill was ordered to fence his quarries, otherwise compensation had to be paid. The lack of any further reference to the cases suggests the notices were obeyed. At last there was a mechanism for controlling the grazing on the common but the difficulties of successfully enforcing the new measures continued well into the next century.

As the nineteenth century unfolded the necessity for regulation became more and more apparent, not just for the local inhabitants. A large number of them claimed right to the common. Even in 1695 85 freeholders from Bishop's Cleeve had been prepared to defend their common grazing rights. An unknown, but obviously much smaller, number from Southam agreed to do the same. In 1847, when the open fields of the ancient parish were enclosed after a process which had taken nearly a decade, 159 people made claim to Cleeve Common. The demands of traditional use on this valuable resource were still considerable, and the new and different demands issuing from Cheltenham increased pressure on the land. This was paralleled elsewhere, especially around London as explained in the Introduction. The 1845 General Enclosure Act had made it easier to enclose such land, to the detriment of the common grazing rights of farmers and labourers. Over 600,000 acres were enclosed during the following twenty five years. The management of Cleeve Common towards the latter part of the nineteenth century can be viewed as a series of steps taken in an attempt to respond to pressures such as these. What were these steps?

In 1868 the freeholders met in Bishop's Cleeve church to set up a committee to enquire into the future uses of the common. It reported that the responsibility for fencing the quarries belonged to the lords of the manors, who owned the mineral rights and that the position of haywarden should be reinstated, as noted above. They also recommended that a subscription list should be opened to pay his wage, and other expenses. A rare statement of account survives from 1885. Total receipts came to £32.2s.9d., mostly from payments for shepherding of the flocks (£18). The haywarden received £30.12s.6d. for his work and so there was a modest profit.

By this latter date the ad hoc committee was unable to deal with the pressures being placed upon the common, and the commoners took the decision to apply for the uses of the common to be regulated under the 1876 Commons Act. A provisional order was acquired but opposed by the local labourers because they feared for the loss of their rights of access. Pressure from outside, resulting from the desire of Cheltenham Corporation to safeguard access for its inhabitants, had split the local community into those in favour (landowners and farmers) and those against (labourers). At two public meetings held in Bishop's Cleeve in 1886 140 commoners objected to the order, fearing the pressure of visitors from Cheltenham would seriously affect their grazing rights. After some amendments to the original proposals a parliamentary enquiry was held in Bishop's Cleeve in March and April 1890. Its minutes throw much contemporary light on the uses of the common, and attitudes towards those uses.

We read of some familiar features: of upward of 900 sheep and 200 cattle plus a small number of horses and donkeys pasturing on the common's 1,000 acres; of uncertain stinting arrangements; of stone quarried as and when required; and of the failure of earlier attempts to reconcile conflicts. We are also given different perspectives on familiar themes. Horse training disturbed the sheep, but the sheep sheltered behind the hurdles erected as practice jumps, and several had been killed when the horses landed. Individual commoners had extracted illegal payments from the horse trainers as a form of blackmail, as much as £25 in one case. Nobody called to give evidence could actually state what had happened to the money given to the earlier ad hoc vestry committee. There is a striking similarity in the evasiveness over answering such questions with the witnesses called in the Elizabethan court cases three centuries earlier.

The result of the enquiry was the passing on 4 July 1890 of the *Commons Regulation (Cleeve) Provisional Order Confirmation Act*. Under its terms the common was to be managed by a Board of Conservators. This did not affect the ownership of the common which continued to be in the hands of the lord or lady of the manor of Bishop's Cleeve and of Southam. The Board comprised three conservators from Cheltenham Corporation; three from the vestry of Bishop's Cleeve; two from the vestry of Southam and Brockhampton; two from Woodmancote and one nomination each to represent the two lords/ladies of the manor. All except these latter representatives were to serve varying fixed terms but were allowed to stand for re-election. The vestry representatives became the parish council representatives after an act of 1894 set up parish councils. The make up of the Board remains broadly

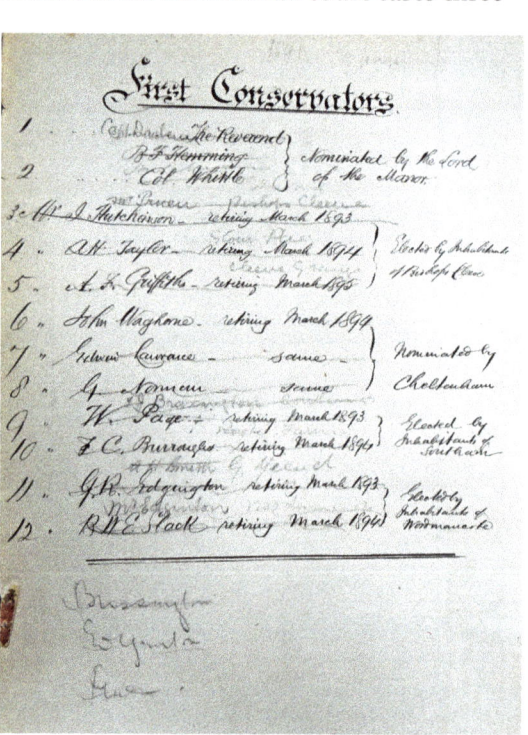

The list of the first conservators (Cleeve Common Trust)

the same today.

The conservators were given wide powers. These included the power to fence quarries and plant trees to protect the animals; to permit the training of horses and the establishment of military camps and military exercises; to drain, level and manure the common to improve the pasture; to allow all local inhabitants right of free access for playing games and other 'reasonable recreation'; and the ability to draw up byelaws to improve their control. In a far-sighted clause they were also empowered to preserve the ancient earthworks on the common, being The Ring and the Iron Age hillfort. This was one of the earliest examples in the country of such protection (the Ancient Monuments Act had been passed only eight years earlier) but too late to save much of the hillfort from being quarried away from the front. They were to receive their income principally from Cheltenham Corporation's £50 per annum and by issuing annual training permits for two guineas for each racehorse. Many commoners welcomed the order but several could only regret the sell-out of their ancient exclusive rights for £50, which gave nearly

The Trust has conserved the Washpool and its sheep dip, providing an information board. This photograph taken in the inter-war period shows its vital importance for dipping the sheep on the common (V. Gardner)

50,000 people the right to the common to exercise their troublesome dogs which were likely to chase the sheep across the downs. The locals only tangible reward was the sheep dip at the Washpool built in 1897 in Watery Bottom by damming the upper reaches of the River Isbourne.

The act also laid down that animals could graze on the common from 25 April to 30 November each year and that the Board of Conservators should meet quarterly to discuss the management of the common. All activities on the common still come under the jurisdiction of the Conservators, now Cleeve Common Trust. Their establishment under the act of 1890 marked a turning-point in the history of the common. On the one hand it has ensured the continued use of the common as traditional grazing ground and went some way towards reconciling the conflicting uses demanded of it. On the other hand it marked the end of its traditional place in the economy and society of the villages lying at its feet. It became, legally, part of a wider context, as a recreational open space for Cheltenham and increasingly subject to national legislation. The nature of its function had changed and the animals on the common in the summer, although important to a small number of local farmers, have become a minor part of the life on the hill. Yet they remind us of a past age. The legislation of the year 1890 played an important part in laying the foundations of the modern uses and perceptions of Cleeve Common which will be examined in the remaining chapters.

Quarrying

The existence of the quarries on Cleeve is a major feature of its landscape, particularly on the face around Cleeve Cloud, and yet their existence also yields little of their history. It has already been explained how their scale of operation was more extensive than intensive, and consequently few records still survive to allow a reconstruction of their development. However a body of documents does survive in the County Archives which covers the three decades before 1850. From these documents the following tale can be told.

These three decades saw some of the busiest years for building in Cheltenham and the demand for Cleeve Hill stone increased sufficiently to make quarrying a more attractive proposition, and a number of quarrymen took on the leases of various quarries which can be found in the Southam manor records. A survey of part of Southam manor taken in August 1829 suggests that there were two areas of large-scale quarrying on the hill, at Postlip and around Cleeve Cloud.

In December 1825 two Winchcombe men, William Powell, described as a quarryman, and Anthony Hampton, a wheelwright, took out a lease on a quarry near Cleeve Cloud. The terms provide a rare and interesting glimpse of the conditions of a quarrying lease: 'The said William Powell and Anthony Hampton to work such quarry fair and not to do any wilful or unnecessary damage and to clear away all Rubbish and make good the Soil as they go, and so fence and guard such Quarry that nothing depasturing on the said Common can receive any Injury therefrom'. The Delaberes thus put their responsibility for fencing, as lords of the manor, on to their lessees. A clause in the lease forbidding haulage of stone along the Southam Road between October and February on pain of a £5 fine indicated the poor condition of the roads and the problems of haulage away from the hill at that time, even along the new lower road of 1823. By Lady Day, 25 March 1831 the lessees were in arrears with their rent to a sum of £67.7s.6d., a not uncommon state of affairs. William Powell seems also to have rented the Postlip Quarries for at some time in the early 1830s (the actual date is unclear) we find that Henry Gaskins took over Powell's quarries at Postlip, which he then sublet. The quality of the stone from Postlip meant it was used extensively in Cheltenham. Arthur Price, the expert on Cotswold stone, has identified that the exterior of the prestigious Pittville Pump Room, completed in 1827, was built of Postlip stone as was the Rotunda (now The Ivy) in Montpellier, completed in the previous year.

Henry Gaskins' name appears most frequently in the court rolls as a lessee of the quarries. He built Laburnum Cottage, just above Spring Lane, on land stolen from the common, and was

Pittville Pump Room in Cheltenham was built from Cleeve Hill stone, completed in 1827

allowed to keep it because his quarry leases were a source of profit to the lords of the manor of Southam, the Delaberes, to whom he paid £30 annual rental. When the Delaberes sold the manor to Lord Ellenborough in 1831, Henry was leasing all the quarries on Lord Ellenborough's estate. In 1832 they were described as freestone quarries 'on the way to the racecourse' which identified the location around Cleeve Cloud. Henry seems to have taken his first lease in 1826, possibly taking over from the Hawkers at Nutterswood, and then paid £50 per annum for them. In 1837 he supplied Lord Ellenborough with a large quantity of stone and lime as his lordship remodelled and enlarged Southam House. Then in 1842 Henry defaulted on his rent and was ordered to demolish his lime kiln. Soon after that the quarry's lease passed to William Denley of Upper Bottomley and then to Thomas Yeend in October 1845 for £30 per annum. Part of the agreement was that Thomas should not undercut overhanging rock, which again indicated the quarries were located along the Undercliff towards Nutterswood. The importance of the quarries to the manors can be measured from two entries in the court rolls. In 1828 Gaskins was excused his rental because he was supplying the Coxwell manor with stone; in 1831 Lord Ellenborough also excused him his rental for the same reason.

The stone for Lord Ellenborough's mock-Norman tower at Southam House was built of stone from his quarries on the hill

The Cleeve Cloud and Postlip Quarries produced freestone of quality good enough for making ashlar blocks. A visitor to the latter quarry in 1865 commented that a mine had been opened to better access the stone, but not all the stone was of such quality. Roadstone was taken from quarries on the top of the hill. In 1890 the enquiry into the common recorded the opening of a new quarry there, possibly Roadstone Quarry. The enquiry also recorded the quarries were by then little used

Roadstone Quarry lies on the White Way. The stone was used for repairing the local roads in the days before tarmac came into use in the 1920s

and the stone of poor quality, not worth taking three miles. This seems a particularly pessimistic view of the quarries. Gravel continued to be extracted on a small-scale from several places, such as that which led to the King's Beeches archaeological excavation in 1902.

We know little of how the stone was used. However, the details of the building of the old school in Bishop's Cleeve, now St Michael's Centre, have survived, and from the rather confused accounts we can understand a little about using the stone. The school was built in 1845 by the National Schools' Society to replace the schoolroom above the church porch. The stone came from Postlip Quarry and was roughly cut to shape before being brought to the school site, where it was finished and stacked or use. The accounts provide a further example of the problems of haulage. Five hundred cubic feet of good quality freestone cost £21.10s. to purchase at the quarry, but £46 to haul down into Bishop's Cleeve. The building of the new school exemplified the problems which faced the exploitation of the quarries throughout our story.

St Michael's Centre. The two gables mark the extent of the original National School

Woodland

By the early nineteenth century a pattern of woodland had been established which has remained largely intact until today, although the modern neglect of woodland has destroyed the regular coppicing of the scarp woods, and many timber trees have fallen through decay and have not been felled for use. However, with the exception of the wood at Wontley discussed in the next section, the extent of the woodland has changed little in the past two centuries, apart from that lying below Nutterswood (See Chapter 8).

Ring dating of ash trees felled on the lower edge of Stutfield Wood suggests they were planted or emerged as seedlings about 1830, the time when Lord Ellenborough was buying the Southam manors. We know that he considered the valuation of the timber on the Coxwell manor to have been too high at £2,176, but this included trees in hedges and along the roadsides in addition to Queen's, Stutfield and Thrift Woods.

Settlement

The main feature of changes in settlement during this period was the continuing encroachment around the edges of the common by families stealing a small piece of land and settling there. The 1847 Enclosure map shows the situation in mid-century. Mention has been made earlier of how the Kitchen family had taken in land from the common by 1793 (plot 1030); how Henry Gaskins had been allowed to retain his enclosure (1029); of the future Captain Barnett's training stables (1040); and how in 1866 George Stevens purchased a cottage

Bishop's Cleeve Enclosure map of 1847 clearly shows encroachments along the lanes and on the common (Gloucestershire Archives Q/RI/45)

built on land taken from the common before 1716 (528).

Encroachments alongside the lanes leading to the hill, particularly Gambles Lane and Stockwell Lane, continued and were consolidated. Along the latter lane, the narrow plots on the northern side of Richard Barnes' fields (518, 522) show this process underway. The house on one of these plots still carries the name Horses Green to remind the passerby that two centuries or more ago this lane was wider and flanked by wide verges where animals could graze. In the 1891 census the addresses of all the houses in this part of Stockwell Lane were given as Horses Green; Post Office Lane had not yet been built. Without exception all the heads of households living here at that date identified themselves as labourers. Encroachments can also be observed along the earlier turnpike route across the hill, particularly where it passed through plots 1022 and 1025. Here the chief transgressor can clearly be identified as Thomas Belcher (1024).

Horses Green on Stockwell Lane – a reminder of the roadside encroachments

The whole of the adjoining area, as indicated by its name, Hillground, had at some earlier date been stolen from the common. By 1826 Thomas had built a house and outbuildings at the rather large cost of £210 near a small quarry he was working. In 1833 Lord Ellenborough offered to buy him out for £84 but Thomas refused. He actively added to his land by encroachment, and in the Southam manor court of 1855 he was accused of encroaching four feet on to the old turnpike road, and ordered to demolish his wall. He obviously ignored the order because he was presented for the same offence again in 1861, presumably with the same results, for Spring Lane exists now as a very narrow footpath. Even the tighter manorial control in Southam in the mid-nineteenth century lacked the real power to re-assert community interest over the interests of the individual. The decisions by Lord Ellenborough's court to receive rents from the Kitchens, Gaskins and also the Hawkers at Nutterswood rather than evict them, is clear evidence of this change in attitude.

Such examples show how difficult it proved to control what is traditionally known as squatters' settlement, even where tight manorial control lasted into the relatively late date of the second half of the nineteenth century. This is apparent in the Enclosure map from the pattern of land-owning. Note how the northern (upper) part in Bishop's Cleeve has many names placed across the fields signifying a fragmented pattern of landownership with many encroachments, while the southern part in Southam, shaded blue, belonged solely to J.S. Packington, the owner of Haymes.

The ancient boundary between the manors of Bishop's Cleeve and Southam is shown by a dark line. It was uncertain where it ran at the top of Rising Sun Lane. By building exactly on the line of the boundary families could claim to have built in the other manor. Hannah Kitchen managed to avoid paying rental to Southam manor until 1834

Rising Sun Lane with Sunnyside to the left and Giles Carter's tower house in the centre

when her claim that she lived in Bishop's Cleeve was finally rejected. However she declared she had no objection to paying 6d. annual rent to Lord Ellenborough. On what is now Rising Sun Lane, Giles Carter, had built his tower house on the edge of a plot of land which had been earlier described as a garden. Giles was a solicitor from Winchcombe. In the 1842 list of Southam residents on Lord Ellenborough's estate, his name has been added in pencil and so that gives us a date by which the house had been built. He was paying his lordship a shilling a year as quit rent. In the 1851 census he was described as a fifty seven year old widower, living with his thirteen year old daughter Victoria and one servant. Giles' Gothic folly would seem to be the first house built on the hill for somebody who was not economically dependent upon its resources. A variety of myths surround the house, but the fact is that it was built straddling the manorial boundary. On 12 October 1855 the perambulators of the Southam boundary kept to their route by forcing a window to follow the boundary through the house. He was away when this happened, and his reaction is not recorded although he was forced to swear in the manorial court that he would be present the next time the boundary was perambulated. As with many residents who did not need to live there for their livelihood, soon after that date he left.

An inter-war postcard of the Rising Sun Hotel (G. Cocks)

CLEEVE HILL

This, then, was the nature of the community on Cleeve Hill until the middle of the nineteenth century. It comprised a small population mostly made up of the families of agricultural and general labourers with a smattering of quarrymen and stonemasons. The houses of this period are still recognizable today. They were originally unpretentious, rather low Cotswold stone houses, devoid, with the notable exception of the Tower, of any embellishments. They appear as evidence of the period when Cleeve Hill and its common still held economic importance for a small number of people on the periphery of the parish. But the situation was beginning to change and already the Rising Sun Hotel, 'newly built' in 1829, stood as an early exception to this localised economy, taking its living from passing trade. It had developed as a hotel halfway between Cheltenham and Winchcombe where the summit of the road of 1823 crossed Gambles Lane.

The 25 inches to the mile Ordnance Survey map of 1883 recorded the changing nature of the traditional community. Captain Barnett built his riding stables at Cleeve Lodge c.1850. In the 1881 census the trainer

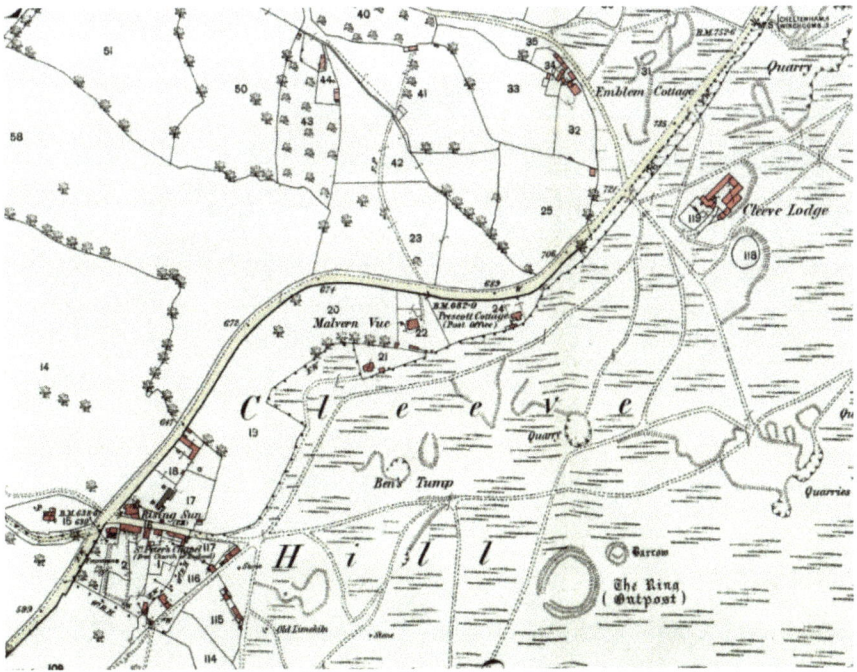

The 1883 Ordnance Survey map also shows the milepost mileages at the top and an old lime kiln at the bottom (National Library of Scotland)

John Holman was living there with his wife Jane and daughter Evelyn with two servants and six stable lads. Ten years later eight stable lads between the ages of ten and nineteen lived there. They must have added colour to the local community. Prescott Cottage carries the date stone 1877 and at the time of the 1881 census was the home to Edward and Susanna Watts, postmaster and mistress. Ten years later they still held those positions but had moved next door to the Malvern View which was being built on 3 April when the census of 1881 was taken. The convex rather than straight style of the stones of Prescott Cottage set the precedent for the shape of the stones of the later houses. At The Rockery in Rising Sun Lane, Henry Taylor, of independent means, had converted his laundry into the church of St Peter which was affiliated to the Free

The Rockery (now called Adderstone too) and Adderstone House in Rising Sun Lan

Church of England, an Evangelical movement which had split from the established Church of England in 1844 in protest at the increasing influence of High Church Anglo-Catholicism. He was still living there ten years later when he was recorded in the census as a lay reader of the Church of England. The cross at the end of the roof of the former church still serves as a reminder of the building's former function

The census of 1891 evidenced the changing nature of the community on the hill from one based upon the land to one which chose to live on the hill for its location to enjoy the peace and quiet of the countryside, but not too far from Cheltenham. The census recorded that Gambles Lane and Stockwell Lane were still the home of families depending upon the area for their employment and livelihoods, but

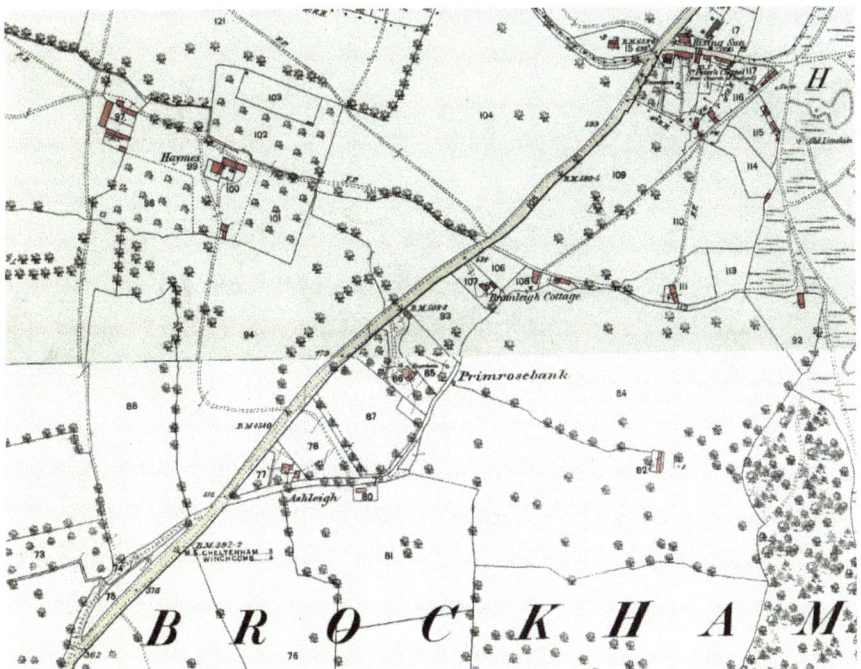

The lower slopes above Southam shown on the 1883 Ordnance Survey map (National Library of Scotland)

this was changing as new influences were creeping up the road from Southam. Ashleigh House was the home of a retired army colonel; Primrose Bank a widowed silk draper; at Bramleigh Cottage the head of the family was absent but his eldest daughter was recorded as a draper's assistant. All employed servants, but they were a mobile population and none was living there ten years later.

None of the people were farmers, for the poor quality land in small fields could not, by themselves, sustain a farm. The possible exception was Longwood Farm on Nottingham Hill, which carries a date stone of 1718. In 1779 Samuel Rudder, in his county history, recorded that the proprietor was prospecting for coal on his land. In 1881 it was the home of Henry Smith, a seventy one year old bachelor living with Mary Richardson described as his servant, aged thirty eight. Henry farmed 80 acres employing three labourers. So, in searching for farmers we must now return to Wontley, Cockbury and Haymes as the former fields of the Medieval settlements continued to bring hope and despair to successive occupiers and owners.

The fields of Wontley continued to belong to the Lawrence family of Sandywell Park. In 1828 West Wood and Wontley/East Wood were purchased by John Prince for £3,500. He seems to have been responsible for building the now ruined farmhouse. Yet again another owner hit hard times. This led to the clearance of Wontley Wood and some replanting in order to raise capital, but unsuccessfully, and in 1833 he sold the holding to Walter Lawrence for only £3,000. The outline of the former Wontley Wood can still be recognized in the field boundaries. The arable land thus grew to 321 acres, which were leased later in 1833 to John and George Lane for ten years at £150 annual rental, together with 34 acres of West Wood for £25. The 1839 Tithe map recorded the nature of the farm at Wontley; 236 acres of arable; 88 acres of pasture; and 66 acres of West Wood reserved to Walter Lawrence. With the clearance of the woodland in the early 1830s the landscape around Wontley had taken on much of its present appearance. The 1851 census recorded three small households at Wontley, of an agricultural labourer, a shepherd and a farmer. The 1881 census recorded the same but gave the farm's acreage as five acres, which suggests most of its land was being farmed from elsewhere, possibly from nearby Westwood House. Ten years later just two agricultural labourers were recorded. Three of John Hall's children were recorded as scholars, although it must have been a long walk to school, presumably in Winchcombe. The isolated nature of the farm was emphasised by the reference that it was approached via Andoversford.

Cockbury fared better. It remained a tenanted farm, with a

mixed economy belonging to the Coxwell Rogers family of Dowdeswell. The Tithe map recorded 140 acres elsewhere in Bishop's Cleeve parish farmed by its tenant, George Hone, who, unlike the tenants at Wontley, played a prominent part in parish affairs during this period. The Hone family came from Stoke Orchard. By 1881 the farm seems to have been passed on to his grandson Edward who was then farming 400 acres and employing five men, two of whom lived at Cockbury, plus four boys and two women. Ten years later the farm was still in the same family but the occupier of the farmhouse was George Hone, described as a farmer's son. A shepherd and a carter lived in the two cottages.

Looking across to Haymes before the building of the mushroom farm in 1965. The farm buildings below the house are those marked on the 1883 Ordnance Survey map

Haymes continued to function as a farm into the twentieth century. Recorded on the Tithe map as a 234 acre farm occupied by William Holder, from a well-known local farming family, it was owned by the MP for Droitwich, J.S. Packington, who played a leading rôle in the Tory governments of the mid-nineteenth century. In 1874 he was ennobled as Lord Hampton. He provided yet another example of how foreign capital was used to exploit the potential of the hill by making money for absentee landowners. In 1871 he sold the estate to Joseph Lovegrove, the County Coroner, another absentee. At that time it was being farmed by Joseph Minett from another well-known local farming family, who had entered into his tenancy in 1863, paying £403 per annum. In 1881 it was being farmed by John New, but the land holding had shrunk to 94 acres, which he worked with two labourers. Ten years later the farmer was Henry Holliday who owned the farm jointly with his brother Charles. They were well-known Cheltenham butchers with a shop in Pittville Street.

Recreation

At first glance it might seem unnecessary to include here a section on recreation, having taken a whole chapter to investigate Cheltenham races on Cleeve Hill, but those were not the only recreational activities taking place in the nineteenth century. From the evidence to the select committee which led to the act of 1890, people from Cheltenham came to the hill for football, cricket and other games in addition to walking across the common for the enjoyment of the open space. We have no record of how many people or how often they came, except it was too often for the commoners. However, we do have evidence for one particular type of visitor, which provides the focus of this section.

In July 1846 a small number of county gentry, clergy and would-be gentry met together to establish a society with the aim of 'seeking Nature in her remoter haunts', five or six times a year. Thus was born the Cotteswold Naturalists' Field Club. Inevitably one of the remoter haunts was Cleeve Common and their minutes record several visits between 1846 and the end of the century. In 1852 and 1857 they visited Postlip and Cleeve Cloud Quarries respectively in a search for fossils. At the latter date part of the membership went searching for butterflies over at Postlip. In May 1859 another visit started with breakfast at The Lamb in Cheltenham's High Street, then by omnibus to the foot of Cleeve from where the geologists walked to Rolling Bank Quarry. We find in the society's minutes further interesting detail on quarrying, for in 1859 Rolling Bank had been newly opened; the members returned again in 1863 and 1865 at which former date they examined a tunnel from which stone had been extracted and stacked up. This provided a rare reference

Rolling Bank Quarry with its information board lies to the south of Cleeve Lodge

to the mining of Cotswold stone on the hill, although in 1865 one of their number, Thomas Wright, recorded that at Postlip Quarry a mine had been opened from which 'a large quantity of good rock had been obtained' and it was stacked up outside the entrance. Arthur Price has studied these and other Cotswold stone quarries around Cheltenham and explored the extensive mines at Whittington and Syreford barely two miles to the south of West Down, the stone from there being used extensively in the building of Cheltenham in the nineteenth century.

Another similar county society, the Bristol and Gloucestershire Archaeological Society, was founded in 1876. It attracted the same type of membership as the Field Club. The minutes of their meetings record only one visit to the hill during the period covered by this chapter. In summer 1889 over 100 members and friends visited 'Cleeve Camp' on their way to Winchcombe, Spoonley Roman Villa and Whittington Court. The foremost county archaeologist of the day, G.F. Witts, addressed the party on the latest thinking on the nature of the camp.

Such visitors were learned, serious-minded and aware of their position as visitors to a valuable economic resource. They just overlapped with the last of the races on the hill and contrasted starkly with the more usual visitor seeking an open space for fun and games, although probably not as extreme as the following extract from the *Cheltenham Chronicle* recorded. In July 1841 it thundered, "On the afternoon of Sunday last the Downs exhibited a scene of debauchery, drunkenness and fighting; the holy stillness of the Sabbath was completely lost sight of." The new conflicts which were first recorded emerging during the years studied in this chapter, were only partly resolved by the passing of the regulation act of 1890. This new leisure-orientated conflict replaced the older ones over manorial rights and land use which had provided the driving force throughout most of the hill's history. The final two chapters investigate the attempts to balance such conflicting demands to the present day.

FURTHER READING

The secondary sources detailed at the end of the last chapter provide the general background to this chapter also. Arthur Price's book *Cheltenham Stone* (Cottswold Naturalists' Field Club, 2007) is essential reading about Cotswold quarries. Michael Cole's *Southam and Prestbury* (Prestbury Local History Society, 2020) details the family history of the Delaberes and also Lord Ellenborough's life at Southam including his career as a politician, especially his controversial holding of the office of Governor General of India 1841-44. Most of the primary sources have been consulted in the County Archives. These include Bishop's Cleeve vestry minutes, tithe and enclosure awards (P46). Further details of the 1847 enclosure are catalogued under D2216. Southam manor records in D2025, Boxes 31/69/70 contain material on the quarries. Bishop's Cleeve school details were found in D2186/13; and Wontley details in D444 collection. The Ordnance Survey boundary books were consulted at their headquarters in Southampton; the parliamentary enquiry minutes at the House of Lords, viz: *Report from the Select Committee on Commons; together with the proceedings of the committee and minutes of evidence dated 17 April 1890*. The proceedings and transactions of the two county societies can be consulted in Cheltenham or Gloucester libraries. As noted earlier all but the most recent volumes of the Bristol and Gloucestershire Archaeological Society are now online, as are the census returns at Ancestry and Find My Past websites.

7
'THE COTSWOLD HEALTH RESORT'
(1890-1918)

Cleeve 'ill is a town consisting of several bungalows, one hotel, one stables, two hundred and forty three stone walls, one golf links, one post-office, one hill, and a large number of other useful Institutions, such as a tin church, a sanitory, and a tramline.

Selina Jenkins' Letter,
Cheltenham Chronicle and Gloucester Graphic, 18 April 1903

Context and Perceptions

Most people who come to Cleeve Hill reach it along the Cheltenham to Winchcombe road. It is certainly no ordinary Cotswold village, and even if it no longer quite corresponds to the fictitious Selina Jenkins' satirical description at the turn of the last century, it is still recognisably the same place. This chapter tells the story of the great changes which took place in the three decades at the turn of the last century, transforming the small, rather poor hamlet towards the peripheries of the parish of Bishop's Cleeve into an affluent suburb and favourite holiday and day-trip resort for the people of Cheltenham and further afield. In these three decades, within the lifetime of those alive to experience it, the hill saw its greatest changes since at least the creation of its modern agrarian landscape at the end of the Middle Ages or even, arguably, since the original clearances before and during the Bronze Age. Why did they happen so rapidly in these years?

WINCHCOMBE DAME *(who has got as far as Cleeve Hill for the first time since the tramway was commenced)*: Lawks-a-muurssy; what be they posts and wire for, Jaarge?

HER HUSBAND: The 'lectric tramway, o' coorse! The papers calls it "the overhead trolley" —— zummat.

WINCHCOMBE DAME: Well, if they runs trolleys on they wires, I doon't wonder they ooverturns, and I'm afeared the lighter cars they talks aboot woont be mooch beeter.

An old attitude in a new guise – the contrast between the sophistication of Cheltenham and the rusticity of Winchcombe's inhabitants is reflected in this cartoon concerning the arrival of the tramway on Cleeve Hill. The reference is to the fatal crash in Southam on a test run in July 1901 (Cheltenham Library)

The growing use of the common as Cheltenham's 'lung' was explored in the previous chapter. Cleeve Hill was readily accessible, even on foot, to the people of the expanding town, but as improvements in transport occurred, then accessibility improved and this enticed more people to enjoy the air and the freedoms brought under the 1890 Act. From September 1891 horse-drawn buses ran to Southam; three years later they climbed to the Rising Sun Hotel; in August 1901 electric tramcars started to run to the Malvern View Hotel at the end of a line from the Midland Railway station, now Cheltenham Spa station. Built by the Cheltenham and District Light Railway company it had cost £4,000. According to the *Cheltenham Examiner*, 10,000 passengers were carried on the first Sunday of operation. Taken literally, a fifth of the population of Cheltenham moved out of town for the day. So the context of life on Cleeve Hill was increasingly 'Cheltenhamised'. Not only did a significant number of Cheltenham traders and merchants with their families come to live on the hill, but also a vast amount of Cheltenham capital was invested in the rapidly growing settlement. At all periods the importation of 'foreign' capital has been a powerful force for change.

As a result of the crash, single-decker tramcars were ordered for the service to and from Southam, where passengers transferred to the Cheltenham tram

Cleeve Hill became a fashionable place to live for more affluent people, ironically, seeking peace and quiet after making their money in the town. Many owned their houses, but others rented. The 'trippers' who followed took short holiday lets and day trips. They each had their own perceptions of the place. Even today the visitor can still seek out the turn-of-the-century mansions, expressions of the wealth and self-confidence of self-made men who with their families looked down on humanity, not now from the ramparts of the Iron Age hillfort, but from the wooden balconies of pine villas. They shared with the day tripper the desire to escape to the common, to breathe the air, to walk the downs. And, even if they played golf while the latter played football, they shared the often held view that the commoners' animals were mere nuisances intruding into 'their' landscape.

Wealth, however, did bring privileges not available to the day tripper. Private transport if the tram was crowded, tea on their own lawn rather than in a crowded tea garden and comfortable rooms rather than cramped lodgings as demand outstripped supply. Selina Jenkins recorded how she was given a room which could only be reached through the bedroom of another guest. She also remarked on the discarded orange peel, broken ginger beer bottles and used tram tickets which littered the roadside. Clearly the 'Cotswold Health Resort' had different perceptions for the different people intent on enjoying its life and facilities. When the desirability of the tramway was debated in Cheltenham's council chamber in 1898, the golfers and the horse trainers, themselves comparative newcomers, condemned the proposal. It would bring 'the scum of the earth' to strew empty beer bottles around. They were just two more groups trying to protect their own self-interest against outside intrusions. Like the others, they failed. A month before the trams arrived in July 1901, the *Cheltenham Chronicle and Gloucester Graphic* described the resort in these terms:

> and every little shed and shanty has invested in a pennyworth of cardboard, on which the classic legends 'Tea and Hot Water', 'Aerated Waters', 'Furnished Apartments', and so forth are inscribed in fearful and wonderful characters to entice the simple trammist. Enormous tradesmen's mansions erect their ponderous walls on the hill slope, bungalows spring up in every corner like mustard and cress, the most improbable sites are staked out and divided

into streets and alleys by the prospective builder, the land goes up in price 500 per cent.

The vitality and excitement of these years comes across well, but why so much interest then? In searching for an answer to this question, it is necessary first to examine how the hill came to be associated with healthy living.

The Cotswold Convalescent Home

This story originated in Cheltenham. On 25 May 1892 a small group of public-spirited townspeople met in the Victoria Home in St James' Square to establish a convalescent home as a charity for inhabitants of Cheltenham recovering from free hospital treatment but

Victoria House in St James' Square in Cheltenham

without the means, financial or domestic, for a period of convalescence. A subscription list was opened, a site investigated, and enquiries made of suitable builders. With speed difficult to understand today, within two months £600 had been raised by subscription, a further £100 promised and a gift of £1,200 made available. The committee therefore were able to accept a tender of £1,284 from Messrs. Billings to build the home. By the following March, the building was well under way. The site had to be in an elevated position away from the less healthy vale and so a disused quarry by the main road on Cleeve Hill was bought for £150. The only reason for this choice seemed to be that it was available at a satisfactory price. Would the subsequent history of Cleeve Hill have been the same if it had been built elsewhere, perhaps on Leckhampton Hill which was also considered?

The convalescent home was formally opened by the local MP Sir John Dorington on the second Saturday of July, less than fourteen months after the initial decision to build had been taken. The home catered for six men and six women during the summer months from April to the end of October. Then it closed for the winter because it was felt the cost of running the home in the cold months would be too great. Ninety nine patients stayed during the four months of its first season. Welcome as any period of convalescence must have been to its patients, the régime prompted comparison with that threat to all working-class aspiration and endeavour, the Union Workhouse. This is well-illustrated by the following timetable:

> Morning prayers: 8.15
> Breakfast 8.30
> Dinner 12.30
> Tea 4.30
> Supper 8.00
> Prayers 9.00

Male and female residents were not allowed to talk or walk with each other and had to keep to their side of the grounds. They were not allowed to go home without permission nor allowed to visit a public house or the house of a friend.

The parallel with the workhouse can be developed a little further. The first concern of the Poor Law Guardians was the cost, not the comforts of the workhouse inmates. The highlight of the year at the home was the annual subscribers' tea, held in the summer on the lawn. It followed a brief inspection and even briefer formal meeting (fifteen minutes long in 1895). This was a large affair, attended by 100 subscribers and guests, headed by the mayor. There could have been no greater symbol of the influence of Cheltenham. From the poorest to the most affluent, the townspeople could claim Cleeve Hill as their own, at least until 1899 when the subscribers' tea began to be taken in Cheltenham.

Yet we must not dismiss unfairly the efforts of late-Victorian philanthropy. Within two years four more beds had been established to meet the obvious need for the home and the idea was only kept alive by generous giving. The annual subscription of a guinea gave the right to nominate one person for a two week stay for a maximum charge of 5s. per week. As the home had a close connection with Cheltenham General Hospital, many patients were able to stay at no cost to themselves at all.

The Convalescent Home about the time of the First World War

These arrangements for the running of the home lasted until the First World War. From 1902 it remained open until the end of November and in 1909 the building was extended as the result of an appeal in memory of H.T. Carrington, who had been treasurer and secretary of the home for many years. The 1911 census recorded two patients, both young women from Cheltenham. Then, on the outbreak of war in 1914 the committee briefly offered the home to the War Office, before changing its mind and offering it to the Red Cross, who immediately sent to it sixteen wounded Belgian soldiers in November 1914. It was run as part of the Red Cross hospital at New Court in Lansdown Road. For the first time in its history, there was no winter closure. Miss Eleanor Adlard of Postlip House had already offered £25 to keep it open in the winter. She also provided the Christmas meal. During 1915, 217 British soldiers, 17 Belgian soldiers, 4 sailors and 33 civilians spent time at the home. The latter were still nominated by the subscribers and the rest were paid for by the Red Cross. In 1916 the war came closer when the windows were blacked out and an insurance against air-raids taken. The paddock was dug up to grow potatoes. When the military finally left in January 1919 the home closed until April, as usual.

Building the Health Resort

Of all the periods which have left their mark on the hill, that of the Cotswold Health Resort is probably the most obvious and the easiest for the visitors of today to discover and interpret for themselves. This part of the story of the landscape is the easiest to see; it is one of the most difficult to disentangle from the mass of written evidence which survives.

Our starting point can be the Ordnance Survey maps shown here. The 1883 map recorded a community very similar in size and nature to that analysed for 1847. The 1901 map shows the community growing

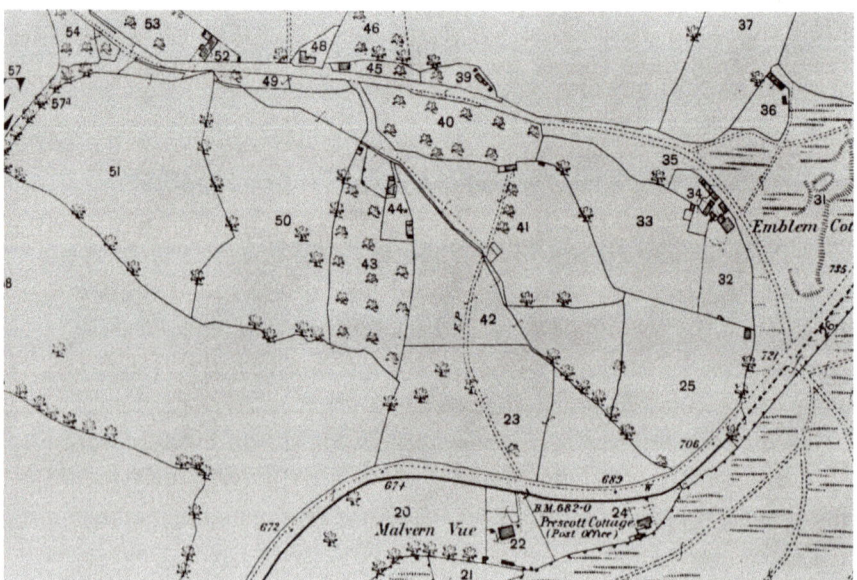

Cleeve Hill on the 1883 Ordnance Survey map (National Library of Scotland)

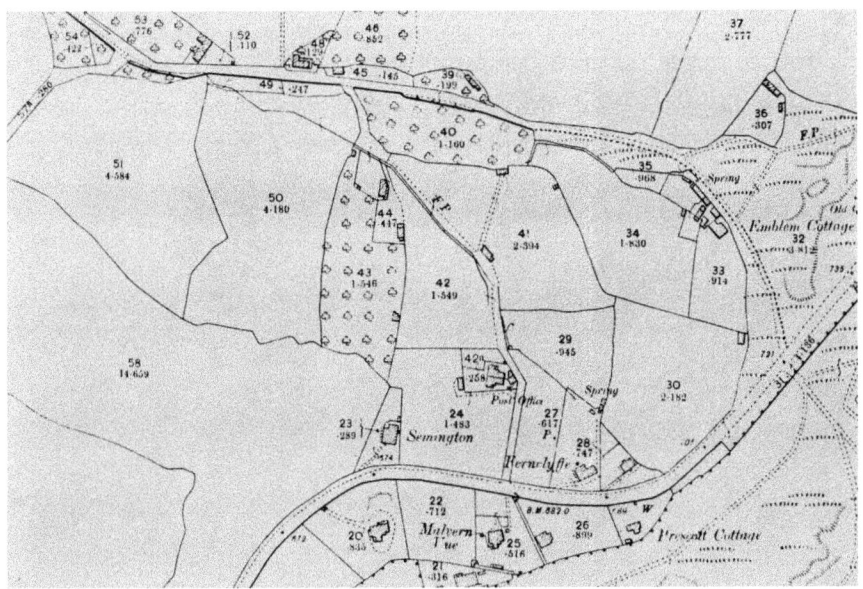

*The 1901 map shows the growth since 1883
(National Library of Scotland)*

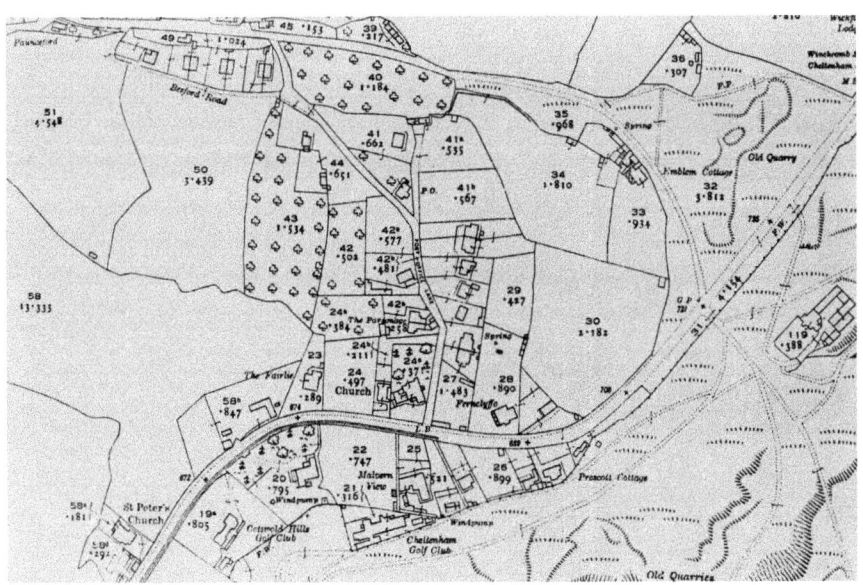

By 1921 the main outlines of the present settlement had been created (National Library of Scotland)

and by 1921 the modern shape of the community on Cleeve Hill had been formed. Developments since then have reinforced the pattern which had largely been established by 1918. So the purpose of this section is to outline the processes of change which have so clearly left their mark in today's buildings.

The catalyst for the development was improved transport, which enabled a variety of people to seize the opportunity to make money by building on land bordering the main road, particularly the narrow strip lying between it and the earlier turnpike road. Most of the houses were built as speculation, financed by capital from the purses of wealthy Cheltenham entrepreneurs. Cleeve Hill became integrated into Cheltenham in both visible and invisible ways.

Before considering some of these developments in detail, it is worth pausing for an overview of the nature of the settlement which grew up during these years. In his budget of 1909 David Lloyd-George, the Chancellor of the Exchequer, proposed to introduce a windfall tax on the unearned increase in the value of land. Returns for Gloucestershire survive in the County Archives and since the first edition of this book, have been made available online with a very useful search facility. For Cleeve Hill the returns cover the years from 1911 to 1915, identifying individual land holdings, giving their extent and value with the names of the occupier and owner. For a number of reasons it is not now totally complete, but this does not invalidate the conclusions. Fifty two properties can be identified, ranging from Haymes Farm through the large villas of the Health Resort, to shared properties at Nutterswood. 28 were owner occupied and 24 were rented. Of these latter, seven were owned by people with addresses in Cheltenham, six on Cleeve Hill, four in Bishop's Cleeve, Southam and Woodmancote and three much further afield, including Brighton. For some properties the subsequent sales were recorded. These reinforce the transient nature of the population for at least 35 properties had changed hands during the next ten years.

The development of the Cotswold Health Resort may also be traced from two other sources: Kelly's directories, and the records of local estate agents Bayleys, who seemed to have possessed a near monopoly of the house and land transactions on the hill at this time. Neither source is without its problems. Kelly's directories continued to include outdated information. In 1863 it still carried the statement that Cheltenham races were held on Cleeve Common, eight years after the final unsuccessful attempt to restart them after a gap of thirteen years. However, the inclusion of Cleeve Hill as a separate entry in 1894 did mark a recognition of the growing separateness of the embryonic resort, now becoming noticeably different from the rural nature of Woodmancote with which it had previously been linked. In 1889 it simply recorded, 'Cleeve Hill, which includes several scattered farms and other houses'.

The difficulties with the Bayley's records lie in the identification of the separate houses and building plots. Geographical descriptions are imprecise, but more importantly the rapid turnover of residents led to frequent renaming of properties and consequent problems of continued identification. This can only really be done when other sources, particularly deeds, can be consulted. The name of Adderstone House, which stands at the bottom of Rising Sun Lane, has been altered several times in its history. In 1872 it was called The Rockery, by 1897 it had been renamed Upmeads, by 1918 Petra, and by 1924 Heron Rock. In 1926 the name changed to Adderstone and to Adderstone House in 1966. This is an extreme case but illustrates well a major feature of the new settlement, the transient nature of residents and owners of the properties. Emblem Cottage has retained its distinctive name since George Stevens' ownership, but after his son sold it in 1888 it had changed hands a further five times before being sold for £1,000 in 1916, to a Mrs Pearse, the wife of a colonel in the Indian Veterinary Department. Only one of these owners actually lived at Emblem Cottage. George Yiend, quarryman, bought it for £400 as the sitting tenant in 1888 but had to sell in 1897, being unable to pay off his mortgage. The history of Emblem Cottage also illustrates well how the ownership of the existing buildings moved to the wealthy of Cheltenham, and even further afield. It also illustrates again the transient nature of the population; Mrs Pearse in turn sold the cottage in 1921.

The existing houses were insufficient for the demand. Although it is impossible to trace here the building of all the houses which appear on the later Ordnance Survey maps, an indication of the process can be given in outline. The Malvern View Hotel was actually being built at the time of the 1881 census. Its neighbour Prescott Cottage has a stone dated four years earlier. Ashleigh House, lower down the hill in Ashleigh Lane towards Cheltenham, was newly built in 1886. Upper Colletts (Plot

Laburnum Villa (now Cloud's End) and Laburnum Cottage

20 on the map of 1901) was built a decade later for a local magistrate C.C. Turnbull of College Lawn, as a holiday residence and for letting. He sold it for £2600 in 1918, which made it one of the more sought-after properties compared to a three-roomed cottage owned by Solomon Hawker in Nutterswood, which had sold the previous year for £90. One local person who did enter into this housing speculation was the stone mason George Yiend, who lived in Laburnum Cottage on the common. He had Laburnum Villa built in his garden as a letting property. In 1900 it was let for £35 per annum. In 1911 his widow Fanny was still living in the cottage whilst Janet McGraith of private means was living with her daughter and a servant in the villa; just another example of how the hill was an increasingly attractive place of residence for outsiders. The architectural difference between the labourer's cottage and the speculative mansion is still very evident today despite more recent alterations. All these houses were built out of Cotswold stone, a tradition which was carried on into the twentieth century. Flagstaff, opposite the former Malvern View Care Home, is said to have been the last property to have had local stone used on its construction, in an extension built shortly before the Second World War.

The similarity of style and stonework of many of the Cotswold stone houses betrays their common origin. They were built by Arthur

Arthur Yiend in 1935

Yiend who moved from Winchcombe in 1897 and who rented quarries on the common. He was most active in the two decades before he retired in 1920. He seems to have taken the distinctive style of his stone work from Prescott Cottage, which pre-dated his developments. He laid out Post Office Lane, where he lived at Denewood, which is marked as the Post Office on the 1901 map. His family was one of only two recorded in the 1901 census still living on the hill in 1911, albeit having moved a few yards down Post Office Lane to Glendale, which he built in 1907. In 1912 Arthur bought land from Rose Farm lower down Stockwell Lane in Woodmancote for £500 and created Besford Road, which he constructed at the same time as he was providing the stone for Besford Court, near Pershore, hence its name. The houses he built are hand-drawn additions onto the Lloyd George Land Tax map indicated they were under construction during the years of the survey. It seems he built for rent and then slowly sold them off by 1920. During the First World War Rochdale (now Barnfield), the last house in the road, was used by a Miss Waghorne as a private school. Two more instantly recognisable Arthur Yiend houses are Paunceford and Holleybank in Stockwell Lane, the former carries the date 1906 and the latter advertised rooms for holiday let in 1911. When the census of that year was taken on 2 April, although only possessing five rooms in total, Alice Gaskins at Holleybank, living with her husband, two daughters and a son, was recorded as having two boarders. Her

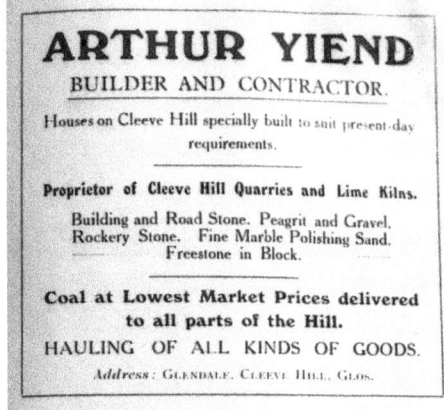

An advertisement from Burrow's 1909 guide book to Cleeve Hill evidences Arthur Yiend's many interests (Gloucester Library)

View to Nottingham Hill c.1900 showing Post Office Lane in the foreground and Henry Taylor's short-lived Reading Room in the distance on the left

The style of the houses in Besford Road is typical of those built by Arthur Yiend

husband and one of the boarders worked on the greens for the golf club; a new source of employment as the Cheltenham influence grew stronger.

The distinctive appearance of the hill as a health resort did not, however, depend upon Arthur Yiend's houses, for in their stone construction they shared a continuity with the past. The impression of a health resort is rather to be found in the prefabricated pine villas which were constructed at the turn of the twentieth century. The first to appear were erected by T.W. Stephens, who had a picture frame making establishment in Winchcombe Street in Cheltenham. He put two, Cotswold Chalet and Cotswold Bungalow, quite literally in the front garden of his own home, Ivybank in Lye Lane, for holiday letting in 1897. Advertised as only a ten minute walk to the bus stop, the Bungalow was 45s. per week with special terms for the rest of the year. Two years later Walter Dicks, who owned a large soft furnishing emporium in the Lower High Street in Cheltenham, had a much larger pine house erected on part of a plot he had recently purchased. He named it Semington. Today it is known as Highfields. Three more similar houses soon followed. Walter built and owned Ferncliffe which became the home of Henry Norton, who owned an ironmongers which later became a

THE COTSWOLD BUNGALOW, CLEEVE HILL, CHELTENHAM.

THE COTSWOLD CHALET, CLEEVE HILL, CHELTENHAM.

The back of this postcard advertised both long and short-term lets of the Cotswold Bungalow and Cotswold Chalet

Walter Dick's pine villa, Semington, built in 1899 and photographed in 1975

motor depôt on the corner of the Bath Road and the Strand in Cheltenham. Unsurprisingly Henry became the first resident on the hill to own a motor car. His car, registered in 1906 as AD769, was a Humber open tourer. By that date he had already been buying and selling cars for two years at his motor depôt. Greenmount was another pine villa, built in the grounds of the Malvern View Hotel for holiday letting by Harold Swift, its owner. The fourth example was Hillcrest next to Prescott Cottage. These houses still help to give the hill its atmosphere of a holiday resort.

The division of the fields into building plots can also be traced in Bayley's records. The earliest reference to such plots in their records can be found in 1896, when half an acre near the Rising Sun Hotel went on

Hillcrest with Prescott Cottage in the garden of which Hillcrest was built

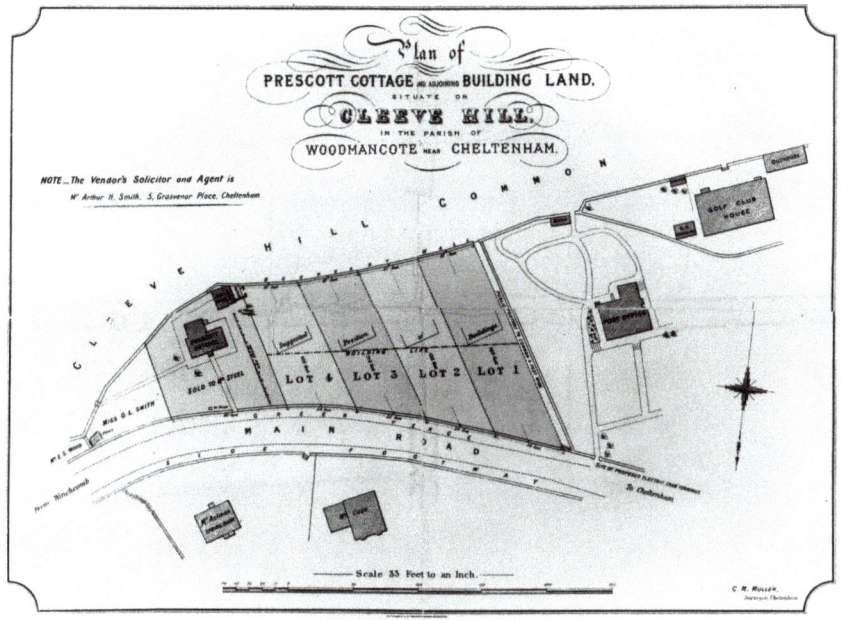

The process of development is captured in this plan from the deeds of Prescott Cottage. The importance of the tramway for such developments is obvious (J. Wilson)

the market for a 100 guineas freehold. The land market speeded up with the arrival of the tramway in 1901, as the plan of Prescott Cottage evidences. Unsurprisingly there is no evidence to support the claim in Selina Jenkin's satirical letter quoted at the head of the chapter, that land prices rose by 500 per cent. Building plots costing £300 in 1896 were similarly priced in 1903, but rather easier to sell as the Health Resort developed.

The changes in the type of the person living on the hill can be studied in detail by examining what was happening on Haymes farm. In these years the owners were William and Charles Holliday, the butchers from Cheltenham. They seemed to have been intent on selling off small plots of their land for profit. The consequence was the creation of a new road, Haymes Road, along which a small number of houses were built reflecting the changes happening on a larger scale higher up the hill. In early 1904 they sold a four acre plot of land to William Baker for £1025. However the transaction could only go through once the new road was completed. William was a school master at Cheltenham

By the time this photograph was taken c.1970 the houses in Haymes Road had been joined by newer houses below them towards Southam (T. Curr)

College and originally from Suffolk. On his plot bordering on the main road he built a handsome house of twelve rooms called Greystone (now Mulberry House). On census night in 1911 he was living there with four children and three servants; presumably his wife was away. In January 1906 the Hollidays sold a smaller plot to Charles Smith for £150. He built Springfield (now Laurentides) where he was living with his wife Emily, a daughter and a single servant in 1911. He was described as a bank cashier originally from Nottingham. Also in January 1906 the adjoining plot, presumably Inglenook (now Swift's Place), was sold to a Mr Cresswell also for £150. Two years later at the end of 1908 the land for Haymesgarth was sold to Charles Bailey from St Annes on Sea in Lancashire for £600 for the building of a house 'to cost not less than £500'. Charles built a substantial house of twelve rooms. He was a retired shipping merchant aged 72 living there in 1911 with his wife Hannah and two servants. Between Haymesgarth and the main road James Welsh was living in Cleeve Hill House (nine rooms) with his wife Elizabeth, one son and three servants. James had undisclosed private means. By

1915 only one plot between Haymesgarth and Springfield remained undeveloped. Amos Wilson the Cheltenham builder constructed Cleeve Hill House, Greystone and Haymesgarth. By their architecture they reinforced the break with the traditional houses on the hill, even those houses built by Arthur Yiend. Thus in this small way the changes taking place higher on Cleeve Hill were reflected on its lower slope. But what of Haymes farm itself?

The 1901 census records that it was the home of tenant farmer William Walker and his wife Mary who employed a single servant. Ten years later it was home to Philip Bodington, his wife Elsie with a son and daughter and two servants. Philip's occupation was given as a schoolmaster employed by the county council. Presumably these people were tenants because Charles Holliday was living there in 1912 and farming its 96 acres.

Whilst such developments were taking place at Haymes, the other two large farms on the hill carried on their traditional rôles. Wontley continued under the ownership of the Lawrence family at Sandywell Park until 1921 when it was sold for £4290. In the Lloyd George survey entry, dated 1912, the occupier was a Mr E.F. Watts who was farming it from what is now Westwood House, which was also on the Lawrence estate.

This postcard of Cockbury Court showing the house and barn was sent in 1915 (G. Cocks)

However the acreage of the farm, 333 acres, still reflected the extent of the land of the Medieval settlement.

In the previous chapter it was explained how Cockbury was still in the hands of the Hone family in 1891. By 1901 this had changed and the farmhouse had become the home of Samuel Swindell, described as a retired club steward born in Yorkshire. The presence of John Hall, described as a shepherd, and his family in one of the cottages and his son Isaac, described as a carter, indicated the land was still being farmed. In 1911 Charles Snow was living there with his wife, three children, a groom and a cowman. He described himself as a farmer and his son, also Charles, as a professional cricketer. The house was recorded as having twelve rooms. By 1912 the size of the farm had shrunk to 86 acres by which time it was owned by W. Lloyd Evans who lived at The Park in Cheltenham. The influence and money of Cheltenham had even reached Cockbury.

We must not, however, think that every building venture was successful as far as the speculators were concerned. The best example of this was that part of the Wickfields lying opposite the Convalescent Home. In 1896 eight acres were purchased by C.B. Dix. He not only ran a builders' merchants and ironmongers in the Bath Road but was also landlord of many houses in that area of the town. He bought them for £500. Shortly afterwards he put the land back on the market as four building plots at £150 each plus six acres at £150 per acre. His profit would have been three times the purchase price. There were no takers and when the venture was repeated in 1903 it again failed. Today's visitor is perhaps thankful that not all speculation succeeded.

In the same way that the commoners of Bishop's Cleeve, Southam and Woodmancote found their traditional claims to the common being swamped by the trippers from Cheltenham demanding open space for their recreation, so the few families who had made a traditional living from the hill found themselves swamped by the newcomers. This can be summarised in general terms by taking the occupations of the adult population from the censuses of 1891, 1901 and 1911. The percentages of the adult population recorded as either an agricultural or general labourer plus those working in the quarries or as stone masons fell from fifty five per cent in 1891 to thirty one per cent in 1901 and to twenty seven per cent in 1911, at which date there were more people

A suburban villa at Nutterswood, advertised as newly built in 1908. The architect, Thomas Malvern, had his business in Winchcombe Street but lived at Ivydene on the lower slopes of the hill (T. Curr)

living off private means than in any of the three traditional occupations. This trend can be illustrated by examining the detail from some of the returns. In 1901 ten stone masons were living on the hill, by 1911 only three were recorded, all living in Nutterswood, but even here modernity was making its presence felt. At 2 Cleeve Cloud Mary Innes, a retired teacher from the Ladies College, was living with Margaret Dudley, of independent means. Mary had been born in India. In 1911 a handful of agricultural labourers still lived in Gambles Lane and Stockwell Lane but the new developments in Post Office Lane and bordering the main road were the homes of people like Richard Sanders at Treganna, now Top of the Hill, in Post Office Lane, the managing director of a drapery company with neighbours Lucy Lutman and Herbert Baillie, both of private means and all employing domestic servants, which did, however, provide some employment for the young women from the more established families.

Along the main road George Bick, retired portmanteau maker, lived at Ivybank and Charles Barnett, fish, poultry and game dealer, lived at Bramleigh. Both employed two servants to look after their family. The main feature of this new life on the hill was its transience; remarkably only Walter Dicks and his family at Semington were living in the same house in 1911 as in 1901. However, by 1915 even he had moved, back to his other residence in Hewlett Road in Cheltenham, and he then let out Semington until it was sold in 1938. Other Cheltenham merchants who chose to live on the hill at this time included J.J. Banks the bookseller on The Promenade who lived at The Shanty and published *From a Cotswold Height*; Thomas George, bootmaker, who lived at Greenmount; J.S. Friskney who had a toyshop in Pittville Street and lived at Thrift Cottage; and Thomas Malvern, architect and surveyor, of Ivydene. They made their money in Cheltenham and enjoyed looking down on the town. Butchers and bakers fell over themselves to make life on the hill as comfortable as possible. By 1911 the residents were well served by frequent visits on rounds from Cheltenham with butchers Holliday and Page even offering to send urgent orders by tram.

One other development in these years is worth noting. Alice Gaskins in Stockwell Lane was not the only person offering lodgings

The "Geisha" Tea House which later became Gresham House

to people spending a few days or even months in the Health Resort. Her near neighbour Mary New at The Orchards had two boarding guests when the census was taken in 1911. On the main road towards Winchcombe, Charlesville (now Flagstaff) and Wilcote, each with eight rooms, were newly-built as boarding houses. In the busier part of the village stood The Geisha, a Japanese-styled tea house where Anna Smith would serve the visitors tea and in 1909 was offering accommodation from Saturday until Monday morning for 10s.6d. despite having only five rooms in total. In 1901 Herbert Theyer and family were living at the Malvern View with two servants. He was described as a joiner, although in the Kelly's Directory of 1902 he was letting out rooms as apartments. Ten years later Harold Swift and his wife Lilla were running a boarding house there with three servants. The census recorded they had five guests. At the Rising Sun Hotel Walter and Charlotte Knott employed four servants and had eight guests. The hotel provided another example of Cheltenham money influencing developments on the hill. The Original Cheltenham Brewery in the town's High Street obviously saw the market potential of the nascent health resort, for in 1891 it took on the lease of the hotel and in 1903 bought it outright. The brewery eventually became part of Whitbread in 1963, since when the hotel has been enlarged and is now part of the Greene King brewery company of Bury St Edmunds. For visitors in 1911 who only wanted refreshments having travelled by tram for the day, there stood opposite the Rising Sun Hotel the Cleeve Hill Café and Tea Gardens, which in 1909 was advertising 'parties of 200 catered for at the shortest notice'. It had opened in 1902 on land bought

An advertisement of 1910 for the Malvern View Hotel, where the tram terminated (S. Weir)

In 1909 the Cleeve Hill Café offered to cater for parties of up to 200 'at the shortest notice' (G. Cocks)

by C.J. Davies, a grocer of Suffolk Road for £200 the previous year and was run by Ernest Batstone, a pastry cook from the Bath Road. In 1913 Edward J Burrow, the prolific Cheltenham publisher of guide books and post cards, invested £500 into the business; yet another example of the impact of Cheltenham influence and money affecting the developments on the hill.

All these developments led to the introduction of utilities which underpinned the lives of residents and visitors and which today are taken for granted. The first to arrive was the telephone in 1899. In July of that year the National Telephone Company started to pay the Board of Conservators an annual payment of 5s. for a pole erected on the common. The Rising Sun Hotel, Upper Colletts and Ivybank appeared in the first telephone directory. In 1912 the GPO was created and a telephone exchange was built at what was Treganna in Post Office Lane where it stayed for fifty years before the growth of Woodmancote and Bishop's Cleeve led to a new automatic exchange being built off Gotherington Lane in Bishop's Cleeve. Sewerage followed in 1908 and by 1914 gas had arrived. Although Woodmancote had taken a water supply from Wickfields in 1896 and Cleeve Hill residents were paying water rates by 1898, they were complaining bitterly they had no mains supply. The supply of water came from a number of springs. In 1907 the Conservators agreed to the Rising Sun

Hotel taking water from the common. In 1920 the spring water which Arthur Yiend had provided for Besford Road was declared safe to drink. In 1921 Haymesgarth was still depending upon a wind pump to supply spring water to the house. In 1931 the workmen presumably laying what was the main pipe found the remains of the skeleton on the roadside at the top of Stockwell Lane.

By 1918 the nature of the present village of Cleeve Hill had been established. Within a few years it had become an affluent outer suburb of Cheltenham and a holiday resort. It was publicized by an enormous variety of picture postcards and, from 1909, a series of guidebooks. They captured for us the spirit of the age and provided important clues for the understanding of the period. Many of the new residents on the hill were affluent retirees or had businesses down in Cheltenham. They tended to move in to enjoy the wealth they had created, moving out when advancing years or, ironically, ill-health forced them into more accessible locations. Unlike the local families, the Gaskins, Hawkers and Yiends, this was a transient population and as if to compensate for this transience, the newcomers made attempts to establish institutions which would bind the community together and create for it an identity independent of the individuals who might at any one time belong to it; these met with varying success.

The Institutions of the Health Resort

Selina Jenkins noticed three institutions in her 'visit' in 1903. The 'sanitory' and tramline have already been discussed; the third was the tin church, known locally as 'the tin tabernacle'. The type of people who came to live on the hill were the backbone of many a church and chapel at the turn of the century but there was no place of worship on the hill until Henry Taylor, converted his laundry at The Rockery in Rising Sun Lane into a chuch, as explained in the previous chapter. When he left in 1896 the services stopped and for a time the worshippers shared in the morning services conducted in the Convalescent Home by the Reverend Thomas Jesson, the rector of Bishop's Cleeve. This did not meet their demand in the winter months when the home was closed and so in an attempt to establish a permanent place for worship, Mr and Mrs Thomas Astman made their home, Springbank, available for a Sunday School and an evening service between June and November 1900. Then Walter

Dicks of Semington offered his stable loft for the winter months, but the congregations had grown so large that it was decided to build a proper church. A committee was established and Walter became the secretary.

From the start the local traders played a large part. Walter himself gave land out of his garden at the cost price of £50, Arthur Yiend built the foundations for £65 and the whole congregation contributed the £250 paid to the firm of James Lee of Manchester, who won the contract to build the church with a patent lightweight design, necessary because of the potential instability of the site. The affluence of the congregation meant that finance was not a problem and the total cost of £650 had been met by the opening. On 26 June 1901 the evangelical Cleeve Hill Interdenominational Church was opened by Sir John Dorington, the local MP, who announced that the Bishop of Gloucester, Dr Ellicott, sent his blessing. Here again the influence of Cheltenham was paramount. Of the eight original trustees recorded in 1908 only Walter Dicks lived on the hill, six gave addresses in Cheltenham and one in Clifton near Bristol.

The tin tabernacle. The architect has taken considerable licence in flattening the slope of the site

The church had an interesting mixture of Anglican and Nonconformist services; the former on Sunday morning, the latter in the evening, thereby catering for all people, who on their own could not sustain any one type of church, although the morning services did not start until the November to avoid clashing with those held in the Convalescent Home. Walter Dicks and his wife set up a Sunday School with their daughter Olive taking the infant class. Before the First World War numbers varied between 50 and 60 with children reported to be attending from a wide area. By that date meetings of the Band of Hope (a national movement set up to discourage children from drinking alcohol) were taking place each Wednesday at 6pm, followed by a service at 7pm and choir practice at 8pm. How much of this continued during the war is impossible to discern from the surviving minute book.

For the first eight years of its life the church had no resident pastor, services being taken by visiting preachers from the Cheltenham area. Their first pastor, the Reverend William Edwin Lewis from Leicester, took up his post in October 1909 after two others had turned it down. When he left in 1913 six ministers refused the living before a successor was found. It was not an easy congregation to minister to, but clearly a need was served. Over a hundred people regularly attended the annual teas held on the lawn of Ferncliffe, the home of Henry Norton.

CHURCH GATHERING ON CLEEVE HILL.

The affluent congregation of the tin tabernacle at the annual garden party in July 1912 (T. Curr)

That Edwin Lewis was appointed in 1909 was the result of two factors: one internal to the church, the second external. The internal factor concerned the arrival on the hill in 1904 of Major-General and Mrs Richard Oldfield, late of the Indian Army. Mrs Oldfield soon became superintendent of the Sunday School and later organist and choir leader, whilst her husband took on the rôle of treasurer and from there preferred to contribute in less obvious ways. He was the anonymous donor who in March 1909 promised a manse, Sunnyside (now The Parsonage) in Post Office Lane, and a £100 annual stipend for a resident pastor. By the end of the year Mr Lewis was living in the manse next to the Oldfield's own home, Inglecroft. Arthur Yiend had collected his furniture from the former Cleeve railway station in Stoke Orchard and made no charge.

The church had been set up largely by affluent merchants who knew what they wanted and liked to get their own way. Such people formed the committee and were generally successful in steering the church, but some petty feuds can be discovered in the minutes. In November 1910 Olive Dicks resigned as the organist, claiming that several people refused to attend church because of the poor quality of the singing which reflected on her playing. A year later, her successor Kitty Rose resigned because her name came only second in the list of officers in the church magazine. In November 1912 the pastor Edwin Lewis resigned because of growing uncertainty over his salary and his intention to train for the Anglican ministry. At least five clergyman refused an invitation to be the new pastor before Dr Warren accepted it in October 1914 at a salary of £50 per annum. He obviously worked hard and in his first year he visited 750 people living in Cleeve Hill and Woodmancote. When he resigned in January 1917 a replacement was not found until July 1918 when the Rev Stanley Mercer was appointed. He served until May 1931.

The second, external factor concerned the opening of St Peter's Mission Church by the Anglicans in January 1907. The *Cheltenham Chronicle* explained it thus, 'At all events it did not astonish one to find that this little tin church ran on interdenominational lines should fall very short of the ideal of many local Church people residing in the higher part of Bishop's Cleeve parish.' As early as October 1901 the committee running the Convalescent Home had offered a site in their grounds for an Anglican chapel of ease, but the offer was refused. A new bishop in Gloucester seems to have instigated the venture but it was strongly pushed forward by the rector of Bishop's Cleeve, Reverend Thomas Jesson, who called together a small committee in January 1906 to consider the building of such a church. The *Cheltenham Examiner* published a vitriolic correspondence between the two sides once word was out that an Anglican church was to be built. Under a pen name, 'Anglican' considered 'a second-hand blessing from a Bishop' hardly constituted a proper dedication of the tin tabernacle, whilst 'A Loyal Churchman' called the services there as 'nondescript' and its preacher 'lacking in the ability to give spiritual aid'. At least the defenders of the church had the courage to put their names. Major-General Oldfield refuted the assertion that the late Bishop of Gloucester's blessing had been second-hand. Robert Ley-Wood, one of the trustees, argued that three of the nine trustees were Anglicans and that the Anglican church at Southam was only a mile away. Nevertheless, these were just words and the construction soon began.

The name St Peter's reflected the earlier church in Rising Sun Lane and was obviously associating its location on the hill with the play on the name Peter being called a rock by Jesus in the New Testament. Led by W.M. Baker, a master of Cheltenham College who lived at Greystone, the decision was taken to engage the Frazzi company, which had patented a hollow terracotta brick to give strength without weight, to make the best use of a sloping site almost opposite the Rising Sun Hotel. The final cost of around £550 was met by private subscription and a church grant. The building work was carried out by Amos Wilson and the interior was heavily influenced by the Arts and Crafts movement fashionable at the period. After it was opened, the congregations at the tin church fell, and their response was to appoint their own pastor. St Peter's, of course, was served by the parish clergy from Bishop's Cleeve. Thus by 1914 the hill was served by two places of worship. Ironically the institution chosen to bind the community together had, in fact, split it into two, but the personalities

The attractive Arts and Crafts interior of St Peter's church (G. Cocks)

involved had made their mark by being successful in a competitive environment.

Another institution which Selina Jenkins mentioned on her visit in April 1903 was the golf course. There was no clearer statement of Cheltenham moving out of town than the establishment of the golf course and the two clubs which played over it. They provided no benefit to the traditional inhabitants on the hill, except as green keepers and caddies, but they introduced a new conflict with the traditional users of the common.

There is no doubt the golf course originated in the wishes of Cheltenham gentlemen to take advantage of Cheltenham's right to recreation on Cleeve Common as laid down by the 1890 Act. Eighty four people attended a public meeting at the Queen's Hotel in the town on

The Queen's Hotel in Cheltenham where the Cheltenham Golf Club was founded

6 March 1891 for the purpose of setting out a golf course and forming a golf club. Cheltenham Golf Club came into being with Lord Eldon of Stowell Park as president and James Tynte Agg-Gardner, MP for the town, as one of the committee members. Prestbury Park was soon dismissed as a potential location in favour of Cleeve Hill. The Board of Conservators negotiated an annual fee of £35 for the privilege. D.

CLEEVE HILL

The original first tee outside the clubhouse

Brown of Malvern laid out the course and four rooms were rented at Rock House to serve as the club house. The club had originally wanted to purchase neighbouring Upper Colletts, but Gertrude Warrell wanted £4,250 for the property and the club was only prepared to offer £2,500. The launch of the club took place in July with a lunch in the Rising Sun Hotel. It already had a membership of 112 gentlemen and 20 ladies, but only 30 of them were described as active golfers. In the Victorian age it seemed quite proper to allow lady members to be elected without allowing them use of the club house. Lord Eldon's daughter, Lady Margaret Scott, won the monthly medal in September 1892 by beating eighteen gentlemen but could not use the club house. The situation was not fully resolved until a new club house was opened in the grounds of Rock House in

Rock House and the 1904 club house, now private residences

April 1904 when the ladies were allowed to use the original rented rooms there. The new club house now forms two private residences.

Cheltenham Golf Club was a club for gentlemen and their ladies. Membership was exclusive, the entrance fee cost four guineas and the annual fee cost two guineas. A round of golf cost 2s. Ironically the new type of resident on the hill, being mostly merchants and traders, could not join. Wealth could not buy status. In 1895 a few of these middle class gentlemen began to play over the course and as numbers increased they rented a shed in the grounds of the Malvern View Hotel to serve as their club house. They called themselves the Cheltenham Town Golf Club and later the Cotswold Hills Golf Club. The arrival of the tramcar in 1901 brought many more people to the hill and partly as a consequence of this growing popularity, these golfers met at Bayleys', Cheltenham's auctioneers and estate agents, offices in the Promenade on 12 February 1902 to formalise the situation. George Bayley, Henry Billings, the builder whose company had built the Convalescent Home, and Harold Webb, brick maker with offices in The Colonnade at the bottom of the Promenade, were the driving forces, creating more Cheltenham influences on the hill. It entered into an agreement with the Cheltenham Golf Club, paying it 10s. per member. Its first home in 1902 was a small, wooden bungalow, on the same site where a

The Cotswold Hills clubhouse with the first clubhouse of 1902 on the right (Cotswold Hills Golf Club)

permanent club house was built three years later, which is now known as 1 and 2 Cleeve Hill after the club moved out in 1937. James Agg-Gardner was invited to open it and in 1911 he accepted the invitation to become the club's president. Here the annual subscription was a mere 30s. and golfers could play over the same course as the gentlemen for only 1s.6d. Such was the demand that within five years of its opening, accommodation was offered in the club house to members and their friends; 10s.6d. a week for a bed or 2s.6d. for one night. By 1910 they could camp in the grounds for 2s.6d. a week. Our understanding of the development of the two clubs and their impact on the landscape has to be rooted in the class values of late Victorian and Edwardian society. When the caddying was performed by the locals, it confirmed their lowly status on their own common.

The arrival of the golf course with two clubs introduced yet another conflict into the uses of the common and again it was the established users who found themselves under increased pressure with

This cartoon of 1904 neatly sums up the problems facing the golfers (T. Curr)

little recourse to redress. Even the Board of Conservators struggled to enforce its byelaws to protect them. Writing in the *Golf* magazine in 1895 a visitor commented favourably on the course's location but was critical of the course itself. He recommended that the ruts caused by the cart tracks be filled in to prevent golf balls from landing in them as there was no room for the golfer to swing a club to hit them out. He criticised the green inside the hillfort as being too small and 'it would be easy work' to increase its size by flattening the banks. Fortunately in this case the Board had authority under the 1890 act to prevent such damage. The golfers frequently complained of the damage caused to the course by the horses training across the common. On the other hand the commoners complained about Sunday golf and the attitude of the golfers towards them. The clubs themselves did not encourage, but did nothing to prevent Sunday golf, although it was not until 1921 after the war had ended that the Cheltenham Golf Club opened its clubhouse on a Sunday. By then an uneasy peace reconciling these new demands on the common had emerged. The succeeding century would show a pattern had been set.

Finally, there is one institution which Selina Jenkins did not mention, the Reading Room, built in 1893 by Henry Taylor of The Rockery as a place of improving recreation for the working classes. At his own expense he provided books, newspapers and games. We must not be surprised she failed to mention it, for by 1897 it had already closed. Why did it not long survive his departure from the hill in 1896? The reason is not difficult to discover. He built it along Wickfield Lane on Nottingham Hill, almost a mile from the growing settlement of Cleeve Hill. Our real surprise should be why he chose to build there, as he had already shown goodwill towards the residents by converting his laundry into St Peter's church in the much more convenient location of Rising Sun Lane. We will probably never know his reasons but at least someone seemed to be providing for the local working people whose traditional way of life had become so obviously swamped by the incomers during this period of rapid change immediately before the First World War. Whether they felt patronized or pleased is always likely to be another unanswerable question.

The Quarries

The traditional life of the common continued under increasing pressure from the new demands of the early twentieth century. Not only did these include the burgeoning recreational use of the common, but also the increased quarrying activity which brought some conflict between it and the communal rights for grazing. Again there is a lack of detailed sources which tell the full story. As Selina Jenkins commented, quarrymen who worked in a 'quiet, genteel, any-time-will-do style' were unlikely to keep detailed records for future historians. Their scale was seemingly so limited that they were barely affected by recent legislation. The Quarry Fencing Act of 1887 ordered the fencing of all quarries lying within 50 yards of a public highway. No quarry fell into that category, which resulted in the lords of the manor considering they had no responsibility for fencing the quarries. In 1894 a Quarries Act required registration of all open workings over twenty feet deep. Only one quarry was ever registered. Calling it simply 'Cleeve Hill', Arthur Yiend made the registration in March 1897, at which time he recorded the employment of two men.

The 1890 Act imposed on the Board the requirement to fence the 'upper sides' of the quarries, but they seemed in no hurry to do so in any systematic way. In 1902 stone was being extracted from Milestone, Ring,

The demand for freestone meant that Wickfield Quarry was one of the last to be worked. It is seen here in 1901. Today it is used as a car park (T. Curr)

Sidelands, Hardstone, Freestone, Rolling Bank and Wickfield Quarries in Bishop's Cleeve manor, but only the first had adequate fencing. Gravel, mortar and sand were being taken from the King's Beeches where the Iron Age occupation site was discovered. Two sand holes were producing white sand, used in making pottery and polishing marble. Trains of pack donkeys were said to have taken sand to Staffordshire in the late eighteenth and early nineteenth century. The sand used for polishing marble went to the famous H.H. Martyn and R.L. Boulton companies in Cheltenham. On Southam manor, stone was being extracted from Cleeve Cloud, Middle Hill and Postlip Quarries and gravel from the Middle Hill gravel pit. Most of these also needed fencing. From Captain Daubeny's book it is known that at this time Arthur Yiend was renting the rights to all the Bishop's Cleeve quarries for £35 per annum. George Yiend was renting Southam quarries for £30 per annum. References to fencing in the Board's minutes are very irregular. In 1903 £28.15s. was spent on hurdles, in 1905 four dozen were ordered and in 1912 24 hurdles were placed around Milestone Quarry, presumably to replace earlier fencing. However the Board was active in controlling the workings of the quarry. In 1909 Arthur Yiend agreed to stop quarrying there, where dynamite had been used since the 1860s, as it was encroaching on the old turnpike road. By then the 'mounds' shown on the plan of the King's Beeches excavations (see Chapter One) which were most likely to have been Bronze Age round barrows, had been destroyed with no record kept. The Board then became concerned at Arthur's activities near the hillfort, especially as he was using dynamite there also. In 1911 they consulted the county's leading archaeologist G.B. Witts to give his opinion on the damage being caused. After a heated meeting with a committee set up by the Board, Arthur had to agree to stop quarrying there and he was even forbidden to remove the stones he had already quarried. Two years later he turned from poacher to gamekeeper as he joined the Board and served on it for 31 years, latterly as the chairman.

Much local stone went into the building of the houses on the hill and keeping the local roads in some state of repair before the use of tarmac. Details of other uses are few, but their diversity is surprising. Arthur Yiend supplied stone for Cheltenham Ladies' College and in 1914 for repairs to Tewkesbury Abbey. He built Bishop's Cleeve and Gotherington stations for the opening of the local railway line in 1906.

Besford Court near Pershore, built by Arthur Yiend (H. Denham)

He also supplied stone for work in Magdalen College, Oxford; Romsey Abbey; Winchester College; and for restoration work in several churches over the Welsh border in Gwent. The difficulties of transporting the stone can be measured from his contract to supply stone for Besford Court, near Pershore. At one time thirteen teams of horses and a steam traction engine were employed. Such transport problems, the skill and increasing costs needed to extract the stone and, above all, the availability of alternative materials, led to the abandonment of quarrying, as explained in the next chapter. It was responsible for the destruction of much archaeological evidence of earlier periods. It created a conflict of landscape use at least since the Roman period, not only by the quarrying itself, but by the multiplicity of trackways which caused injuries to grazing animals falling into the deep ruts and yet it has given Cleeve Hill its character by which it is so easily recognisable from the vale today.

The Common

The *Commons Regulation (Cleeve) Provisional Order Confirmation Act of 1890* was confirmed by the Board of Agriculture in the following year. The act laid down that the Board had to meet at least three times each year. It had three main responsibilities: to grant free access to the inhabitants of Bishop's Cleeve (which included Woodmancote and Southam and Brockhampton) and Cheltenham, to fence the quarries and to allow the training of horses and military exercises. It also had the right to make byelaws and protect the ancient monuments. To support its obligations £50 each year came from Cheltenham Corporation, plus contributions from horse training and military exercises and any voluntary contributions. A surviving account from 1900 provides a snapshot from the early years. Income derived from £50 from Cheltenham, £42 from horse training licences and £34 from the golf club. Major expenditure included the haywarden's wage of £52, the clerk's salary of £15, rolling and work on the gallops £7 and £7 for the cottage rental for the haywarden. Fencing cost nearly £17. The £10 profit for the year was added to the £95 balance in hand. In October 1891 a Mr Watts had been appointed as full-time haywarden at 18s. per week. This increasingly onerous post was not split into three until 1990, almost a century later.

The first meeting of the Board took place on 22 April 1891 in the rectory in Bishop's Cleeve (now Cleeve Hall). It reflected the traditional older order with the Reverend Benjamin Hemming, rector of the parish and nominee of the Lady of the Manor, Mrs Noblett, taking the chair. The following February there was a request to hold meetings in a public place after having moved to Rosehill House, the home of James Hutchinson who took over as chairman at that meeting. The Board seems to have taken this request literally and the next meeting was held in the now demolished Crown and Harp Inn on Cheltenham Road in Bishop's Cleeve. They soon moved again, to the Rising Sun Hotel on the hill. After January 1896 this location alternated with the clerk's office which was at that time in 5 Regent Street in Cheltenham. Over time more meetings were held at the clerk's office until by 1915 only one meeting each year was held on the hill, at the Rising Sun Hotel. The move of the Board into Cheltenham for its meetings reinforced the perception that the commoners and the local population were losing or even had already lost control over their own common. Six of the original conservators lived in the town which provided further evidence to support the perception. Not until 1990 did the Board meet regularly on the hill, at the Golf Club.

The Board wasted no time in erecting byelaw notice boards at the entrances to the common. However at the second meeting, in November of the same year, they were promising a £10 reward for information leading to the arrest of the vandals who had damaged these boards. Was this a last attempt to object to the new régime or was it just vandalism, which had proved a problem already confronting the Board? At their second meeting they had asked the chief constable for a police presence to keep order on the hill each Sunday. At the outbreak of the First World War in 1914 the Board was still asking for a policeman to keep order on August Bank Holiday Monday. Three years before then the Cheltenham branch of the RSPCA had drawn the Board's attention to illegal cockfighting that had taken place in April on the site of the old race course grandstand. Perhaps a problem more annoying than anti-social was that the Board found itself unable to prevent golfers playing on Sunday in those early years. The many and varied activities on the common which led to these potential conflicts appeared from the earliest days of the Board's existence but conflicts had been going on for centuries.

The 1890 act legislated that animals could graze on the common between 25 April and 30 November, although often the access was less than this for a variety of reasons. In July 1909 fifteen people laid claim to rights of common and 1079 sheep and lambs, 84 cattle and 64 horses were counted, but still individuals over stocked it. In 1910 a Mr Adcock had 70 sheep, ten cattle and three horses on the common, which the Board complained could not be sustained on his thirteen acre holding in the vale. It was the haywarden's duty to keep the boundaries in good repair to prevent the animals straying off the common but the problem was that at that time the Board was only responsible for two short lengths of walling; in Padcombe Bottom and between Prescott Cottage and Wickfield Lodge along the main road. The owners of the adjoining properties were constantly complaining that the upkeep of the walls was not their responsibility and were slow to make their walls stock proof. In July 1892 the Board had to spend £5 on barbed wire around 'the worst places', a functional but hardly aesthetic solution.

The popular use of the common for recreation increased the problem of dogs chasing and killing the sheep and lambs, which even today remains a concern. In order to try to keep the problem under control, from time to time rewards were offered for information leading to the identification of the owners of the dogs chasing the animals. This first happened in 1904 when a pound was offered. In November 1917 the haywarden reported to the Board that there were so many dogs on the common "you might think there was a pack of hounds there". Vandalism too continued to be a problem. In 1908 'youths' damaged the Washpool by throwing stones at it.

Yet the minutes of the Board's meetings are not wholly full of problems. In 1897, 1902 and 1911 the Board gave £5 for a bonfire to celebrate royal events. In 1910 they planted the six lime trees near the entrance to Rising Sun Lane to commemorate the coronation of King George V and by 1911 they had provided fourteen seats across the common for the visitors to use. The pattern for the next century of reconciling conflicting demands on the common by trying to accommodate all its varied visitors were clearly apparent in these three decades leading to 1918.

The lime trees at the top of Rising Sun Lane photographed shortly after they had been planted to commemorate the coronation of King George V in 1910

The Board was given the power to charge trainers exercising their horses on the common, especially on the gallops where the races had been held earlier in the century. The licence was fixed at the first meeting at two guineas each horse with 10s.6d. for a hacking licence. The payment by the trainers was to be a source of contention almost to the end of training, even though the licence fee was reduced to one guinea the following year. In September 1908 the trainers withheld their licence fees because of the poor condition of the gallops. The next January basic slag was carried from Andoversford railway station and drilled into the turf. Until the end of the war there is little record of who trained on the common. As they had done in the past, horses came from the neighbouring parishes, especially Prestbury, in addition to those more locally. In 1901 Francis Pratt at Emblem Cottage used the common for training. Joseph Goode was the head groom at the stables of nearby Cleeve Lodge where nine other grooms were recorded.

Finally, another of the responsibilities of the board was to allow military exercises. Such a large area of open grassland was an attractive location for the military and they were not slow to take advantage. The very next month after the first meeting, the Board gave permission to the 2nd Volunteer Battalion of the Gloucestershire Regiment to drill providing it made good any damage. In September of the same year permission was granted to create a rifle range. In May 1893 permission was granted to the army to construct three earthworks for a firing range. This might be the origin of the three trenches on the sloping ground above Milestone Quarry. As the growing national concern with defence increased in April 1912 cadets from Cheltenham College and Dean Close school held exercises across the common and in November over 2,000 members of the West of England Public Schools' Officer Training Corps took part in a 'battle' on the common in an exercise stretching from Andoversford to Bishop's Cleeve railway stations. A year later it was the turn of the OTCs of Birmingham and Bristol Universities to hold their field-day on the common. In August 1914 the First World War broke out, and the manoeuvres became for real. By the end of the year the 9th Gloucesters were marching up the hill every Wednesday for 'practising attacking exercises in open formation'. We know that such wave attacks became responsible for much of the mass slaughter on the Western Front by 1918. These soldiers were experiencing the end of an era. Many of them would be dead after the war, and life would never quite be the same again.

Conclusion

By 1918 Cleeve Hill had been transformed from a small scatter of humble homes into a lively holiday resort and outer suburb of

The Colmore Cup Motor Trials on Cleeve Hill in 1914

Cheltenham. It could cater for residents, long and short term visitors, and the day trippers. Many visitors came long distances and sent home a postcard or two with messages which provide valuable evidence for the historian. Many came on organized excursions.

At Whitsun 1910 an Esperanto congress was held here. It was claimed to have been the first public meeting ever held on the hill. A year later the National Deposit Friendly Society delegates came from their conference at Gloucester for an outing to the hill, using train and tram. The steep gradient of Gambles Lane led to Cleeve Hill being made a stage of the Colmore cup motor trials, which originated in Birmingham, before and after the First World War. These were run for motorcycles and Gambles Lane provided one of the hill climb portions of their trials.

These were the years when the traditional uses of the common, as grazing for the commoners' animals, quarrying for stone and even the training of race horses came under increasing pressure from the growing outside influences. The setting up of the Board of Conservators to control the uses of the common for the benefit of all its users must be seen as an attempt to reconcile all the conflicting interests, which they did and continued to do with varying degrees of success. When they first met on 22 April 1891 no-one could have foreseen the enormous social changes brought about by the First World War. The hill was not unaffected by the

This photograph, which was used on the cover of the first edition of this book, encapsulates the atmosphere of 'The Cotswold Health Resort' before the First World War

war itself and when it ended the vitality and attractiveness of the Health Resort since 1890 would never quite be fully recaptured.

It is not an exaggeration to write that the modern perceptions of Cleeve Hill and its common as a pleasant place to live, stay and enjoy its open spaces were created in these three decades at the turn of the twentieth century. It was a time when the traditional uses of the common and a traditional way of life of those who lived on or around it were rapidly swamped as Cheltenham people and money moved in. Aided by improved transport and publicity campaigns the hill became the popular venue it continues to be. During the First World War, John Henry Garrett, Cheltenham's medical officer of health, lodged with the Yiends at Glendale in Post Office Lane. His descriptions of the hill in *From A Cotswold Height* encapsulates these years and has rightly become a classic.

FURTHER READING

Underpinning the detail of this chapter lie some of the books already mentioned in earlier chapters, i.e., the books by Hart and Jones on Cheltenham; those by Daubeny and Garrett on Cleeve Hill. Hugh Denham's and my books have also much relevant information for the chapter. Contemporary published works have included Kelly's directories; Burrow's guidebooks to the 'Cotswold Health Resort' published from 1909; and volumes of the *Cheltenham Chronicle and Gloucester Graphic* (especially 1901 to 1903) which were issued as a weekly illustrated supplement to the *Gloucestershire Echo*. Copies of all these works can be consulted in Cheltenham or Gloucester Libraries. The website of Cheltenham Local History Society has links to the *Cheltenham Chronicle and Gloucester Graphic* and various directories, https://cheltlocalhistory.org.uk. Much of the information on the golf clubs has been taken from *One Hundred Years of Golf and Good Fellowship* by Patti Cox and Noel Furley (Privately published, 2003). This was supplemented by a history of the clubs found at https://www.golfsmissinglinks.co.uk.

Further information came from collections in the County Archives: Cotswold Convalescent Home (HO 10 1/1), Haymes farm (D5435), the interdenominational church (D4238), St Peter's church (P46/2), Bayleys' catalogues (D4442), the building of Besford Road (DC/SJ57), and some items from Bishop's Cleeve parish council minutes (P46a PC1/1). The Lloyd George Survey of Land Values (D2428) can be assessed online at https://www.glos1909survey.org.uk as the result of an initiative led by Anthea Jones. Most of the deeds used still lie in private hands, and I am grateful to their owners for allowing me to use them. Similarly I have made extensive use of oral history in this chapter and exploited my own collection of pre-war postcards.

8
THE DEVELOPMENT OF THE COTSWOLD HEALTH RESORT SINCE 1918

> Thousands of people visit Cleeve Common every year simply to walk, ride or admire the scenery and views.
> *Gloucestershire Echo*, 2 May 1988

Sources and Contexts

This chapter has been completely re-written and greatly expanded since the first edition, where it was a short piece entitled *Postscript*. This has been made possible by the availability of key sources not available in 1990. The most important has been the minutes of the meetings of the Board of Conservators from 1890 to 2014. In addition the 1939 National Register and a large number of Kelly's directories have been published online. As noted in that original chapter, the Cotswold Health Resort had been firmly established by 1914 and even in the changed world since 1918 its echoes can still be heard even today. People continue to perceive it as a desirable place to visit, live or spend a few days on holiday in its hotels and holiday cottages, but under this seemingly unchanged nature there can be discerned many changes in detail. This last chapter has been divided into two to reflect the title of the book and to bring some order to the charting of the changes.

The People

Settlement

Arguably the greatest change since 1918 has been in the means of transport enabling residents and visitors alike to reach the hill. The last tram ran on 31 March 1930 to be replaced by Cheltenham Corporation's dark red double decker buses on Route 1 for which the turning circle at the top of Stockwell Lane was created. For many years the body of an old tram served as the waiting room. At the start the buses followed the old tram route but from February 1932 the buses ran only to and from the centre. Between 1932 and the outbreak of the Second World War in 1939 the company provided a 'toastrack' bus, with open sides and with the seats running the width of the bus, especially for the weekend trippers to the hill. It was extremely popular but made it very difficult for the conductor to collect the fares. The service ended about fifty years ago. However this was not the only bus service which took people to the hill. From the early twentieth century Gilletts of Winchcombe had offered a horse-drawn service from the town to Cheltenham. The fare was 1s. with an extra 3d. if passengers were not prepared to get out and walk the steepest part. In the 1920s Gilletts bought motor buses and in 1950 it was running three trips a day on Monday, Tuesday, Friday and Sunday with as many as six on Saturday with one less return service each day. It sold out on retirement to Castleways which ran the service until 2014 and then after a period

The resurfacing of the B4632 in September 2018 uncovered stretches of the tram tracks

By the time the first Albion Venturer buses like this one were bought in 1940, Route 1 ran only to and from the centre of Cheltenham (G. Cocks)

of uncertainty the service over the hill was taken over by Stagecoach operating an hourly timetable on Route W.

The years after World War One also saw the increasing popularity of the private car for residents and visitors alike. The problems this created have never been far away. As early as 1914 there were complaints about the thoughtless parking on the road outside the Malvern View Hotel. In 1967 a small car park was created at the top of Stockwell Common despite local opposition. In response to the growing popularity of car transport, Francis Fowler opened his Cleeve Hill garage about 1925 on the site now occupied by The View. The problems of parking associated with visiting the common and also for those who lived in properties adjoining the common are outlined in the second part of this chapter. Finally, since 1970 a few hardened souls have reached the hill along the long distance Cotswold Way which crosses the common.

However they reached the hill and the common in the interwar years, the health resort continued to attract the day visitors and holidaymakers alike. Kelly's directories of the 1930s provide a taste of what visitors were able to enjoy. At the outbreak of the Second World War in 1939, Mrs Hobley, the wife of Arthur Hobley the Cheltenham Golf Club's former professional, was still running her Cosy Corner Tea Gardens at Springbank; the Cleeve Hill Café, renamed as Willow Café, was still open for business; Fanny Yiend's tea garden at Laburnum Cottage had only recently closed. By 1926 John Petty had bought the Geisha Tea House, which he had renamed Gresham House, and in that year he built the Cleeve Hill Hotel in the plot next door so he could

A postcard from Mrs Hobley's Cosy Corner Tea Gardens which was sent in 1928

expand his business beyond a tea garden with just a couple of letting rooms. Gresham House was still being advertised as a boarding house at the outbreak of the Second World War and it continued post-war, for

Cleeve Hill Hotel with neighbouring Gresham House in 1985, before the latter was demolished

in 1952 it was also serving as the post office. It then became a private residence and despite attempts to re-start a café in the 1980s its timbers had suffered so much rot that it was demolished in 1989. Some of its essence lives on in the balconies of the Cleeve Hill Hotel which reflect its original design.

The tradition on the hill of renting out rooms of existing houses for staying visitors was also still alive and well at the outbreak of the war. Ruby Franklin was advertising apartments at Greenmount and Francis Fowler's wife at Upper Colletts was running a guesthouse, having taken over from Gertrude Worrell only a year or two previously. Mary Dempsey had taken over Wilcote from her widowed mother Harriet and was still advertising apartments to rent. At the outbreak of the war The Wickfields, below the lane leading to the golf club, was the home of Thomas Evans but it was then taken over as an American army hospital. In 1971 it was converted into a hotel by Roy Davis and renamed the High Roost Hotel. A decade later it was remodelled into a pub and continued until it closed down in 2003, since when it has reverted to a private residence. Today in addition to the Cleeve Hill Hotel, the Malvern View Hotel and the Rising Sun Hotel offer hospitality to the hill's visitors.

Greenmount, one of the pine villas of the Cotswold Health Resort, was taking guests in 1939

The hill continued to attract visitors but it also continued to attract residents. The numbers can be traced from the list of private residents listed in successive Kelly's directories: 40 in 1919; 44 in 1927 and 91 in 1937 and these do not include the commercial entries. In the 1939 National Register 113 households were counted between Haymes Road and Cockbury and descending down the hill to the junction of Post Office Lane and Stockwell Lane. Today there are about 125 houses in that area.

In September 1939, soon after the outbreak of the Second World War, the government organised a National Register of its citizens as part of its wartime footing concerning the issue of identity cards and organising conscription. In theory it was kept up-to-date until 1991 and as a consequence names have been blanked out under the hundred year rule because that person might still be alive and his or her details available to everyone. Fortunately, as far as can be discerned, all the blanked out entries for Cleeve Hill cover children or domestic servants, which does not affect the key details of each household. Like the census it gave the names, addresses, ages and occupations of everyone on the list. Unlike the census it did not give place of birth and neither did it leave the occupation blank. This led to full-time housewives being quaintly described as carrying out 'unpaid domestic duties'. So what can be learnt from the register about the residents of Cleeve Hill in 1939?

Two conclusions stand out. The traditional means of earning a living on the hill had been overwhelmed by the changed nature of the settlement since its origins as the Cotswold Health Resort. Secondly it was a very transient population with barely a handful of families remaining since the 1901 census. 46 different occupations or statuses were listed for the head of each household across 113 households, of these 27 were retirees, fifteen living off private means, eleven

Cleeve Hill Stores and Post Office, now Hilltop

housewives, seven hotel or boarding house proprietors, five managers, four motor engineers, three gardeners, two chauffeurs and two company directors. There were single examples of such varied occupations as doctor, school teacher, postman, tax inspector, university lecturer and policeman. The police station was at Silverdale in Besford Road which opened in 1929 and closed c.1962. Edith Edmonds kept the only shop, 'The Stores', at Hilltop near the Rising Sun Hotel and that suggested that residents' needs were met elsewhere by travelling away from the hill. It was not a self-sufficient community and reinforced the conclusion that it had become an outer affluent suburb of Cheltenham. The changed nature of that community was complete; there was no farm labourer, only one stonemason and only one farmer, the latter being Arthur Yiend, now 67 years old, whose main career had been as a quarry man and builder during the years of the health resort's foundation. Fifteen households were recorded as having domestic servants but only two of them had two, the rest a single person.

The study of individual entries provides fascinating details of the lives of some of the residents. People were still visiting and staying on the hill even though the war had begun. A flying instructor with the RAF was among the seventeen guests staying at the Rising Sun Hotel. At the Cleeve Hill Hotel five of the seven guests there were recorded as living off private meals. Four guests were staying at Gresham House, three at Wilcote kept by Mary Dempsey and her brother John. The nursing home had three patients. Kate Nottingham at the Malvern View Hotel had described two of her daughters as waitresses but there no guests. Ruby Franklin at Greenmount had two guests, a retired builder and someone living on private means.

The turnover of residents noted in the last chapter and partly explained by the number of rented properties serving as investments for people living outside the community, continued. Of those who could be identified as having moved to the health resort as it became a desirable place to live, Henry Norton at Ferncliffe was one survivor from 1901. Now aged 76 his description as a retired ironmonger did not do justice to his long ownership of his garage in The Strand in Cheltenham and as a pioneer of motoring in the area. Arthur Yiend was another long-term resident, still living in Post Office Lane. The Dempseys with their boarding house at Wilcote and the Denleys at Upper Bottomley were also stayers. Walter Denley described himself as haywarden but Upper Bottomley was also a smallholding. Apart from the Denleys, the other stayers forming the last remnants of the traditional life of the common lived, perhaps not surprisingly, mostly at Nutterswood. Thomas Yiend recorded himself as the sole stone mason living on the hill, whilst his younger relative and neighbour William Yiend worked on the railway as a ganger. William encapsulated this changing world for as an eighteen year old in 1901 he was learning to become a stonemason. Charles Kitchen listed as a retired general labourer was still living at Nutterswood. He and his wife Georgina together with Mary and Alfred Gaskins, one of the two families living at Sunnyside at the top of Rising Sun Lane, were all described as OAPs (Old Age Pensioners). This suggests they were the

Thomas Belcher's Hillground stretched from the line of Lye Lane and Spring Lane to the common. This area has been much developed since 1939

only ones living solely on the state pension which had been introduced in 1908. Presumably all the other heads of household recorded as retired were living off private pensions. Haymes Road continued to be the location of the more affluent, a retired stockbroker, a retired Indian civil servant, a company director and Beryl Donaldson, a lady of private means with two domestic servants.

The nature of the community on the hill portrayed in the 1939 register has changed little in the years to the present. Houses have continued to be built to accommodate more residents, many of them having been built along Lye Lane and Spring Lane on that enclosure called Hillground, stolen from the common by Thomas Belcher by the middle of the nineteenth century. Only four houses were recorded in Lye Lane in 1939. By 1924 one house had been built on Wickfields almost opposite the Convalescent Home, along a road which was originally called Wickfield Crescent but was changed to Petty Lane in 1995 to commemorate Georgina Petty, the daughter of the Pettys of Cleeve Hill Hotel who lived at Westridge (now Heron Haye) in the lane from 1944 until her death in 1991.

In addition to this new housing and infilling in the gardens of existing houses, several houses were converted from earlier buildings. The first example was the conversion of the Cotswold Hills Golf Club house into 1 and 2 Cleeve Hill after the golf club moved to the existing clubhouse in 1937. In 1979 the shop at Hilltop closed and the whole building was converted into a dwelling. The YHA hostel, which had been a conversion of the Cheltenham Golf Club house after its closure in 1935,

The View was built on the site of Francis Fowler's garage in 2017

was itself closed in 1995 and converted into two dwellings. After the Cleeve Hill garage closed, the plot was landscaped and the four houses of The View were built there in 2017. St Peter's church just reached its centenary before its last service in July 2007. Since then it has been transformed into another dwelling and in so doing the approach to it has destroyed the last vestiges of the terraced gardens of the Cleeve Hill Café. The most imaginative building conversion was of the Tewkesbury Borough Council toilets at the top of Stockwell Lane after they had been closed in 2009. The name 'Lou's Views' serves as a reminder of its former

Wilcote was rebuilt in 2018

use. More recently, the Dempseys' Wilcote boarding house has been completely rebuilt. Finally, Phoenix House represents another type of conversion, given away by its name. In 1980 Samarkand, itself a post-war house, started sliding down the hill on unstable ground. It had to be totally demolished and was replaced by Phoenix House which in its design mirrored that of its next door neighbour, Walter Dick's 1899 timber-framed health resort house, Semington, now Highfields.

Samarkand slid down the slope in 1980 (W. Potter)

Away from the health resort, the long association of Wontley with the Lawrence family at Sandywell Park came to an end in March 1921 when it was sold to a Mr Reynolds together with Westwood Farm. Nine years later a Mr Driver was requested by the Board to repair the stone wall bordering the common. The owners of Wontley were still trying to make a return on their investment but they did not live there and it was hard work. The 1939 National Register listed the families of a stone waller and shepherd living at the farm and its isolated nature is indicated by the address again being given as Wontley, Andoversford. The last person to live there was an eccentric who produced a number of short-lived typed and duplicated newsletters/magazines which he distributed in the local area until *c.*1960. The large barn was given Grade II listed status in 1987 but all the buildings remain ruined and unused as only the fields are cultivated today by the Charlton Abbots estate.

The historical significance of Cockbury Court was recognised by being given Grade II listed building status as long ago as 1960. The description confirms that an original sixteenth-century building has been extensively modified in the succeeding centuries. In a sale catalogue for 1924 it is described as 'of quaint character' which sounds like an estate agent's euphemism. It was for sale then with the adjacent Dryfield Farm and of interest in the sale catalogue is the plot of land on which Wickfield Stud now stands. This was being exploited by Winchcombe Rural District Council as a quarry, presumably for stone for the local roads. The farm was described as being a working farm of 69 acres, all of it to the south of the main road. In 1939 Beatrice Burke of private means occupied the farmhouse and a retired farm worker and a shepherd occupied two cottages. By 1980 eight holiday cottages had been converted from the farm buildings. In 2014 the house was advertised for sale with three acres of land. In 2021 five new houses were built

The brochure advertising the Cockbury Court holiday cottages in 1980

on the site so that the single farm which survived the desertion of the settlement in the later Middle Ages is now at the centre of a community much larger than its Medieval forerunner. The historic farm house which was the successor to the Medieval village is now a private home.

Haymes is another Grade II listed building. On the death of Henry Holliday Haymes was sold as a working farm of 97 acres with the rights of common in January 1921 to Alf Newey, the racehorse trainer. He trained there until 1933 after which the farm passed through a

This view of Haymes was probably taken when Alf Newey was the owner (T. Curr)

number of absentee owners. In June 1940 Walter Redmond of Grange Farm in Bishop's Cleeve took the tenancy for £150 a year from the landlord Reginald Wotton who seems to have been a financier living in Worthing. By 1947 the owner of Haymes was a Mrs Nancy Saunders, another absentee landlord, who had taken over from her deceased husband. Relations between the tenant and landlord were fraught. They deteriorated so much that Walter's tenancy was cut short in 1948 under the Defence of the Realm Act because it was alleged he had not kept the farmland in good repair. Amongst a list of shortcomings was his cutting down of the hedges bordering Gambles Lane rather than having them traditionally laid. The financial aspect of the dismissal was a major problem, trying to work out compensation and rent rebate but unfortunately the records in the archive do not give details of the final settlement.

Once Walter Redmond had gone, the following year Mrs Saunders sold Haymes to Major J.E.M. Bradish-Ellanes recorded at the time as living in Chard in Somerset, another absentee landlord. Old Etonian John Edward Montague Bradish-Ellanes had been born in Cheltenham and had fought in the Hussars in the First World War before serving in the Lifeguards. He led a peripatetic existence and at the time of the purchase he had recently remarried. Shortly afterwards he seems to have gone to India. He died in High Wycombe in 1984, at which date the farm extended to 65 acres. It is not known how long he kept Haymes, obviously an investment, but by 1965 local businessman Peter Deacon had opened a mushroom farm business, which was bought by Garrett O'Connor and his brother in 2005, at which time it was supplying mushrooms to well-known supermarket chains. The business closed in 2018 and the buildings remain empty. They are separate from the house, which sold in 2021 as a family home with just 43 acres of paddocks and woodland.

The Institutions

When the military finally left the Convalescent Home in January 1919 it closed until April, as usual. On reopening, the charge had increased to 10s. per week, which was deeply regretted but unavoidable after the wartime inflation. In November the following year the management committee took the decision that the need for such an establishment had so shrunk since the war that the home was no longer needed and it was sold to Courtaulds, the company pioneering the use of artificial fibres in clothing, for £4,000. The company had a large factory not too far away in Coventry. It added a wing to the left of the original building in 1954 and another to the right in 1960. In turn it sold the property in 1980 to Mr and Mrs R. Cooper and they added another extension in 1992, exactly a century after the idea for such a home was first muted in Cheltenham. An advertisement for the Cleeve Hill Nursing Home in 1990 stressed it took long and short-term patients and provided medical, surgical, convalescent and day care. In 2001 it was taken over by Cleeve Hill Limited, a private company based as far away as Orpington in Kent. Two years later another extension was added so that it could accommodate fifty residents and in the following year the company was renamed Cleeve Hill Healthcare Limited. Between 2004 and 2015 the home also operated Cleeve Link, a home care service which at one stage was responsible for sixty per cent of such services in the county. This part of the company was in financial difficulties before being sold in 2015 and when it collapsed in 2017 many of its workers complained they had not been paid. The home itself took on a new responsibility in 2008 when Winchcombe hospital closed and six of its beds were designated for use under the National Health Service.

The Convalescent Home with the original building at the back and Courtauld's extension on the left and the 1992 extension on the right

From the above it is clear that by the early years of this century, the home which had been built for philanthropic motives and carried on as a family concern had come to be seen as a profit-making institution for its owners through limited companies. This did not influence the standards of care as the Care Quality Commission good reports since 2004 demonstrated. A new company, South West Care Group, took over the home in 2018, at which date the home's address was given as the registered office for four other similar companies. Subsequently the name was changed to the Malvern View Care Home. In the summer of 2023 the company ran into financial difficulties and the staff and residents were given six weeks' notice of its closure which took place in July. Its closure marked the end of an unbroken century-old link to the opening of the Cotswold Convalescent Home in 1893, which had provided the catalyst for the growth of the health resort and the nature of the settlement today.

Two other institutions of the health resort have also disappeared. During the First World War the trustees of the Free Church appointed Reverend Stanley Mercer as their pastor and he served until 1931, the longest serving pastor of the church. In the inter-war years the pattern of services, with Nonconformist in the morning and Anglican in the evening, continued. Sunday School continued to attract the local children and by the time of the Second World War there was a lively youth group which met during the week, but whose members seemed to be reluctant to attend on a Sunday. From c.1950 the Sunday School numbers were swollen in term time by the girls from Oriel School which existed in Southam House until 1972. This was the private school of Miss Bellamy who had moved into the house after the sale of Lord Ellenborough's effects in 1947 with the intention of establishing an alternative to the Ladies College for girls who enjoyed horse riding.

As Bishop's Cleeve grew after the arrival of Smith's Industries in 1939, Derek Drapper, appointed as the pastor in 1955, inaugurated a mission campaign in the village, printing 1,000 leaflets for distribution. The campaign led to the setting up of Bishop's Cleeve Free Church off Station Road. However, despite such enthusiasm, congregations on the hill were beginning to decline and by the 1960s the average size was only half a dozen and dependent upon people coming from Cheltenham. Despite still having a pastor, with this declining congregation the decision was taken to close the church in 1972 and the manse became the parsonage for the pastor at Woodmancote's Countess of Huntingdon's chapel in Stockwell Lane. Although the interior fittings were soon removed, the building itself was not demolished immediately as there were plans to convert it into a residence, but its original lightweight design proved to be incapable of withstanding the natural slumping of the clay fed by a spring on the other side of the road and in 1988 it was demolished. The site has remained undeveloped.

The Anglican chapel of St Peter's had been born out of antagonism with the tin tabernacle's only acting like an Anglican place of worship. For over thirty years they seem not to have recognised, formally at least, each other's existence. Being part of the large parish of Bishop's Cleeve it had the support of an institutional framework which the free church lacked. Hugh Denham suggested that in the 1930s there were plans for a curate's house and even a church hall on the hill, but nothing came of them. Although congregation numbers fell in the 1970s at a time when its competitor closed, numbers recovered almost until the end of the century, when they declined so much that the decision was taken to close, having celebrated its centenary.

Until 1943 there existed a small private school on the hill. This seems to have started *c.*1906 by a Miss Waghorne at an unknown address on the hill before moving during the First World War to Rochdale (now Barnfield) at the bottom of Besford Road. In 1922 the school was taken over by Marie Lawrence who bought next door Silverdale three years later for boarders. She took out a mortgage with the Cheltenham and Gloucester Building Society for £500. When she had paid off the mortgage sixteen years later she moved to what is now Red Roof in Rising Sun Lane. In the 1939 National Register she is recorded as living there with Idris Lloyd, a telecommunications linesman, and a young Spaniard Manuel Munoz. Perhaps he, together with the blanked out young person, were the only boarders at the time. At the very most there were about twenty pupils and most left at the age of twelve. Hugh Denham recounted how Miss Lawrence became more eccentric and former pupils could remember being given endless handwriting practice whilst she cooked meals for the boarders. She was 67 years old when she closed the school in 1943 and most of the children moved to the primary school in Bishop's Cleeve.

Finally a brief mention can be made of Henry Taylor's short-lived Reading Room on Nottingham Hill. Its main use in the inter-war years seems to have been as a shelter for people of no fixed abode, but during the Second World War it served as an observation post for the Royal Observer Corps. At least three men were recorded as Royal Observers in the 1939 National Register. After the war it slowly decayed until nothing can be seen of where it once stood, on the south side of Wickfield Lane on Nottingham Hill.

The Common

Its Changing Management

The years since 1918 have seen the main concerns of the Board of Conservators change from balancing the traditional and potentially conflicting demands of grazing, quarrying, training and latterly of golf and recreation, to the present situation where the Trust is primarily concerned with balancing conservation with recreation through careful management and education. In 1918 the Board only had to work to the criteria laid down in the 1890 act which gave it total responsibility for the management of the common, although it was responsible also for the preservation and conservation of the two recorded ancient monuments of the Iron Age hillfort and The Ring. In the years since then it has been increasingly subject to outside bodies which has brought both positive and negative influences to bear. The main developments can be traced from the Board's minutes.

Apart from the war years, when the common was requisitioned by the military for three years from 1942 to 1945, little change occurred until the 1960s and 1970s. In 1960 the Bronze Age Cross Dyke was declared a protected ancient monument; in 1966 the common became part of the new Cotswold Area of Outstanding Natural Beauty and in 1969 the possibility of inviting the Cotswold wardens, established in the previous year, to assist with the maintenance of the common was first discussed but without any definite outcome.

Then followed a key development, the publication in February 1971 of the report *Use and Potential of Gloucestershire Commons for Outdoor Recreation: Cleeve Common*. This county council report emphasised the problems: the lack of car parking and toilets which limited its uses for many people, the hazards of walking and riding across the golf course, the lack of picnic areas and information boards. Its recommendations caused controversy, the main one being the disbanding of the Board of Conservators to be replaced as managers of the common by the county council and Cheltenham Rural District Council, but ultimately this did not happen. Also in the recommendations was that the Cotswold Hills Golf Club should reorganise the first, seventeenth and eighteenth holes and the ninth green on the basis that the safety of 600 or 700 walkers was more important than the enjoyment of 80 golfers, although it is not clear where these figures came from. Here was the catalyst for the golf club to move to Ullenwood. Although the report made, in effect, little real difference to the management and use of a common, it opened a debate which has continued to the present day. It was only two years after this report that the influence of the county council was brought to bear on the management when its local planning subcommittee refused permission for gliding to take place on West Down. Unrelated to these developments but also important in the historical context of management of the common, in 1974 a significant development was made regarding its ownership as it at last came into the ownership of a single family, where it has subsequently remained, the heirs of the lords of the manor.

In July 1978 the Countryside Commission was consulted in the drawing up of a 'comprehensive scheme for the development of the common'. The next year the Health and Safety Executive (recently formed in 1974) and Tewkesbury Borough Council (also formed in 1974) both expressed concern over the lack of fencing of the quarries. In 1980 it was the county council which forced the issue of using the former quarry at the end of Wickfield Lane as a car park. The 1980s saw the increasing influence of outside bodies in the management of the common. In March 1984 the Board was appalled to discover that the

The former Wickfield Quarry

Ministry of Agriculture had gassed nineteen badgers on the common without its permission, whilst in that same year the Department of Environment brought pressure to bear on the Board to have two holes, which had been dug at the hillfort, repaired. This was done by the person responsible by the end of the year. Then two years later the Nature Conservancy designated the common as a Site of Special Scientific Interest (SSSI) to protect the flora and fauna. On the one hand this resulted in the grubbing up and control of the gorse bushes which became an important part of the management of the common. On the other hand only four months after the designation the Board was forbidden to drain, level or manure the common. In February 1988 the Nature Conservancy insisted all car parking at Nutterswood must be within the curtilages of the dwellings there.

The driving force behind the conservancy's actions was the designation of the common as 'the largest block of unimproved limestone grass in the country', although it could not have included the training gallops in that statement. Despite the increasing restraints on the Board and its actions, one early positive impact of these changes of management came in March 1987 when the Countryside Commission announced it could give 50 per cent grants to approved expenditure, including the wages of a warden if the right person could be found. On the other hand, relations with Cheltenham Borough Council deteriorated in these years as their representative on the board resigned in 1987 which led the Board to complain two years later that they had lacked any contact with the council. It was in that year that the Board first registered with the Charity Commission to establish its charity status. Finally, a small footnote to all these developments in the 1980s was that in June 1985 J. Eric Green resigned as clerk to the Board. He had held that position since 1946, a length of service that has not been beaten. He was replaced by his daughter Jennifer

The following decade brought examples of both the positive and negative effects of the influence of the outside bodies. In 1990 the Cotswold wardens, encouraged by the county council, began to play a larger part in the maintenance of the common. This led to the Cotswold voluntary wardens playing an increasingly important part in monitoring the condition of the common for several years, until many of these functions were taken up by the workforce of the Cleeve

A group of the common's voluntary wardens at the toposcope in summer 2022

Common Trust and its volunteers. In 2000 they reinstated the historic dewpond near the approach to West Down to provide water for the animals. This was only made possible by a grant from the Department for Environment, Food and Rural Affairs (DEFRA), which had replaced the Ministry of Agriculture, Fisheries and Food in 2001. In 1990 the Nature Conservancy interfered with the management of the common as it would not allow the gallops to be fertilised, as had happened over the previous century, but it did eventually relent and allow three small

The dewpond on the approach to West Down (M. Bates)

areas to be so treated. The following year the Countryside Commission offered a grant of up to 75 per cent to a maximum of £4,000 to finance another management plan, but when this came out in 1993 the Board felt it was inadequate as it did not deal with the fauna or the archaeology, it just dealt with the grassland. In 1993 the Ministry of Agriculture, Fisheries and Food, English Nature and the National Grid all made financial contributions towards the upkeep of the common. In March the following year the common was designated an Environmentally Sensitive Area (ESA) which opened another source of funding, offset by even closer control over the upkeep of the common. The use of weed killer on the nettles was soon frowned upon, but in June 1995 the ESA offered a grant of £2,500 which, in the new systems of management, the Board felt it had to consult with English Nature on how to spend it. Later in the year the latter body spent £3,500 in trying to regenerate heather on the common. A long-standing source of income set up by the original act of 1890 was the £50 annual payment from Cheltenham council. This often lapsed with the lack of communication between the Board and the council. In 1945 the Board requested £100 but the council handed over £75. The council paid £2,100 in 1991 but six years later the Board requested two years arrears from the council. This would in reality have made little difference to the income as the accounts for 1999 showed the Board received over £36,000 in grants. Since then payments have been made from time to time.

Yet another management plan came out in 2003 with inputs from DEFRA, Tewkesbury Borough Council, English Nature and others. It also took into account the Countryside Rights of Way Act of 2000 covering rights of way, nature conservation, protection of wildlife and the control of vehicles driving across places such as the common. The Board must have given a sigh of relief when DEFRA confirmed it was still legally operating under the 1890 act and could still update its byelaws by reference to the Department.

By the end of the first decade of this century the changed and changing focus of the management of the common had emerged. A conservation officer and community engagement officer had been appointed to part-time posts. Rangers had replaced the single haywarden and voluntary wardens had been enlisted into keeping an eye on the common and its visitors. The common was now being managed no longer mainly for its livestock and golfing attractions, as the work of the Trust increasingly concerned conservation and recreation. This is evidenced in the annual 2021-22 report which lists its activities in these areas: managing cattle grazing, gorse cutting and scrub clearance under the Countryside Stewardship scheme, conserving critically endangered red hemp nettle and bryophytes (mosses and liverworts), surveying number and health of adders and noting how increased recreational use is affecting the numbers of skylarks and meadow pipits. In addition to the usual recreational activities of walking with or without dogs, horse riding, running, cycling, and kite flying, the common is also used by outside bodies organising such activities as orienteering, charity events and even keep fit exercises. From time to time it has been used in filming and photography, often to promote Cheltenham racecourse which is clearly visible from the escarpment. The Trust continues to be responsible for its herd of belted Galloway cattle (see below) all the year and the sheep grazing in the summer months. Some of these activities bring in small sums of money but of the £127,000 income in 2022, £88,000 came from government grants. These figures indicate just how far the management of the common is now influenced by outside bodies which the original conservators of 1890 could never have imagined.

Grazing

As the First World War ended, 33 commoners or stockholders were recorded as having the right to put animals on the common and in that year 1599 sheep were recorded. During the following century numbers of sheep fluctuated but have always exceeded the number of other animals. In the years of the Second World War, for example, in 1943 1206 sheep, 32 cattle and six horses were recorded on the common. The war years were difficult ones for the stockholders. The minutes record that in 1940 the Royal Gloucestershire Hussars were given permission to exercise three light tanks over the back of the common for six or seven weeks, providing they made good any damage. When an observation post was erected near the existing pylons in the same year, the clerk recommended that horses be removed 'for their own good', although that obviously did not happen. In 1942 the military requisitioned the common and the War Agricultural Committee was given permission to plough up as many as a 100 acres, but again this did not happen. In 1943 the Board received

£16 to repair the walls damaged by firing and £40 for the damage caused to West Down. At the end of the war in 1945 Italian prisoners of war were employed by the adjoining landowners to repair the walls of the common, the military de-requisitioned the common and the following year promised to make good 300 holes which it had created. Probably as a result of these war time experiences the Board refused to allow the common to be used as a post-war training area, but agreed that the war-time radar station could remain. Its reflector stood for more than twenty years.

In 1960 1535 sheep and 94 were grazing on the common and later in the 1990s over 2000 sheep were recorded on several occasions; in 2021 the most at any one time was 1300. During the foot and mouth epidemic of 2001 no sheep were allowed and cattle were allowed only for a short period of two months from the end of August. By this time horses were no longer put to graze and cattle numbers were in decline. Concerned that the absence of cattle meant scrub was spreading, the Board introduced its own herd of Galloway steers in 2006 to improve the quality of the grassland. Four years later a mains water network was installed across the common at a cost of nearly £400,000, funded by Natural England. It meant the cattle could be watered in their enclosures without daily tractor and tanker trips across the common. The herd of between twenty and forty cattle continue to graze throughout the year and have been particularly successful in managing the tougher grasses. The presence of other animals on the common, usually from April to November, although in 1931 animals were allowed until the 31 December and in 1981 stock were only put on the common in July after they had been dipped, has meant that traditional conflicts have continued. The dog worrying of sheep has been a constant issue, although fourteen sheep killed in one week in July 1928 seems to have been exceptional. In April 1953 a hundred notices were printed and from time to time rewards were promised for reports leading to convictions. Animals damaging the greens of the golf course was another continuing area of conflict. In June 1993 the golf club complained that cattle were causing damage. When animals escaped through holes in the boundaries, the Board always maintained the animals' owners carried responsibility for them. Putting more animals on the common than they were entitled to was another continuing problem for the Board. In July 1961 there was yet another attempt to define stinting; one sheep for every two acres of farmland, the 'so-called winter rule'. However, because the number of stockholders had shrunk to three by 1990 the Board decided that a maximum of 40 farmers, designated 'graziers', could also pasture the animals on the common. Stockholders would pay 15p per animal per week and the other farmers would pay 20p. It is no surprise that five years later there were complaints that not everyone had paid; some habits concerning the uses of the common have been well-entrenched. All the charges were dropped after the foot and mouth outbreak in 2001, as the problem of over-grazing in lowland England generally became a problem of under-grazing.

Occasionally the Conservators' minutes recorded other animals on the common, either by accident or design. In 1925 the haywarden confessed his mother had put pigs onto the common without permission. Whether that meant no pigs were allowed or allowed only with permission is unclear. Ten years later Miss Gertrude Worrall left a gate open at Upper Colletts so that not only did her poultry escape onto the common but a number of sheep went through the gate and then her garden to escape onto the main road. Responding to the General Commons Registration Act of 1965, 24 commoners registered their rights. Putting all their claims into effect would have meant that 3050 sheep, 546 cattle, 58 horses, eight goats and three donkeys would have grazed on the common, although it was generally recognised that nationally the numbers of stock compiled as a result of the act, were overstated. There were also reports that geese were sometimes put on the common.

The haywarden had an onerous task; keeping an eye on the sheep, the dogs, the boundaries and keeping the animals off the golf greens. Walter Denley of Upper Bottomley in Gambles Lane was the longest serving haywarden. He was appointed in 1928 and retired fully only in 1971. His immediate predecessor had been sacked for spending too much time in the Apple Tree Inn in Woodmancote and allowing infestations of maggots in the sheep. The Board's minutes not infrequently recorded the complaints that the haywarden was not working the full hours or that he was not doing his job properly, but it appeared a thankless occupation with no fixed hours or even contract until 1937. Fifty years later the Board reported that they did not have

Walter Denley of Upper Bottomley, photographed not long after his retirement as haywarden in 1971

enough money to employ 'the right kind of men'. They sacked the existing haywarden in April 1988 and appointed Cornelius Routledge at an annual salary of £5,000, increased to £6,000 the following year. It was reported that he got on well with the commoners but he was soon complaining his job was very difficult because he had too many masters and that he needed "someone more educated" to take care of the gallops. His contract came to an end in February 1990 when the board at last realised the tasks expected proved to be too much for a single individual and as a consequence responsibilities were split into three so that the haywarden's responsibilities were confined to checking the sheep and the common's boundaries. Five years later the Albutts of Postlip Hall farm took over the responsibility and at that time they were the only farmers with sheep on the common, where they also kept a small number of cattle. In 2021 sheep belonging to four stockholders and two farmers ensured a continuing link with the traditional use of the common as a grazing ground.

Quarrying

Within twenty five years of the end of the First World War, large-scale quarrying had ceased and the exploitation of the underlying minerals which had been a feature of the common for nearly 2000 years had come to an end. Soon after the war ended the Cleeve Cloud Quarries were taken over by Leckhampton Quarries. We know this because in November 1920 they were warned for not giving any warning of blasting. They obviously had high hopes of exploiting the stone because they constructed a stone causeway with a crane at the bottom to transfer the stone onto a cart, or according to local tradition, on to a wagon of a narrow gauge railway, although no written evidence has been found to confirm this. The venture failed almost immediately because the crane collapsed, it is said on the second load. The rotting timbers of the crane

The rusting winch and below it some of the displaced stones of the causeway

existed at the time of the first edition of this book, but today only the rusting winch at the top of the now ruined causeway exists as a memory of another failed speculation.

Quarrying continued at other places on the common. In 1926 the carts carrying stone from the Postlip Quarries were said to be

Freestone Quarry, reached along the White Way just above the golf club, was the last quarry to be worked on the common (G. Cocks)

damaging the tracks they were using. The Strickland Stone Company was exploiting Freestone Quarry, for in 1937 the turf it had cut as the quarrying expanded was ordered to be kept and restored and in 1939 the fences had to be moved back. Quarrying came to an end in April 1941 when the company was ordered to make good any damage it had caused under the threat of a county court order, although the reasons for this are not clear. The Board then stated that only government contracts would be considered in future and eventually, to secure its control over the quarrying, it bought the mineral and sporting rights from the lords of the manor for £200 in 1954. Buying the sporting rights then allowed it to shoot the rabbits which always had the potential to damage the golf greens. Confirmation that quarrying had ceased came much later in 1996 when the Board considered there was no need to register the mineral rights because no quarries were then being exploited.

However the cessation of quarrying did not mean the quarries were no longer exploited. In 1944 before the end of the war, the US Army extracted some stone from unnamed quarries. In 1977 a resident of Nutterswood was given permission to use gravel to repair the track leading to his house. In 1991 stone was taken from Postlip Quarry to

The memorial stone to the 1944 Halifax plane crash was unveiled on 7 December 2022. Left to right: Air Marshall Sir Dusty Miller, President of the Cheltenham branch of the Royal Air Forces Association, Michael Bates, Clerk of the Trust holding a recently found fragment of the plane's wing, Michael Bryant, Chairman of the Cheltenham branch of the Royal Air Forces Association, Colonel Philip Robson, Chairman of the Trust

repair a track across the golf course and in 2022 a stone was taken from Milestone Quarry for a memorial commemorating the tragic plane crash which took place above the Rising Sun Hotel near The Ring in 1944. Early on the morning of 26 August a Halifax bomber returning to RAF Beighton in Yorkshire after a mine-laying operation off La Rochelle in France crashed into the hill. The crew of seven, comprising five Canadians and two British airmen were all killed. Wartime censorship meant the crash was never publicly reported and the cause of the accident has never been fully established.

One legacy of the quarrying was, of course, the need to fence them for safety reasons. The cost of the fencing and arguments about its purpose, whether it was designed to stop people or only the animals from falling over the edge, did not end with the extraction of the stone, especially as many of the hurdles had been donated for the war effort in 1941. In 1979 the Health and Safety Executive expressed concern about the overall lack of fencing. In April 2000 there broke out a heated discussion at the Board meeting as it appeared that the only legal requirement was to fence the quarries which were being worked in 1901. One of the members resigned stating the Board would be responsible for any injuries if accidents happened. Even today fencing around the quarries remains uneven. A second and more positive legacy of the quarrying was the car park at the former Wickfield Quarry.

An unexpected post script to the long exploitation of the mineral resources of the common came in 1963 when the Seismograph Society was granted permission by the Board to investigate the possibilities of finding oil. Unsurprisingly this was a short lived venture, based in Bishop's Cleeve railway station before the station was demolished in the following year.

Woodland

The story of woodland has largely been one of recounting developments on land adjoining the common but since 1918 the story has largely been one of planting trees on the common. The first attempt seems to have been unsuccessful as the Board's minutes record in 1928 that six of the seven trees planted near the Three Sisters had died. More recently, about 50 years ago, the Three Sisters became the Twins after one was blown down. In 1929 a campaign was started to stabilise the sloping area known as The Slips on the western side of Nutterswood by the creation of a plantation of larch trees. More trees were ordered for the area eight years later, both larch and sitka spruce, to cover five acres. The following year the Board complained to the supplier, Forestry Products, that the trees they had supplied were too small. The supplier blamed rabbits for preventing the trunks from growing. The Forestry Commission was called in to adjudicate and found in favour of the supplier but gave the Board a small grant for trees.

Further discussions took place in 1989 when it was decided that the trees planted in 1929 had reached maturity, but the local timber merchant declined the invitation to clear the trees claiming that they had little value and their position made it difficult to fell them. It took a further five years before they were felled, possibly encouraged by the

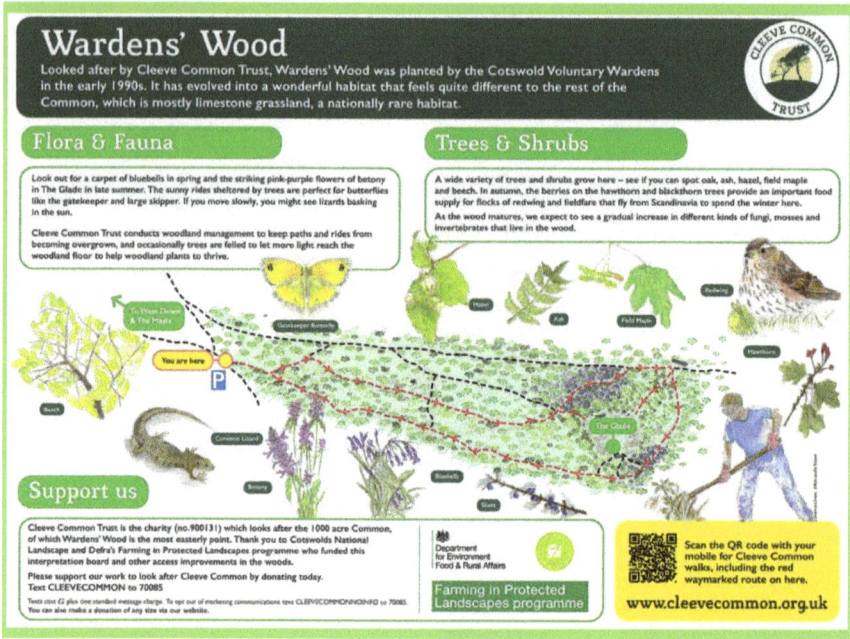

The information board at Wardens' Wood is part of the Trust's commitment to education. (A. Steer)

This photograph of the memorial beech tree with horse riders, a dog walker and a cyclist encapsulates the modern uses of the common

county council offering funds for replacement. The council had already shown an interest in growing trees on the common, having spent £400 on planting 200 trees at the end of West Down as a shelter belt. The main tree planting activity at the end of West Down was the creation of the Wardens' Wood by the Cotswold Wardens starting in 1995. Three years later the work was highly commended in a national award. Since that date the Trust and the wardens have continued to develop the wood as an asset to encourage people to visit this extreme edge of the common. Another small area of woodland was planted by Wheeler's Gate early in this century to commemorate Hugh Denham who died in 1999. Hugh not only wrote *The Woodmancote Book*, but was chair of the parish council for many years and a campaigner for the charity, the Council for the Preservation of Rural England. Finally, although not exactly woodland, since 2012 the single beach tree, the sole survivor of a small group of trees on these harsh uplands, and reputed to be the tree growing at the highest elevation in the Cotswolds, has been the centre of a memorial wall with plaques commemorating those who once enjoyed the space and tranquillity of the common.

Horse Training

In the years since the end of the First World War managing race horse training seems to have been the biggest challenge faced by the Board until regular training came to an effective end in 2005. The twists and turns of the relationship between the Board and the trainers can be followed in the Board's minutes and what follows is a summary of some of the recurring themes.

Immediately after the war the trainers were complaining about the state of the gallops, situated mostly over the old racecourse, which had been unused during the war. Arguments continually went to and fro between the trainers and the Board over who was ultimately responsible for keeping them in usable condition. In 1931 trainers were told it was their responsibility and the Steeplechase Club was given permission to cut the gorse, but during the Second World War in 1942 it was the Board which made good the damage caused by the military. Twenty years later the trainers refused to pay the licence fee because of the poor state of the gallops. The situation must have been desperate for in the following year the Board asked Cheltenham racecourse to take over as a possible solution, but they refused. In 1971 the trainer 'Frenchie' Nicholson from Prestbury offered to chain and harrow the gallops, but the Board turned him down. He did it anyway the following year when the board complained he had done it without their permission. Not until 1989 did the racecourse respond to the Board's requests when Peter McNeile, who was its operations' manager, was co-opted in direct response to the haywarden declaring he needed "someone more educated" to manage the gallops at a time when the trainers themselves were at loggerheads over its management. In that year also the 'cantering loop' which ran round the common to the north of the gallops towards Postlip was drilled and reseeded; the only time this longer course was mentioned in the minutes. Two of the trainers offered to take over the running of the gallops in February 1995, but the number of trainers using the gallops was declining and so the condition of the gallops no longer featured in the minutes except for a note in January 2004 that they were unusable as a result of vandalism. The following year Owen O'Neill from Cleeve Lodge, who had been training on the hill for 40 years, ceased training, since when the gallops have no longer been regularly used. Occasionally the Grassick stable at Dryfield Farm has trained its horses there.

Lionel Densham on Fieldmaster was photographed on the gallops in 1935 (B. Mustoe)

The number of horses being trained at any one time fluctuated since 1918. In 1923 70 to 80; in 1927 34; in 1953 as many as 88; in 1991 44 and by 2004 only Owen O'Neill had a training licence. In 1974 he had been training 30 horses. The minutes of the Board contain details of the number of trainers and licences issued between 1927 and 1939 and provide an insight into some of the most famous trainers of the day. In 1927 twelve trainers were using the gallops. This had reduced to five in 1939. Foremost amongst their number was Alf Newey from Haymes farm from 1921 to 1933 when he moved to Woodmancote Farm for a further five years. As a jockey his greatest achievement was winning the 1907 Grand National on 'Eremon' despite losing a stirrup at the first fence. From at least 1925 to 1952 Charles Piggott, the great uncle of the famous jockey Lester Piggott, trained from Cleeve Lodge on the common, whilst Ben Roberts ran his stable in Mill Street in Prestbury from at least 1926 to 1946. Arthur Saxby, who had ridden over 300 winners, brought his horses from his stables at the Old Farm in Bishop's Cleeve during the 1920s and early 1930s. The stables continued into the 1960s and in 1963 launched the career of trainer Jenny Pitman, the first female trainer to win the Grand National with 'Corbière', exactly twenty years later. By far the most successful trainer in later years was Herbert 'Frenchie' Nicholson of Lake Street in Prestbury. As a jockey he won the Cheltenham Gold Cup in 1942 riding 'Medoc II' but as a trainer he also trained such successful jockeys as Pat Eddery and Brough Scott. The most recent stable to be built for training on the hill was Wickfield Stud on Wickfield Lane in 1985.

There had been an uneasy relationship between the commoners and the trainers concerning the impact of training on the grazing, but the main concerns of the Board focused on chasing the trainers to pay for their training licences. Although the cost of the licence was quite modest for many years, three guineas in 1949, £10 in 1985 rising to £20 per horse in 1992, the minutes are full of complaints. Trainers just refused to pay until threatened with court action; in 1966 eleven trainers were threatened. Another complaint was that they trained more horses than they had licensed. When the haywarden carried out a census in November 1953 he counted 88 horses of which only 39 were licensed. In 1974 and again in 1975 there was the added problem of 'strangers' training horses on the common. In the former year the Board refused to accept a payment of £25 from a trainer from Ross on Wye who had been caught training on the hill and a summons was issued. In 1975 two men from Gretton were similarly treated. Unfortunately the minutes do not record the outcome, as in so many cases of threatened prosecution. In 1977 the continuing problem of reluctant payers led the Board to ask Ray Gould, the racing correspondent of the *Gloucestershire Echo*, to write a column designed to shame them into paying; a desperate action by the Board. Another common complaint was that trainers took out hacking licences as they were cheaper, usually about a third of the cost. In 1987 the board insisted each rider should exhibit a badge to indicate the licence had been paid. It was no surprise it met with varied success. In 1992 the Board hoped to have solved the problem by entering into an agreement that Wetherbys would be responsible for collecting the fees, however the following year the Board declared the licences were not meeting the cost of the upkeep of the gallops and the annual fee was doubled to £60 a horse. This was reduced in 1994 to £45 as the trainers finally agreed to take on the upkeep of the gallops. Ten years later the decline in the number of licences issued was given as the reason that the gallops were in such poor condition, but this was the last year of regular use of the common for training horses. The existence of better all-weather training facilities elsewhere was an important factor in the decline.

Hacking licenses are needed if horse riders wish to ride off the bridle paths onto the grassland. As the number of training licences declined, the number of hacking licences increased. Since the Covid epidemic numbers have doubled, with 110 being issued in 2021. The legacy of the gallops, themselves the legacy of Cheltenham races in the nineteenth century, is now fulfilled by horse riders on the common for the purpose of recreation, not the more serious business of training race horses.

Golf

Dividing the chapters in this book at 1918 is a convenience for the historian rather than a key date for any of the developments affecting the common, including the golf clubs, and so it was no surprise that pre-war issues were soon recurring, especially complaints about the damage to the all-important greens. In 1920 this occurred most unusually as the result of an unauthorised polo match organised from Postlip, but the usual damage caused by training the horses continued to be a problem and the Board was less than helpful by the its refusal to allow fencing around the greens. It also refused to pay for the damage caused by the commoners' animals and refused to allow the golfers cars to be parked on the common. Relations were definitely cool at this period as the Board refused the many requests which arose from the difficulties the clubs faced in playing over common land with public access. However, one positive development for the clubs themselves in these immediate post-war years was the setting up of a Joint Green Committee in 1921 to enable them to work together more closely. One negative development affecting the Cheltenham Golf Club was the opening of the Lilleybrook course in 1922 which attracted away a significant number of members.

The early 1930s were times of change for the clubs and their members. In 1933 a new club was established, the 'Cleeve Hill and District Artisans Golf Club' at the Apple Tree Inn down in Woodmancote. Limited to 50 members, the entrance fee was 2s.6d, the annual subscription 5s. and the club paid 5s. per head to the Cheltenham Golf Club to allow members to use the course. Harold Smith from Woodmancote, who became the green keeper, would now be able to play over the course he tended. By this same date the Cheltenham Golf Club was in financial difficulties, having lost so many members, and so it requested a reduction of the annual payment of £100 but the Board declared itself "not sympathetic" in a crucial meeting in 1935. This

The 1937 golf club building was photographed in April 2021. It has captured the short period when there was a pop-up coffee pod on the lawn to provide refreshments as the covid restrictions were easing, but the club house was not yet able to open

situation led to discussions over the merging of the two clubs but to no avail and at the end of the year the original Cheltenham Golf Club folded. Fifty members joined the Cotswold Hills club which then took on the failed golf club's financial obligations to the Board. The clubhouse was taken over by the YHA as a youth hostel two years later.

The Cotswold Hills Golf Club then explored the possibilities of a new clubhouse and entered into negotiations to purchase The Mount, reached off Wickfield Lane, but the Board would not agree to allow parking on the common so as a result the club bought two acres of land next to The Mount where they built a new clubhouse. William Harbrow Ltd of South Bermondsey was the contractor and the total cost came to £3,778. The old clubhouse on the main road was sold for £1,500 and converted into two houses. The position of the new clubhouse meant the start of the course became too inconvenient so that the first and second holes were re-positioned; new greens and bunkers were also allowed by the Board. Its attitude seemed to be changing and in April 1938 it did allow parking on the common for the opening tournament and so a precedent for parking had been set. At that date the club at 450 members.

The golf course was barely unaffected during the war years 1939-45. Obstructions were placed on three fairways to prevent enemy planes or gliders landing and the putting green was dug up to grow potatoes but relations with the Board improved. For an exhibition match in May 1941, which included such famous players as Henry Cotton, and which raised a record £450 for the *Daily Sketch* war relief fund, the Board again allowed car parking. Relations between the golf club and the Board were becoming more cordial and in that month the Board began holding its meetings in the clubhouse, recording its thanks in the minutes. During the war the annual rental was reduced to £25 but subsequently raised after the war. However, when the board demanded an annual fee of £200 in October after the war had ended in June, the golf club threatened to quit and a compromise of £150 per annum payable for the next three years was agreed. At that meeting in October it was announced that the army had de-requisitioned the common which allowed the course finally to return to normal.

Golf was played on the common with little change for the next 25 years until soon after 1971, the year in which the county council produced its report on the present state and future of the common. This foresaw increased visitor numbers demanding greater public access, leading to the re-positioning for safety reasons of some of the holes on the golf course. This served as a catalyst for the Cotswold Hills Golf Club to investigate a move from the common and it was no real surprise when in December 1972 the club announced it was planning a move to a new course at Ullenwood on the other side of Cheltenham. The Board moved quickly to reassure the Artisans that they would not be affected by the move. Two years later the club took out a new agreement with the Board for just two years until the new course was ready, paying £900 each year. As a result of this move, Cheltenham Rural District Council agreed to take over the golf licence but as a result of local government re-organisation, the common became part of Tewkesbury Borough and it was this council which took over the licence in December 1975 paying annually £1,200 for the next three years. In the following May the 700 members of the Cotswold Hills club moved to Ullenwood. Under Tewkesbury Borough the course became a pay and play course but the council moved out of direct management in 1983 and the clubhouse and course were leased out.

The handbook issued by Tewkesbury Borough Council

Five years later the council was allowed a representative at the Board's meetings; it had not been in existence in 1890 when the Board of Conservators was established. In 1990 it agreed to pay a much increased fee of £20,000 per annum plus one per cent of green fees. Since that date it has continued to provide the largest locally-sourced annual income to the Board, which is now £25,000. However there were difficulties in this period. In 1990 Ron Wheeler, the chief executive of Tewkesbury Borough Council, complained the clubhouse needed complete refurbishment or demolition and rebuilding. The golfers were complaining that the course had deteriorated since 1976, but the lessee responded that they did not pay enough for a round of golf to finance proper maintenance. In

In May 2023 the PGA organised a Cleeve Hill Masters Tournament over the course

1994 and again in 2011 plans were put forward for a new clubhouse but nothing developed. Then in March 2021 the golf club operator became insolvent and there was a worrying wait for the golfers as the borough council debated whether to continue with the course because of the great demands on the Trust's management of the grassland, but the continuation of a historic feature and the health benefits of playing the golf won the day. A new company, the Cotswold Hub Company, took over in April 2021 with plans to redevelop the club house site and the course became ranked in the top 100 courses in the United Kingdom and Ireland. Today's golfers are heirs to a tradition which goes back to 1891 and with it the beginning of the regulated uses of the common for recreation.

Recreation

The act of 1890 provided free access to the common for recreation for the population of Cheltenham and this is now the principal reason for people visiting the common. Three years after the ending of the First World War the Conservators' minutes record 'the common is now used by the general public as a recreative health resort much more than in former days'. Seventy eight years later in 1999 they recorded 'it is obvious that the Common is a priceless recreational aid'. In the annual report for 2022, under the heading *Outdoor Recreation*, can be found the following 'the Trust seeks to promote physical health and mental well-being by enabling recreational use of the common by a myriad of users'. This is unlikely to change in the future as the Trust's website states clearly 'in 100 years time, visitors to Cleeve Common will enjoy the same sense of space and tranquility with the diversity of plant and animal life, as they do today'. Since 1918 the range of recreational uses has expanded significantly. Walking, with or without dogs, remains the most popular and it was no surprise when in 1970 the long-distance Cotswold Way footpath was routed across the common. Orienteering, cross-country running, mountain biking, rock climbing, horse riding, picnicking (but not barbecues) attract many to the common and during this century the Trust has organised walks on subjects from archaeology to zoology.

Together with the recreational uses of the common since 1918 have come some continuing problems for the Board to address. In 1983 a sixth former from Cleeve School, Jill Clark, carried out an 'A' level study which identified thirteen conflicting interests held by visitors to the common. These ranged from walking, golf and horse training to model aeroplane flying, driving cars across the common and sheep grazing. At the Stockwell Lane entrance she identified eight conflicting uses in that one area. Problems of erosion, litter and degradation of the grazing were here at their most acute. The balance of the seriousness of the problems for the Board has changed during the last forty years, but at many times the problems seem to have dominated their meetings. Litter has been one constant problem. The first litter bins were not put up until 1977 and the first bins for dog waste in 1999. Abandoned cars became an increasing problem and when four were dumped in March 2004 the Board also complained that the recovery vehicles were causing too much damage to the turf. Less damaging but probably a more serious problem was that visitors failed to shut gates so that animals on the common could escape. In 1935 'Please Shut the Gate' notices were fixed to the entrance gates but with little success. Not until cattle grids were installed in the early

The installation of the cattle grid at the top of Rising Sun Lane in 1991 (G. Cocks)

1990s was that problem solved. Vandalism has also been a continuing concern. On August Bank Holiday Monday in 1923 the Washpool was so badly damage that the Board requested a police presence the following year. Petty vandalism including lighting fires, destroying notices and damaging fences has continued to be a problem.

On the other hand the Board has been proactive in addressing the needs of visitors, installing metal seats since 1922. After the end of the Second World War, in 1947 the minutes record the need to increase the number of seats as visitors to the common had increased. One facility which took a long time to build was the provision of toilets. First proposed by Southam Parish Council in 1959, none were built until 1986 when the block at the top of Stockwell Lane was erected, despite vehement local opposition. Since their closure in 2009 visitors have had to use the toilets at the golf club. A toposcope explaining the views from the common was sponsored by Cheltenham Rotarians in 1973. In 1998 the first leaflets explaining the common for visitors were produced, followed in 2005 by a geological trail map brochure. Further leaflets were produced in 2013 as part of an educational programme after the appointment of a community engagement officer. The first website appeared in 2000 and the Board opened Facebook and Twitter accounts in 2014; all designed to enhance the enjoyment of visitors to the common.

At present there are many recreational uses of the common that could not have been foreseen

The disused drinking trough next to the cattle grid at the Rising Sun Lane entrance was placed there by his children in 1939 in memory of Alfred Taylor, a Cheltenham merchant, who was an original conservator. He served for many years, latterly as chairman

The current visitors' guide to the common gives details of the common, its life and attractions

in 1890 and the last century has seen the Board trying to cope with these new demands. Visitors arriving by cars created the most difficult new development to address, especially when they attempted to park on the common. The requests from the golf club to allow parking on the common were not the only ones to be turned down, in 1929 Mr Sabbatella was not allowed to park his ice cream van on the common. 'No parking' signs were placed at West Down in 1934 and by the late 1950s it had become such a problem that in 1961 the Board felt it had to place a warning in the *Gloucestershire Echo,* but it was fighting a losing battle. As a result of this pressure, a proposal was made in 1967 to use Wickfield Quarry as a car park, but the county council insisted on planning permission and nothing happened immediately, and so it was ironical that thirteen years later the county council itself suggested the quarry should be used as a carpark.

An episode which brought into focus the limitations of the Board's powers concerning the illegal driving and parking of cars on the common was well-illustrated by an incident in 1985 which even reached the national news. In the summer of that year a 'Rainbow Village' of two to three hundred 'hippies' set up camp on West Down. The conservators had responsibility for enforcing the byelaw prohibiting the driving of vehicles across the common, but had no power to evict the travellers. The maximum fine they could impose was just 40s. After lengthy legal discussions a court order was taken out by the lords of the manor who, as owners of the freehold of the common, were the only people who had the right to evict. This was done and the 'village' quickly disappeared. Two years later a parking area was set out by the radio masts and in the following year licences to park were at last issued to the inhabitants of Nutterswood after many years of conflict between the inhabitants and the Board. The car parks made it easier for visitors to reach the common and enjoy taking recreation over it but nothing could prevent the wilful driving over the common. In the middle years of the 1980s the Board worked with the police to prosecute offenders, until in 1987 the police withdrew, maintaining they had better things to do. In January 2005 trenches were dug at West Down to try to prevent this but the Trust's 2022 report recorded that a 4×4 vehicle had damaged one of the golf greens, which led to rising bollards being installed at the Wickfield Lane entrance. The

Trust noted, however, that nothing could stop the illegal driving of motorbikes across the common.

There have been a myriad of recreational uses which could not have been foreseen in 1890. Gliding was one of these and although it was not allowed in 1948, attitudes gradually changed and 23 years later the Cotswold Gliding Club was given permission to fly at weekends. In 1977 hang gliding was not permitted but four years later model aircraft could be flown. By that date Castle Rock had become a popular location

Rock climbing on Castle Rock (G. Cocks)

for climbers. In 1988 mountain bike riding was allowed but paragliding refused in 1997. In the early 1990s the local scouts and guides organised a 'Sun Run' which involved running from the top of the hill to the top of the Malverns in the time it took from sunset to sunrise. In 1992 the Board agreed it had been much better organised than the previous year. The year 2000 brought an entirely new activity to the common, geocaching. First developed in the USA, anyone can hide a small container and log its position on the geocaching app on a mobile phone for other people to find it using the GPS (Global Positioning Signal) on their mobile phone. The container has an item to exchange and/or a log book to record the discovery by the finder. At the time of writing there are three such containers hidden on the common. However, what nobody could have foreseen was that in April 2001 the outbreak of foot and mouth disease meant the common was closed completely for six months. Conversely, in the Covid epidemic of 2020-21 local people living within walking distance used it as an escape from lockdown and visitor numbers more than doubled.

One visitor on Sunday, 13 January 1957 propelled the common into the national news headlines. That morning Harry Thierons from Bishop's Cleeve set out with a few friends to explore Isaac's cave above Nutterswood for the thirteenth time. It was an unlucky number and unlucky date for Harry. He set out alone and having explored further than he had ever done before and reaching the end of the cave, when he decided to return he became trapped as he tried to squeeze past a boulder 80 feet from the entrance. His friends heard his cries for help, went to release him but failed and so the police, fire and ambulance were called. They could not reach Harry either as the entrance to the cave was very small and the passage inside was very constricted. Even a specialist mine rescue team from the Forest of Dean failed to reach him as their equipment was too bulky.

Flashlight photo of interior of Cleeve Cave, which extends 150 feet into the hill.

[Taken from interior; looking outward.]

The interior of Isaac's cave photographed in 1910 (T. Curr)

There was only one person small enough to do so, thirteen year old Tim Hamblett from Nutterswood. He kept Harry's spirits up by taking him brandy, sandwiches, hot water bottles and blankets. He even tried to pull him out by greasing the visible part of Harry's body and tying a rope round his foot, but without success. The only solution was to enlarge the hole where Harry was stuck, so Tim's older brother Pat spent three and a half hours of energy sapping effort chiselling away at the stone to enlarge it. Eventually Harry, who had been stuck for over twelve hours, was able to wriggle free. Amazingly he had only a few minor cuts and bruises. Pat collapsed from his efforts and both were taken to Cheltenham General Hospital and kept overnight before returning home.

This human interest story with a good ending was widely reported. It appeared on the front page of the *Daily Herald* and *Birmingham Daily Post* and as a news story throughout the United Kingdom in the *Belfast News-Letter*, Cardiff's *Western Mail* and the *Edinburgh Evening News*. Tim was even interviewed on the BBC Panorama programme. The potential for further incidents as thrill-seeking visitors came to investigate the cave led the Board of Conservators to take the decision to block up the cave at their meeting in April to prevent the possibility of any repeat. Isaac's cave is one of nine naturally-formed limestone caves identified as existing on the common by the Bristol University Spelæological Society in 2004. None of these caves is accessible to visitors.

Today's visitors seeking recreation are heirs to those who gained their access in 1890. Although recreation is a recent use of the common in its historical context, it is by far the most important use today and the work of the Trust has to focus on meeting the needs and demands of the visitors seeking their recreation along with the other pressures on this valued upland open space. This places emphasis on the Trust's programmes of education to ensure all the visitors can appreciate and enjoy their time on the common.

Conclusion

This greatly expanded chapter compared to the 1990 edition of the book has enabled a much more detailed analysis of how the impact of those factors and trends which had emerged during the years of the creation of the Cotswold Health Resort continued throughout the twentieth century and into the first two decades of the twenty first, to mould the people and the landscape of the hill and its common. This would not have been possible without the access to significant archives not readily available thirty three years ago. Since 1918 the changing means of transport and expansion of housing in the local area have led many more people coming to enjoy the hill to enjoy its fresh air and wide open spaces away from the pressures of everyday lives. This

This cartoon appeared in the first edition of the book, but it still has relevance today (Gloucestershire Echo)

chapter has charted the growth in the recreational use of the hill as the old traditional uses have faded except for the sheep which still graze there for half the year. Yet conflicts still arise, although largely different in nature from those examined in earlier chapters. It has also shown that although the Trust is no longer its own master, it continues to work hard for the benefit of all the common's users.

FURTHER READING

This chapter could not have been expanded without access to the Conservators' minutes 1890-2014 held by the Trust. Its accounts since 2017 are published on the Charity Commission website and all the current details of its work can be found on the Cleeve Common Trust's own website. The books used in Chapter Seven have again been used. A fascinating glimpse of life on the hill was found in *Gloucestershire Countryside* for April 1940 in Cheltenham Library (CE/G052). The 1939 National Register can be consulted on the Ancestry website. The Care Quality Commission website has reports on the former Convalescent Home from 2004. Further use has been made of the Gloucestershire Archives' collections also listed in Chapter Seven, with the following additions: Cockbury sale 1912 (D2299), details of commons and commoners under the 1965 Commons Registration Act (K1887, K2051), various house sales (D4858/2/4), various press cuttings concerning the common and hill c.1920-2010 (D12676/7/2/1,3). I have also used my own knowledge of the common and hill since 1960.

THE FINAL WORD

This story has covered five thousand years, yet like any good story the end has yet to be written. During this time a landscape has been developed. It is possible to read that landscape for clues to its own history, to identify continuities, changes and conflicts, and within them three main turning points, in the Bronze Age, the later Middle Ages and at the end of the nineteenth century. In every age there have been some new developments but the present perception and uses of the common can be dated to the last of those turning points and the creation of the Cotswold Health Resort. Cleeve Hill with its common is a fascinating piece of landscape, still very much a treasured resource in a crowded countryside. Those who visit it; those who live there; those who have responsibility for its future ought to be aware of its past. Increasing that awareness has been the ultimate purpose of this book.

FIRST EDITION ACKNOWLEDGEMENTS

A work such as this could not have been written without the wholehearted cooperation of a large number of people. Wherever possible I have already acknowledged them in the text and the captions. However, it has not been possible to thank in this way all who have helped me, and I gratefully acknowledge their assistance here. My research has taken so long that many might have forgotten their contribution, and several are no longer with us to enjoy the results of their help and advice. I apologize for any who might have inadvertently been omitted despite my careful recording of all the assistance I have received over the years.

Readers will already be aware that local records in the County Record Office have provided the backbone to this study. I thus start by thanking the County Archivists, Brian Smith and his successor David Smith, whose staff have dealt with many enquiries and requests with unfailing courtesy over many years. To the staffs at the other two major record repositories in the county, at Gloucester and Cheltenham libraries, I also extend my thanks. If my use of Bishop's Cleeve and Winchcombe libraries has necessarily been less, the assistance I have received there has been equally appreciated. Steven Blake at Cheltenham Museum has drawn my attention to the variety of material held there which has been relevant to this study, and I am grateful to him for that. Jackie Taylor and Tony Jones of the Planning Department at Shire Hall, Gloucester, have provided information on the current plans for Cleeve Common.

Further afield, I wish to record my indebtedness to the staffs at the following repositories: Bodleian Library, Oxford; British Library, London; British Newspaper Library, Colindale; House of Lords' Record Office, London; Ordnance Survey (Boundaries Division), Southampton; Public Record Office, Chancery Lane, London; Worcestershire Record Office, St Helen's, Worcester.

I am indebted to Steven Bassett of Birmingham University and Joan Thirsk of Oxford University for discussing some of the ideas in Chapters Two and Four respectively. Mick Aston of Bristol University has commented upon my manuscript, as has Christopher Dyer of Birmingham University, to whom I stand further indebted not only for allowing me to use his transcripts of the Bishop of Worcester's medieval court rolls, but also for accompanying me in search of the hidden medieval landscape. He also drew the plan of Wick.

Many local people, many of whom have known the area for far longer than myself, have given freely of their time and knowledge to fill in the gaps in the written record. I give my thanks to the following or their surviving relatives: C. Arno, T. Ballinger, P. Deakin, J.T.C. Denley, H. Gaskins, J. Garrett, E. Green, S. Hora, W. Humphries, A. Lunt, J. Mead, D. Oakey, G. Pitt, H. Smith, O. Stinchcombe, D. Waters, E. Way and W. Yiend. I am especially grateful to Vera Gardner, Vi Pearce and John Yiend who commented on the closing chapters to prevent my making too many obvious errors in my reconstruction of more recent events.

Just one person has been with this study since its inception. I have already acknowledged through the captions the enormous debt I owe to Tim Curr for his photographic work. But the debt is far deeper, for through four decades we have walked, talked and argued over Cleeve Hill, its common and its people. His continuing enthusiasm has been the necessary spur I needed to put the results in print. I hope he is not disappointed.

Finally, to my family, Margaret, Peter and Timothy for their forbearance and encouragement, particularly during the hectic recent months of turning notes into text, I once again give my thanks. The text itself has been transformed from illegible and confused manuscript to perfect typescript by Pat Freeth. She has cheerfully performed wonders in a very short time and no gratitude can be too great.

If any fault still remains after the help and advice of everybody listed here, I alone remain responsible.

NEW EDITION ACKNOWLEDGEMENTS

In October 2019 my school friend Tim Curr passed away. I was fortunate to receive his collection of photographs, not only those he had taken himself, but also those he had copied for other people, keeping a copy for himself. I have used many of these in the book, but realise that as he did not keep records of the copied images I have been unable to establish the original sources. I would be happy to do so in any future edition. Where appropriate I have gratefully acknowledged the source of my illustrations in the captions.

My greatest thanks go to Michael Bates, the clerk to the Cleeve Common Trust, and Phil Robson, chairman of the Trust, for allowing me access to the Conservators' minutes, without which this new edition would have been much the poorer and much shorter. Michael has also advised me on matters relating to the work of the Trust both now and in the recent past, for which I am also grateful. Giles Alder, the Trust's Conservation Officer, and Nicola Daw, its Community Engagement Officer, have helped me to understand how the Trust works in ensuring the common continues to be a special place to visit.

I am indebted to Paul Evans and the search room staff of Gloucestershire Archives and to the staff of Bishop's Cleeve library for their unfailing helpfulness and advice.

I am also indebted to individuals who shared their knowledge and expertise with me: Travis Anderson for discussing Haymes; Steven Bassett for sharing with me his researches into the land charters for Bishop's Cleeve; Bruce Clayton for his observations on Cockbury; Tim Copeland for sharing his knowledge of the archaeology of the common and commenting on the first draft of Chapter 1; Gill Cocks for allowing me to select from her collection of historic postcards; Chris Dyer for exploring Wontley with me; Mike Edwards for explaining the horse training on the gallops; Noel Furley for discussing the history of the Cotswold Hills Golf Club; Anthea Jones for guiding me through the

Lloyd George Land Tax records; Richard Jones for allowing access to Wontley; Derek Maddock and Stephanie Duensing for guiding me round the excavations at Sudeley; Sue Weir for information on the Malvern View Hotel; Rob White for information on Arthur Yiend; Will Williams of Cleeve Bookshop for encouraging and supporting my writing.

    Arthur Price has generously answered all my questions on the nature and uses of Cleeve Hill stone. Fellow members of GlosArch have made possible the investigations at the hillfort, The Ring and the racecourse grandstand: Neil Cathie, Les Comtesse, Phil Cox, David Jones and Mike Milward. John Chandler of Hobnob Press has been a very supportive publisher. Finally, my wife Margaret has again shown forbearance and patience during the long period it has taken to write this book and she has also commented upon the drafts. To all the above I give my heartfelt thanks, but I alone remain responsible for what I have written.

GLOSSARY

Acre an area of land approximately half the size of a football pitch
Assart a piece of woodland cleared and converted to arable land
Bailiff the lord's estate manager
Coppice woodland where the wood was cut periodically, usually after no more than eight years, to provide wood for handles, poles, hurdles, wattles
Commoner a person with rights to the common
Copyhold the right to rent a property by a copy of the manor court roll
Cotlander a Medieval peasant holding about six acres and working on the lord's demesne as rent
Croft a small plot of land usually attached to a house
Cruck a pair of curved timbers which support the roof of a building
Curate an assistant to the parish priest
Demesne land retained by the lord of the manor for his own use and not rented out
Enclosure the process, usually by an act of parliament, by which the land of the open fields and some commons was converted into smaller fields with boundaries, also called enclosures. These became private property
Estate historically all the manors belonging to one person or institution, later a housing development
Fallow land not ploughed in any one year to regain its goodness
Freehold the right to do what the person wished with his/her land without any obligations to the lord of the manor
Hide originally the amount of land ploughed in a year by a team of eight oxen
Manor an area of land over which the lord of the manor had control, also the house where the lord lived
Messuage a house or farm with other buildings on a small plot of land
Open field farmland divided into strips without hedges or fences and

divided among the tenants with agreed routines for growing and harvesting crops

Pannage the right to feed pigs in the manorial woods

Rector the person entitled to receive annually all the tithes from a parish, usually, but not always, the parish priest

Reeve a person appointed by the tenants to represent them to the lord of the manor

Ridge and furrow the corrugated surface of fields today which represents the strips of the open fields

Stinting the number of animals a commoner could place on the common according to local regulations, usually based on the number of animals his/her own land could support

Tithe a tenth of the produce of the land given to the rector; changed to a money payment in 1836

Underwood the produce of coppicing, also used as fuel

Vestry an unelected body of the main landowners which governed the village before being replaced by an elected parish council in 1894, also the room where they met

Yeoman a term of status from the sixteenth century identifying a better-off farmer

INDEX OF PLACES

Ashleigh Lane 69, 187
Belas Knap 3-7, 11, 16, 22, 25, 49
Ben's Tump 25
Besford Court 189, 213
Besford Road 189, 190, 201, 227, 236
Bishop's Cleeve xii, xx, 3, 7, 11, 14, 19,
    24, 29, 30, 32, 33, 34, 39, 40, 49,
    51, 52, 55, 56, 62, 66, 67, 74, 97,
    102, 109, 110, 111, 114, 115, 118,
    119, 130, 133, 140, 143, 147, 150,
    151, 152, 154, 155, 156, 157, 158,
    163, 165, 167, 168, 173, 177, 186,
    196, 200, 201, 204, 205, 212, 214,
    217, 220, 232, 235, 236, 249, 253,
    263
    Cleeve Hall (formerly the Bishop of
        Worcester's manor house and later
        the rectory) 24, 74, 106, 119,
    Cleevelands 3, 7, 10, 11, 20, 35
    Church Road 20, 24
    Dean Brook 110
    Dean Farm 3
    Gilder's Paddock 20, 24
    Greenacre Way 20
    Home Farm 24, 31
    Homelands 10
    Lower Farm 11, 30
    Maxwell Place 20
    Manors 35, 50, 52, 54, 55, 56, 59, 61,
        62, 63, 64, 67, 68-73, 74, 76, 78,
        82, 85, 86, 88-94, 99, 102, 106,
        111, 118, 119, 157, 158, 167, 168,
        211, 212, 214, 238, 247, 261
    Old Farm 89, 90, 253
    St Michael's Centre 163, 164
    St Michael's church 33, 50, 74, 96,
        112, 157
    Stoke Road 3, 11, 20, 28, 31
    Tesco 10, 20, 24, 31
    Tithe Barn 56
    Town Meadow 110
Bittemoor 71, 110, 112, 113, 115
Blockley 55, 56, 67
Bottomley 113, 114
Bredon Hill 21
Brockhampton (in Southam) xii, 34, 133,
    156, 158, 214
Castle Rock 262
Charlton Abbots 14, 39, 41, 51, 65, 231
Cheltenham xvii, xxi, 10, 12, 16, 25, 28,
    32, 86, 87, 95, 99, 117, 118, 123,
    124, 127, 129-147, 150, 154, 155,
    156, 157, 158, 159, 160, 161, 169,
    171, 174, 175, 177, 179, 180, 181-
    184, 186, 187, 191, 192, 193, 195,
    196, 198, 199, 200, 201, 202, 203,
    205, 206, 208, 210, 212, 214, 215,
    217, 219, 222, 223, 227, 229, 233,
    235, 237, 239, 241, 242, 251, 254,
    255, 256, 257, 258, 264
Cleeve Cloud 17, 34, 75, 90, 126, 197
Cleeve Cloud hillfort 17, 18, 19, 21, 25,
    123, 133, 145, 159, 180, 210, 212,
    237, 239
Cleeve Hill Café and Tea Gardens 199, 223
Cleeve Hill 'camp' 9, 123, 175
Cleeve Hill Hotel 224, 225
Cleeve Prior 35
Cockbury 29, 43, 45, 49, 51, 75, 78,
    79-80, 83, 95, 104-110, 115, 117,
    118-119, 120, 172-173, 195, 196,
    225, 231-232
Cosy Corner Tea Gardens 223, 224
Cotswold Convalescent Home 181-184,
    196, 201, 202, 204, 208, 229,
    233-235

Cotswold Way 259
Cross Dyke 13-14, 26, 70, 71, 237
Dewpond 240
Dry Bottom *xiv*, 13, 39, 46, 71, 90, 121
Dryfield Farm 38, 104, 231, 253
East Wood *see* Wontley Wood
Gambles Lane 71, 75, 97, 110, 114, 166, 169, 171, 197, 219, 233, 245
Gloucester 21, 25, 30, 45, 48, 51, 56, 87, 122, 129, 154, 219
Gotherington *xviii*, 12, 21, 34, 38, 50, 118, 124, 131, 212
Golf course 206-210, 254-258
Gotherington Lane 10, 200
Granna Lane 12, 21, 38, 45, 124, 125
Grinnell Lane *see* Granna Lane
Hailes Abbey 75
Ham Hill 13
Haymes 2, 5, 16, 22-24, 25, 30, 31, 34, 75, 80, 81, 83, 92, 110-115, 117, 118, 119, 127, 128, 167, 172, 186, 173, 193-195, 225, 229, 253
High Roost Hotel 225
Hillground 166, 228, 229
Houses on Cleeve Hill
   1 and 2 Cleeve Hill 209, 229
   2 Cleeve Cloud 197
   Adderstone House 187
   Ashleigh House 171, 187
   Barnfield 189, 236
   Bramleigh 171, 198
   Charlesville (now Flagstaff) 188, 199
   Cleeve Hill House 194, 195
   Cleeve Lodge 147, 149, 169, 175, 217, 252, 253
   Denewood 189
   Emblem Cottage 115, 116, 149, 187, 217
   Ferncliffe 191, 203, 227
   Gambles Cottage 115
   Glendale 189, 220
   Greenmount 198, 225
   Gresham House 223, 224
   Greystone (now Mulberry House) 194, 195, 205
   Haymesgarth 194, 195, 201
   Highfields 191
   Hillcrest 192
   Hollybank 189
   Horses Green 166,
   Inglecroft 203,
   Inglenook (now Swift's Place) 194
   Ivybank 191, 198, 200
   Ivydene 197, 198
   Laburnum Cottage 161, 188, 223
   Laburnum Villa (now Cloud's End) 188
   Lou's Views 10, 230
   Paunceford 189
   Prescott Cottage 170, 187, 189, 192, 193, 215
   Primrose Bank 171
   Red Roof 236
   Rochdale 189, 236
   Rock House 207
   Semington (now Highfields) 191, 192, 198, 202
   Sheep Way 115
   Silverdale 227, 236
   Spring Cottage 116, 117
   Springbank 201, 223
   Springfield (now Laurentides) 194, 195
   Sunnyside (now The Parsonage) 117, 167, 203, 228
   The Mount 256
   The Orchards 199
   The Rockery (now Adderstone too) 170, 187, 201, 210
   The Shanty 198
   The Stores (now Hilltop) 226, 227
   The View 223
   The Wickfields 225
   Thrift Cottage 198
   'tower house' 167, 168
   Treganna (now Top of the Hill) 197, 200
   Upper Bottomley 162, 227, 228, 244, 245
   Upper Colletts 187, 200, 207, 225, 244
   Westridge (now Heron Haye) 229
   Wickfield Lodge 215
   Wilcote 199, 225, 227, 230

Huddleston's Table 46, 47, 48, 49
Hyde Brook 34, 41
Isaac's cave 263-264
King's Beeches 5, 8, 9, 15-16, 22, 25, 163, 212
Langley Brook 38, 80, 105
Lilleybrook 255
Longwood Common 66
Longwood Farm 172
Lye Lane 97, 112, 123, 191, 229
Malvern View Care Home 188, 234-5
Malvern View Hotel 170, 179, 187, 192, 199, 208, 223, 225, 227,
Memorial beech tree 250
Nottingham Hill *xiii, xviii,* 9, 12, 19, 24, 25, 38, 49, 61, 63, 64, 67, 75, 81, 95, 104, 119, 125, 131, 172, 190, 210, 236
Nutterswood 17, 25, 46, 74, 92, 115, 116, 162, 164, 167, 186, 188, 197, 228, 239, 247, 249, 261, 263
Padcombe 29, 39, 40, 43, 46, 77, 103, 215
Post Office Lane 166, 189, 190, 197, 200, 203, 220, 225, 227
Postlip 13, 14, 39, 43, 45, 51, 65, 77, 97, 102, 110, 117, 118, 119, 121, 123, 135, 174, 184, 245, 252, 254
Postlip Warren 65, 66
Prescott 38, 110,
Prestbury *xviii,* 41, 45, 51, 101, 103, 122, 135, 138, 145, 150, 217, 252, 253
Prestbury Park 131, 136, 138, 141, 143, 144, 145, 206
Quarries
   Ash 74
   Cleeve Cloud 45, 73, 74, 96, 160, 161, 162, 174, 212, 246
   Freestone 212, 247
   Hardstone 212
   Middle Hill 212
   Milestone 9, 10, 11, 125, 211, 213, 217, 248
   Postlip 13, 39, 72-73, 97, 98, 161, 162, 163, 174, 175, 212, 246, 247
   Ring 211
   Rolling Bank 174, 175, 212
   Roadstone 162, 163

Sidelands 212
Stables 5, 16, 22
Queenwood 45, 122
Queen's Wood 26, 41, 44, 64, 100, 101, 103, 123, 141, 164
'Rainbow Village' 261
Reading Room 190, 210, 236
Rising Sun Hotel 25, 58, 169, 179, 192, 199, 200, 205, 207, 214, 225, 227, 248
Rising Sun Lane 5, 8, 13, 71, 167, 168, 170, 187, 201, 205, 210, 216, 229, 236, 259, 260
St Peter's church 170-171, 204-205, 210, 236,
Sandywell Park 103, 143, 172, 195, 230
Sapleton 50
Sevenhampton *xviii,* 14, 40, 41, 51, 93,
Southam *xii, xx,* 33, 34, 35, 43, 44, 45, 47, 50, 51, 57, 62, 67, 72, 79, 81, 84, 86, 88, 89, 95, 97, 100, 101, 102, 121, 123, 126, 133, 135, 147, 150, 152, 154, 155, 156, 158, 167, 171, 178, 179, 186, 194, 196, 205, 214, 260
   Bentley 92
   Bentley Lane 20, 126
   Kayte Farm 145
   Manors 25, 51, 55, 67, 68-73, 79, 80, 86, 87, 88-94, 95, 96, 100, 101, 104, 106, 110, 115, 130, 155, 158, 161-162, 164, 166, 167, 168, 211, 212
   Muckmead 34, 35, 100
   New Road 123
   Ratcliff Lawns 100
   Southam House 88, 91, 125, 128, 138, 162, 235
   Southam Lane 145
   Sunset Lane 126
Spoonley 175
Spring Lane 71, 97, 117, 123, 161, 167, 228, 229
Stockwell Lane *xv,* 10, 20, 75, 81, 97, 115, 119, 121, 147, 149, 166, 171, 189, 197, 199, 201, 222, 223, 225, 230, 235, 259, 260

Stoke Orchard 34, 80, 133, 173, 203
Stutfield Wood 44, 45, 64, 100, 102, 164
Sudeley Castle 98, 99
Tewkesbury *xviii*, 20, 21, 56, 75, 97, 117, 131, 212, 230, 238, 241, 257
The 'Geisha' 198, 199, 223
The Hewletts 123, 133, 144, 146,
The Ring 8, 16, 17, 159, 237, 249
The Slips 249
Three Sisters (now The Twins) 47, 122, 126, 249
Thrift Wood 44, 45, 64, 75, 90, 100, 126, 164
Timbingctun 33, 35, 36, 42, 43
'Tin Tabernacle' 201-204, 236
Tyrl 33, 34, 41
Ullenwood 238, 257
Undercliff 162
Wardens' Wood 39, 250, 251
Washpool *xv*, 39, 159, 160, 216, 260
Watery Bottom *xiv*, *xv*, 39, 160
Welsh Way 45, 47
Wendlescliff 33, 45
West Down 11, 13, 40, 41, 42, 43, 44, 45, 49, 69, 71, 77, 93, 124, 125, 129, 131, 133, 175, 238, 240, 243, 251, 261
West Wood 39, 42, 44, 65, 77, 172
Westwood House 172, 195
Wheeler's Corner 40, 45, 122, 251
White Way 13, 45, 47, 90, 125, 163, 247
Whitehall 104
Whittington 102, 136, 139, 145, 175
Wick 75, 81-84, 106, 115
Wickfield Crescent (now Petty Lane) 229
Wickfield Lane 43, 80, 110, 124, 210, 236, 238, 253, 256, 261
Wickfield Quarry 211, 212, 238, 249, 261
Wickfield Stud 231, 253
Wickfields 83, 107, 117, 119, 196, 200, 229
Winchcombe 32, 34, 36, 38, 39, 43, 45, 47, 51, 56, 64, 65, 71, 72, 74, 76, 78, 79, 87, 88, 95, 97, 98, 102, 109, 117, 118, 119, 121, 122, 123, 124, 135, 161, 168, 169, 172, 175, 177, 178, 189, 199, 222, 231, 234
  Deepwood 65
  Humblebee 5
  Humleyhoo 65
  White Hart Inn 123
Wontley 22, 26, 29, 39, 40, 41, 45, 47, 59, 60, 63, 64, 68, 69, 70, 71, 76-79, 80, 83, 84, 91, 93, 102-104, 105, 110, 115, 117, 120, 164, 172-173, 195, 230-231
Wontley Wood 39, 42, 44, 64, 77, 100, 102, 172
Woodmancote *xii*, *xx*, 15, 34, 56, 59, 63, 75, 81, 82, 83, 84, 86, 88, 89, 91, 92, 93, 120, 126, 133, 147, 152, 154, 155, 158, 186, 187, 189, 196, 200, 204, 214, 244, 255
  Apple Tree Inn 244, 255
  Bushcombe 62, 63
  Bushcombe Lane 2, 20, 57, 63
  Bushcombe Wood 61, 62, 63, 103
  Butts Lane 62, 119
  Kerr's Hill 63
  New Road 113
  Rose Farm 189
  Sheephouse/'Tobacco Barn' 119
  Woodmancote Farm 253
  Yew Tree Farm 2

www.ingramcontent.com/pod-product-compliance
Lightning Source LLC
Chambersburg PA
CBHW061246230426
43662CB00021B/2441